Global Ethics

This book is dedicated to all of my students, past and present, and to the great pleasures and rewards of teaching.

Global Ethics

An Introduction

KIMBERLY HUTCHINGS

polity

First published in 2010 by Polity Press
Reprinted 2010, 2011 (twice), 2013, 2014 (three times), 2015 (twice)

Polity Press
65 Bridge Street
Cambridge CB2 1UR, UK

Polity Press
350 Main Street
Malden, MA 02148, USA

ISBN-13: 978-0-7456-3681-8
ISBN-13: 978-0-7456-3682-5(pb)

A catalogue record for this book is available from the British Library.

Typeset in 10.5 on 12 pt Sabon
by Toppan Best-set Premedia Limited
Printed and bound by CPI Group (UK) Ltd,
Croydon, CR0 4YYl

The publisher has used its best endeavours to ensure that the URLs for
external websites referred to in this book are correct and active at the
time of going to press. However, the publisher has no responsibility for
the websites and can make no guarantee that a site will remain live or
that the content is or will remain appropriate.

Every effort has been made to trace all copyright holders, but if any have
been inadvertently overlooked the publisher will be pleased to include
any necessary credits in any subsequent reprint or edition.

For further information on Polity, visit our website:
www.politybooks.com

Contents

Acknowledgements

I am grateful to several people and groups of people for enabling me to write this book. Thanks are due to David Held for encouraging me to do it, and to the two anonymous readers at Polity who gave me valuable feedback on the original proposal and on a draft of the text. Particular thanks are due to Joe Hoover and Henry Radice who very kindly gave up their time to read and comment on a full version of the manuscript. Above all, I am grateful for the feedback of the many students I have taught on courses on global and international ethics over the years at Wolverhampton, Edinburgh and, most recently, at the London School of Economics. Without what I have gained from all of those classes and tutorials, this book would not have been possible. Needless to say, any faults and errors are my responsibility alone.

Kimberly Hutchings
July 2009

List of Abbreviations

ANC	African National Congress
FGM	female genital mutilation
ICTY	International Criminal Tribunal for Yugoslavia
IGO	international governmental organization
INGO	international non-governmental organization
GDP	gross domestic product
MDG	millennium development goal
MNC	multinational corporation
NATO	North Atlantic Treaty Organization
TRC	truth and reconciliation commission
UN	United Nations
UDHR	Universal Declaration of Human Rights
UNSCR	United Nations Security Council Resolution
WTO	World Trade Organization

1
What Is Global Ethics?

Introduction

The words 'global' and 'ethics' are familiar to most English-speaking people from everyday conversations about public events and private behaviour. We've all heard, read or used expressions such as 'global warming' or 'globalization' in the context of discussions about the environment or the world economy. We've all heard, read or used terms such as 'ethical' and 'unethical' in the context of people's actions in their personal or professional lives. But what does the 'Global Ethics' in the title of this book mean? *Global Ethics* (always capitalized when used in this sense) *is a field of theoretical inquiry that addresses ethical questions and problems arising out of the global interconnection and interdependence of the world's population.*

In contrast to other fields of theoretical inquiry that come under the broad heading of Applied Ethics, which are usually clear about the nature and reality of the field of application (for example, Professional Ethics, Environmental Ethics, Medical Ethics), within Global Ethics the term 'global' is deeply contested. Not only is its meaning debatable, but scholars also differ over whether it refers to something, i.e. globalization, which actually has happened or is happening. This means that theorists engaged in Global Ethics do not just disagree about ethical theory but also about what significance, if any, is to be attached to the term 'global'. The purpose of this chapter is to sketch out the terrain, and some of the defining disagreements, of Global Ethics as a field of theoretical inquiry. Subsequent chapters will flesh out the arguments touched on here in much more depth and detail.

The first part of the chapter will focus on the constituent terms of Global Ethics. First, we will examine debates over the meaning of 'global'. Second, we will examine the term 'ethics', the distinction between 'Ethics' as a mode of philosophical inquiry and 'ethics' as sets of substantive principles and values, and the relation and distinction between 'ethics' and 'morality', 'ethics' and 'politics'. Having done this, we will look briefly at the variety of understandings of Global Ethics and of the range of questions and issues that come within its scope. On this basis we will arrive at a working definition of the field of Global Ethics and its key concerns. We will then examine how world religions claim to provide answers to the questions raised by Global Ethics. We will conclude, however, that the questions and issues identified as the subject matter of Global Ethics cannot be resolved on the basis of religion. The chapter will end with an outline of the rest of the book and some advice on how to use this book as an aid to learning.

Defining our terms

Global

The word 'global' is generally used to signify something pertaining to the world as a whole. If something has global causes or global effects, then the suggestion is that either its causes or its effects are worldwide. This may mean 'world' in the sense of the terrestrial globe of the earth (as in global atmosphere), but it may also mean 'world' in terms of humanity, and the humanly organized terrestrial space of homes, villages, cities, nations, states and regions (as in global economy). The applicability of the term 'global' is a matter for debate amongst natural scientists when it refers to the earth, but it becomes a matter for debate amongst social scientists and philosophers when the reference is not simply to the material globe, but to people, and to the situation that people have constructed in relation to that materiality. People have always lived in a global world in the first sense, but there are ongoing arguments as to what extent and in what ways, if at all, their situation is, has been, or will ever be global in the second sense.

So, when global is used in the second sense, what does it signify? Here I suggest we can distinguish between two distinct but related dimensions of meaning. On the one hand global signifies a worldwide scale of commonality and, on the other hand, it signifies a worldwide scale of interconnection. In the first sense, when we are told that we live in a global (or globalized) world, we are being told that we live in a world in which all humanity shares a common situation. Whereas in the past, our scale of commonality with others may have been that of our tribe, our city or our state, we are now in a world in which there are significant commonalities across all borders of collective identity, linguistic, cultural, legal or political. Examples of this kind of claim for worldwide commonality across people and peoples include statements in which 'we' signifies humanity as such, such as: 'we are participants in a world market'; 'we are all subjects of international law'; or 'all of us have certain basic human rights'.

Related to, but also distinct from, claims about global sameness or commonality is the second dimension of the meaning of global, in which it refers to the worldwide interrelatedness of humanity. The claim here is that humanity's situation is a global one, because we are interconnected at a global level and therefore the actions (individual or collective) of people in one part of the globe affect, and will be affected by, the actions of people in other parts of the globe to an unprecedented degree. Another way of putting it is to say that human beings are now involved in interdependent and reciprocal relations with each other on a global scale. For example, my purchase of a shirt depends on the cheap labour that produced the shirt, which is in turn dependent in one direction on the international bank that finances the mortgage on the shirt factory's premises, and on the other on the foreign child whose labour is so cheap. Each of these actors is in turn dependent on my actions as a British consumer. Economically, socially, culturally and politically, we are embedded in, and depend on, relations with strangers from all parts of the world.

A global world, therefore, contrasts with a world in which the economic, social, cultural and political relations between people are confined within discrete local communities. In a global world, local events are affected by global processes (for example, in the global financial crisis of 2008). But it is not just that the global affects the local; in a global world the distinction between the local and the global becomes much more difficult to draw. At the level of everyday life, from eating habits to religious beliefs, in a globalized world strangeness and strangers are no longer at a distance; they are living in the neighbourhood. And social, economic and political activities that originate locally have intended and unintended global implications. This phenomenon has led to the label 'glocalization' being used to describe the effects of globalization, which both transform and are transformed by local actors (Robertson and White 2003; Watson 2004).

At a commonsense level, then, the claim that we live in a global age is the claim that the earth's human population shares a common situation in significant respects, and is deeply interdependent and interconnected. Within the social sciences, however, the meaning and status of this claim has been the subject of ongoing analysis and argument. Scholars have examined the nature and extent of globalization in different sectors of human activity, and differ fundamentally about whether our age is indeed global and, if it is, whether this is a recent development or not (Held and McGrew 2003; Robertson and White 2003; Wiarda 2007). There are those who argue that a technologically and economically driven process of globalization has undermined the significance of territorial distance, cultural difference and, most importantly, the political borders between states. On this view, the state has lost its salience as the key actor in world politics, and as the key mediator between the individual 'inside' the state and the international 'outside'. Instead, multinational corporations, regimes of global governance and a variety of global civil (and uncivil) non-governmental organizations have risen in significance (Held 2004; Mathews 2004; Ohmae 2004). In contrast, others are more sceptical, arguing that the state remains the key mode of economic, political and social organization, and that great powers continue to set the agenda of world politics (Hirst and Thompson 1996). Many scholars, however, hold a more nuanced position, in which globalization is more or less advanced in different sectors (e.g. economic, political, technological, cultural, communicative) or for different regions, peoples or classes of people, and in which the implications of globalization undermine or reinforce state power depending on the particular state and region in question (Rosecrance and Stein 2006).

Reflective exercise

Write down the list of activities you engage in on a normal day. Do any of them suggest that your everyday life is globalized and, if so, in what sense? Think about this in relation to what you are wearing, what you eat and drink, what music you listen to, how you travel, with whom you communicate, how you communicate. Do you see your own life as more or less globalized than that of people in other parts of the world?

Ethics

Scholars may disagree about the nature and extent of globalization, but there is unanimity on the point that, to the extent that the human world is global, this necessarily has implications for human identity and human relations. It is here that *ethical* issues arise and that a link between 'global' and 'ethics' is formed. In everyday language, the word *ethical* is sometimes used as the equivalent of 'morally good', implying that an ethical person is someone who does the morally right thing. In fact, ethics in its original meaning refers to codes of behaviour or sets of values that set out what it is right or wrong to do within particular contexts. An ethical person is therefore someone who aims to act according to such codes or values. When we discuss 'professional ethics' or 'medical ethics', we are discussing what the appropriate guidelines are for practitioners to follow in order to fulfil the aims and goals of their profession. So, for instance, we might raise the ethical question of what it is appropriate for doctors to do when the patient in their care is in a persistent vegetative state and they get conflicting instructions from their patient's living will and their patient's nearest and dearest. But, of course, the everyday meaning of ethics extends beyond the values and principles that should govern behaviour in a particular professional role; it gets applied to all aspects of human behaviour, so that one can ponder, and disagree about, what it is ethically right to do as a parent, a lover, a friend and so on.

Within moral philosophy, ethics has two meanings. Firstly, it is used in a way that reflects our commonsense usage to refer to substantive ethical beliefs, values and principles about what it is right or wrong to do (lower-case *ethics*). Secondly, it refers to the systematic philosophical investigation of the ground and nature of ethical principles and values (upper-case *Ethics*). In its latter sense, philosophical Ethics can be broken down into three distinct but related domains: Meta-Ethics; Normative Ethics; and Applied Ethics. Meta-Ethics is concerned with the most abstract foundational questions, such as the possibility of moral truth or the meaning of moral agency. Normative Ethics, which always relies on certain meta-ethical assumptions, is concerned with the elaboration and defence of substantive moral theories that provide answers about how to determine moral rightness and wrongness in general (see ethical theories discussed in chapters 2 and 3 below). Applied Ethics is concerned with applying Normative Ethics to particular issues and situations (see chapters 4–8 of this book). Within this book, we will be most concerned with Normative and Applied Ethics, but we will also encounter meta-ethical issues and questions along the way, since both Normative and Applied Ethics rely on meta-ethical assumptions about moral truth and moral agency (see Copp 2006, Singer 1993 and Lafollette 2000 for comprehensive mappings of the concerns of philosophical Ethics).

In general, Ethics aims to answer questions such as: *why* is a particular ethical claim convincing or persuasive, for instance, on what grounds should I believe that it is morally wrong to lie or steal (see discussions in chapters 3 and 4)? *What* is or should be the substantive content of ethical values; for instance, should moral principles be based on giving priority to maximizing human welfare or human liberty (see discussions in chapters 3 and 4)? *Who* carries moral responsibility for past or future actions, for instance how much of the responsibility for world poverty is carried by the world's rich (see discussion in chapters 4 and 5)? *How* should this or that ethical principle or value be actualized, for instance, if we think war criminals should be brought to justice, should this be done in an international criminal court or through a truth and reconciliation commission (see discussion in chapter 7)?

Ethics/morality

The everyday meaning of ethics clearly has a lot of overlap with the term 'morality', which we also use to signify matters that concern what it is good and right to do in our relations with others. As words, ethics and morality have similar roots. 'Ethos' refers to the character of a particular community's way of life, and 'mores' to the customary values and standards embedded in particular ways of life. Traditionally, questions of such values and standards have been bound up in religious and cultural beliefs and customs as well as in the specific contexts of particular roles. As we will see, however, in the discussion of different theories in chapters 2 and 3, ethics is, on some accounts, contrasted with 'morality'. For some ethical theorists, *morality* is identified with values, rules and principles that tell us what is right or wrong at a general or universal level for human beings as such, whereas *ethics* concerns human behaviour only within particular roles and contexts.

The ethics/morality distinction has been subject to intense debate within Ethics as a branch of philosophical inquiry. For some thinkers, morality is embedded within ethics, providing a core of common beliefs, values and principles that operate across different conceptions of the good life (see discussion of Küng below). For others, morality provides a, separately derived, critical tool to assess different ethical values (see discussion of Habermas in chapter 2). For others, however, the notion of a morality that exists over and above particular context is incoherent; there is no universal that transcends or underpins ethics, which means that moral issues are always embedded in ways of life (see discussion of MacIntyre in chapter 3). As we will see, the question of whether there is a set of moral standards that is universally authoritative for humanity as a whole (or not) is crucial to much of the debate that comes under the heading of Global Ethics. Since the idea that there is, or should be, a distinction between morality and ethics is contested in the literature, within this book the terms will normally be used interchangeably, except where the work of a theorist who is committed to the distinction is being discussed (essentially the theorists discussed in chapter 2).

Ethics/politics

Ethical questions about what it is right and wrong to do are difficult to separate from political questions about the kinds of laws, procedures and institutions we should put in place to regulate and mediate human action. Moreover, ethical claims do not arise in a vacuum – they are articulated in political contexts of hierarchical power relations, and their implications are likely to have differential effects on different people's interests. Ethics, therefore, in one way or another, always involves politics. Nevertheless, it is important to bear in mind the difference between studying Global Ethics as opposed to examining globalization from the perspectives of Political Science or International Relations. For scholars of Political Science and International Relations, the crucial questions are about describing, explaining and regulating the effects of globalization on intra-state and inter-state politics. These are very different questions from those posed by Ethics, where the focus is not on description or explanation but on *ethical judgement*. Studying Global Ethics means examining, assessing and defending judgements about what is morally right and wrong in our globalized world. You cannot assume that the implications of ethical argument will necessarily be easily realizable or in accord with predominant political realities. When engaging in ethical argument, you need to step back from assumptions about what actually drives political decisions and focus on what *ought* to be the values and principles underlying human interaction. To the extent that you think those values and principles are related to politics, you need to provide an argument for why that is, or should be, the case (see McGinn 1992 and Boonin and Oddie 2005 for examples of ethical reasoning and argument about a variety of issues).

Reflective exercise

- Reflecting on your own moral beliefs, can you distinguish between ones that you think are relative to context, that is, to particular roles or cultural tradition, and ones that are universal, that is, are ingrained in your humanity as such? Does an ethics/morality distinction make sense to you?
- Think about an issue such as the possession and proliferation of nuclear weapons in conditions of globalization. Can you distinguish between what you think about the *morality* of nuclear weapons from your *political* views about current international policies for managing the nuclear arsenals of states? What is the relation, if any, between your moral and your political judgement?

Doing Global Ethics

At the beginning of this chapter, Global Ethics was defined as *a field of theoretical enquiry that addresses ethical questions and problems arising out of the global interconnection and interdependence of the world's population.* On this account, Global Ethics investigates and evaluates the standards that should govern the behaviour of individual and collective actors as members of, or participants in, a global world. However, some of the literatures that contribute to this endeavour do not describe their ethical theories as global, but instead use alternative terms such as *international* or *cosmopolitan*. Within this book, both International and Cosmopolitan Ethics are treated as contributors to the broader field of Global Ethics for reasons explained below.

International Ethics is focused on investigating the morality of relations between nation-states as collective actors, and has a longer history than Global Ethics, especially in relation to moral debates about war and peace (see chapters 6 and 7). Theorists are more likely to give priority to inter-state ethics, when they are not convinced by the argument that globalization processes have broken down the ethical significance, in principle, practice, or both, of the boundaries of political community. However, within this book, *global* is understood to encompass the domain of the *international* as one dimension of globalized social, political and economic relations, which include relations between collective actors such as states as well as relations between collectives and individuals and between individuals. One of the issues that fuels debates in Global Ethics is contestation over the effects of globalization on the ethical status and responsibilities of states. For this reason, theorists who are focused on the ethics of inter-state relations will be included within the field of Global Ethics (see discussions of Rawls, Nagel, Walzer and Miller in chapter 5 and of Walzer in chapter 6).

Cosmopolitan derives its meaning not, in contrast to *global*, from a connection to the earth and the commonality and interdependence of humanity's earthly existence, but from a connection to the cosmos or universe, a material and spiritual order that transcends the actual social and material conditions of humanity. Moral cosmopolitanism or universalism existed long before anyone took the idea of globalization seriously. However, precisely because cosmopolitan ethical perspectives traditionally focused on the moral significance of all human beings, regardless of their specific status and identity, there are many who argue that approaches to ethics in a global world should be cosmopolitan. This has led to the characterization of the field of Global Ethics in terms of a clash between two antithetical approaches: *cosmopolitanism*, essentially any form of moral universalism that takes the human individual as the foundation of moral value; and *communitarianism*, essentially any theory that argues for any form of moral particularism, in which morality is understood as relative to historical or cultural context (Brown 1992; Dower 2007). In what follows I have avoided using this classification as a primary ordering principle. It is certainly the case that clashes between moral universalism and moral particularism are important in debates in Global Ethics (see, for instance, the ways in which virtue, feminist and postmodernist ethics, discussed in chapter 3, challenge moral universalism). However, both moral universalism and moral particularism take many different forms, and debates between different kinds of universalism and different kinds of particularism are also enormously important (see the debate between utilitarianism and deontology discussed in chapter 2). In addition, many ethical theories combine, or claim to combine, universal and particular elements. As we examine different ethical traditions and theories, you will need to think about the *way* each of them is either universal or particular and to identify the fundamental grounds of disagreement between them (Browning 2006).

One of the earliest examples of a thinker using the term global to describe a distinctive field of ethical inquiry was the theologian, Hans Küng. In his book *Global Responsibility: In Search of a New World Ethic* (1990), Küng argues: 'without morality, without universally binding ethical norms, indeed without "global standards", the nations are in danger of manoeuvring themselves into a crisis which can ultimately lead to national collapse, i.e. to economic ruin, social disintegration and political catastrophe' (Küng 1990: 25). Küng bases his argument on the claim that there are economic, political and ecological challenges facing the world as a whole that can only be addressed by globally concerted action and that, for this to be possible, the world as a whole needs a shared ethical orientation. He goes on to argue that it is only in the world's religions that one finds commitment to both the universality and absoluteness of our ethical obligations. He claims, therefore, that the way to establish a global ethic that will command the agreement of all people in the world is through dialogue between the world's religious traditions which will identify and articulate common values that are fundamental to them all. Following Küng, there is now a growing literature on inter-religious dialogue as a way forward for Global Ethics (Sullivan and Kymlicka 2007).

For other theorists of Global Ethics, secular ethical theories provide the resources to address ethical problems inherent in globalization, for example, Peter Singer (*One World: The Ethics of Globalization*, 2004) and Thomas Pogge (*World Poverty and Human Rights*, 2008) (see chapters 4 and 5 for further discussion of Singer and Pogge). For both of these thinkers, as for Küng, we already have the ethical perspectives needed for Global Ethics as a field of ethical inquiry; it is just that they have yet to be applied to the distinctive challenges of globalization. Frost offers a different argument for why we already have the resources to address global ethical questions. In his case, ethical perspectives are understood as reflections of existing or emerging social and political orders. This means that Global Ethics essentially involves tracing and applying the norms already inherent in international society (state sovereignty) and in global civil society (human rights) (Frost 2009). In response to such views about the theoretical basis of doing Global Ethics, a variety of other thinkers have argued that what is needed is a kind of synthesis between existing perspectives which involves bringing the moral universalism of thinkers such as Singer and Pogge together with the contextualism characteristic of Frost's approach (see Dower 2007 and Erskine 2008).

In contrast, there are thinkers who argue for the need for more radical theoretical innovation in Global Ethics. Theorists such as Anthony Appiah (*Cosmopolitanism: Ethics in a World of Strangers*, 2007), Fiona Robinson (*Globalizing Care*, 1999) and Bikhu Parekh ('Principles of a Global Ethic', 2005) argue that existing dominant cultural and philosophical traditions for thinking about ethics and morality are inadequate for dealing with the ethical demands posed by a globalizing or globalized world (see also Cochran 1999 and Hutchings 1999 for attempts to forge new theoretical frameworks for International and Global Ethics).

> Each person you know about and can affect is someone to whom you have responsibilities: to say this is just to affirm the very idea of morality. The challenge, then, is to take minds

and hearts formed over the long millennia of living in local troops and equip them with ideas and institutions that will allow us to live together as the global tribe we have become. (Appiah 2007: xi)

Parekh argues that Global Ethics is neither the continuation of earlier traditions of ethical theory applied to contemporary global issues, nor equivalent to the investigation of existing institutionalized norms and values. He claims that there are two factors that render either of these accounts of Global Ethics inadequate to the challenge of globalization. Firstly, in a global world of plural values in which all are equally implicated in the consequences of globalization, there is no agreed normative or actual standard against which to justify the coercive imposition of some values over others. Secondly, the range of morally relevant players in a globalized world includes all kinds of collective, institutional actors (e.g. states, international non-governmental organizations [INGOs], international governmental organizations [IGOs], multinational corporations [MNCs]) as well as individuals. This rules out traditional moral theories that take the individual as the unit of moral concern and therefore do not take the collective dimensions of moral agency in our globalized condition sufficiently seriously. Although he dismisses religion as a source for a global ethic, Parekh shares with Küng a commitment to dialogue as the way forward to developing a global ethic. But whereas for Küng such a dialogue reveals an inner core of moral truths to which all of us essentially already consent, for Parekh, the dialogue is a messy and open-ended process which will produce, at best, compromise positions that may be agreed to for very different reasons by different participants.

Reflective exercise

Do you think Global Ethics should be about discovering or inventing commonalities of value? How important do you think existing religious traditions are/ should be in this process?

All of the above thinkers are agreed that Global Ethics is necessary in order to think through and address the ethical problems produced or intensified by globalization. But what exactly are theorists of Global Ethics doing when they do Global Ethics? What sorts of question does Global Ethics address? Earlier on in this chapter we referred to the kinds of questions that have been the focus of philosophical Ethics. These encompassed *why* questions about the basis of ethical claims, *what* questions about the substance of ethical claims, *who* questions about ethical agency and responsibility, and *how* questions about the ethical issues raised by the prescriptive implications of ethical values and principles. Doing Global Ethics is about investigating these kinds of question with specific reference to issues of global concern. Throughout this book we will be examining and evaluating different ways of responding to these questions within the Global Ethics literature.

Why should we adopt or reject particular ethical values and principles to guide our actions, or the actions of other individual and collective entities, in contexts of global relations and interaction? This kind of question has always preoccupied moral philosophers, who have been concerned to establish the kind of 'truth' involved in claims about the right and the good. Unlike empirical claims about facts, or logical claims about inference, or aesthetic claims about taste, moral claims are about ethical values. But on what grounds should we accept one account of what are the correct ethical values over another? Within Ethics, there is an established set of arguments in response to the *why* question which ground ethical claims in a variety of ways, from theological arguments that trace the authority of moral principles and values back to a divinity, to accounts that derive from natural law, human nature, human reason, types of contract, dialogue and sentiment (see below and chapters 2 and 3). In the context of Global Ethics, the question of what grounds ethical judgement and prescription is particularly difficult, given the extent and depth of the actual plurality of philosophical traditions involved when we are trying to formulate ethical principles that genuinely apply to everyone. For this reason, theorists of Global Ethics are often particularly preoccupied with the *why* question, about the grounds of validation of their substantive global ethical values and principles.

What is the substance of Global Ethics, what kinds of moral issue or moral claim counts as global? And what is the content of global ethical values and principles? If you examine the literature on Global Ethics, certain substantive issues are very clearly at the forefront. Dower, for instance, focuses on the following list: peace and war; aid, trade and development; and the environment. Küng has a similar list to Dower, and Singer identifies ecological issues, humanitarian intervention and issues of economic justice (Dower 2007; Küng 1990; Singer 2004). In a volume entitled *The Ethical Dimensions of Global Development* (Gehring 2007), the list is extended to cover issues of post-conflict transitional justice and the practice of female circumcision. If we examine the criteria by which a moral issue counts as global or not, then two factors seem to be particularly important: first, whether an issue crosses national borders in its origins and effects, a claim most often made for war/peace, environmental and economic issues in the contemporary world; secondly, an issue can count as global where there are obvious and deep disagreements between ethical values that have been brought together by processes of globalization, for example where international legal norms clash with local values, or where different cultural values clash within a particular local context. It should be noted that, if we accept that dealing with clashes of values that cross cultural borders is part of the concerns of Global Ethics, then issues that have traditionally been counted as part of 'private morality', the morality surrounding reproduction, sexuality and family life, are as much an aspect of the globalized condition as the morality of international aid. In what follows, different theories have different views about the range and depth of specifically global ethical concerns. But they all seek to specify a substantive response to questions about *what* values or principles are most appropriate for resolving or managing these global ethical concerns.

The *who* question takes us to debates, within Global Ethics, about the morally relevant actors within the global ethical field. This includes arguments over whether collective actors, as well as individual ones, have moral status. Such collective actors include most notably the state, which is clearly a being with considerable powers of collective agency in the field of world politics. But they may also include bodies such as transnational or multinational corporations, international governmental organizations, like the World Trade Organization (WTO) or the United Nations (UN), and international non-governmental organizations, from international charities such as Amnesty International, the Red Cross and Oxfam to transnational terrorist networks. Some theories are more concerned with some kinds of actors rather than others, but in all cases the *who* question is wrapped up with a series of further questions about the *nature* of the moral actor under consideration. Without some such account, theorists are unable to move from the *who* to the fourth, *how*, question. This final question asks how moral actors in the global ethical field relate to one another in terms of their ethical identities, entitlements, duties and responsibilities. If one has settled the question of the grounds and substance of global ethical claims and the potential set of relevant moral actors, then one needs to move on to settle the question of who owes what to whom – shifting the focus from philosophical questions about ethical judgement to the domain of prescription and action. Some theorists focus more on the *how* question in relation to individuals but for many the construction of global ethical principles entails action at an institutional, legal and political level.

In summary, in answer to the question about the nature and scope of Global Ethics, in this book it is defined as the systematic investigation of: (a) different accounts of how we are to ground the authority of moral claims about global issues (*why*); (b) different substantive answers to moral questions about war and peace, the global political economy, the global environment, clashes of incommensurate values exacerbated by globalized conditions (*what*); (c) different views about the identity and nature of morally relevant actors in the global sphere (*who*); and (d) different practical implications drawn from the above for the entitlements and obligations of individual and collective moral actors related to each other through conditions of globalization (*how*).

Do we already have an answer to the questions posed by Global Ethics?

As we have seen, theologians such as Küng, mentioned above, claim that we already have the resources to address the *why*, *what*, *who* and *how* questions of Global Ethics within existing world religions. Quite what counts as a world religion is contestable, but is normally seen to incorporate belief systems such as Hinduism, Confucianism, Taoism, Buddhism, Judaism, Christianity and Islam. All of these religions articulate ethical values and principles that should govern human behaviour and, between them, account for a very large proportion of the world's population, so it seems a reasonable starting point for efforts to arrive at global ethical standards. However, if we look more closely at the resources provided by religions for addressing the Global Ethics questions, then certain difficulties becomes apparent.

The first difficulty, which is underlined in Küng's argument, derives from the fact that, in many cases, the claims of religiously based ethics are embedded in a range of other beliefs and practices that refer to modes of existence beyond the material world. This is particularly obvious in religions that, as with the Abrahamic faiths, posit the existence of an all-powerful God and make very clear distinctions between the divine and the human. The *why* question in religiously based ethics is not something that can be answered wholly through philosophical argument or empirical evidence; it also requires faith and trust in a divine authority, which is often seen as scripturally located and/or embodied in certain roles, such as that of a priest. Even where religious traditions do not straightforwardly invoke other-worldly authorities, such as in Confucianism or Buddhism, there is still an established *tradition*, carried through writings and precepts, that in and of itself carries authority for its proponents, without need to refer back to some other set of supporting arguments. This element of faith and trust in the authority of religiously based moral claims has been professed to give such claims a peculiar resonance and persuasiveness (Sullivan and Kymlicka 2007: 238). But it also raises the question of what resources are provided by religiously based ethics for resolving disagreements between religions. Either, it would seem, such arguments are settled on religious grounds, in which case they take us back to fundamental incompatibilities of religious belief systems that only divine or spiritual authority can settle; or they are addressed by reference to philosophical arguments about the nature, purposes and capacities of humanity, and operate within the same vocabulary as secular ethical theories.

The second difficulty to note about religiously based ethics arises from the fact that they not only differ from each other in terms of their nature and scope, but they are also internally contested. Even where religious traditions are explicitly universal in principle (as in Confucianism, Christianity or Islam), as a matter of practice they have historically distinguished between 'insiders' and 'outsiders' and the kinds of ethical values that should govern relations between members of the same religious community as opposed to members and non-members. In addition, none of the religions cited above is a singular, uniform entity; there are deep divisions within religions about what it is that the authorities of scripture or of tradition tell us about ethics. The arguments over ethics within religious traditions, therefore, engage with the same kind of issues and problems that we also find in secular ethical theories.

The third difficulty involved in attempts to establish a global ethic on the basis of religion concerns its substantive content. Following the 'Parliament of the World's Religions' in 1993, which was inspired by Küng's call for a global ethic, the claim was made by representatives of religious traditions that there was a moral core that was common to all those traditions, and that this provided a stronger basis for a global ethic than secular philosophical argument. In the 'Declaration Toward a Global Ethic' that the parliament endorsed, there is a list of ethical commitments that were identified as inherent in all religions (Sullivan and Kymlicka 2007: 236). The principles of this global ethic are outlined in detail in the Declaration. They include as a foundational starting point the so-called 'Golden Rule', that is, the principle that one should treat all other people as one would wish to be treated oneself. Further principles are: commitment to non-violence and respect for life; commitment to human solidarity and a just economic order; commitment to tolerance and truth; commitment to equal rights for all and equal partnership between men and women. When one examines the Declaration, however, two things become clear. The first is that many of the principles are specified so generally that one would need a great deal of further argument to determine how they should be interpreted and applied. Given lack of theological agreement, addressing these questions of interpretation and application would therefore require engaging in theoretical argument. The second is that the Declaration makes clear that there is a sphere of ethics that remains specific to each religion aside from the ground that they share. This suggests a distinction similar to the one between 'morality' and 'ethics' introduced above, but how does one work out what belongs to the universal and what belongs to the particular? Again it would seem that we are back in the realm of theoretical argument.

In summary then, I argue that Küng's project of grounding a global ethic on the basis of consensus between the world religions necessarily involves engaging with the kind of theorizing which is the concern of this book. The religions do not provide us with a shortcut to answering the *why, what, who* and *how* questions of Global Ethics, although they do certainly provide one way into those questions. It is worth noting, for instance, that the theories with which we will be concerned in the next two chapters are largely derived from a western philosophical tradition that owes a great deal to the influence of Christianity.

Reflective exercise

- Compare the 1980 'Universal Islamic Declaration of Human Rights' (www.religlaw.org/interdocs/docs/cairohislam1990.htm) and the 1990 'Cairo Declaration of Human Rights in Islam' (www.religlaw.org/interdocs/docs/cairohrislam1990.htm). Are the moral priorities of these two documents the same?

Continued

- Read the 1993 Parliament of the Worlds' Religions' 'Declaration Toward a Global Ethic' (www. weltethos.org/pdf_decl/Decl_english.pdf, accessed December 2009). How persuasive do you find the case for commonality between the moral cores of different religions?

Outline of the book

Having sketched out the terrain of Global Ethics, it is now possible to explain and outline the structure of the rest of this book, and how it aims to introduce you to the various ways of addressing the *why*, *what*, *who* and *how* questions outlined above. There are two particular difficulties in keeping an introduction to Global Ethics accessible. The first is the extent and complexity of debates surrounding the *why* question in Global Ethics. Most of the contributions to Global Ethics take for granted a variety of reference points to moral theories with their own complex histories and internal debates. In order to grasp, and make judgements about, what differentiates two sides of a particular debate, it is often necessary to have a working knowledge of a range of moral concepts and perspectives, each of which is grounded in specific assumptions about the basis on which we can legitimate claims about right and wrong in the global context. The second difficulty is the sheer breadth of the subject matter. As you will see in the recommendations for further reading throughout this book, there are massive literatures devoted entirely to the ethics of global economic relations or the ethics of war, all of which in turn are dependent on a vast array of empirical as well as theoretical literatures. We can, of necessity, only touch the surface of these issues in the compass of a short book. The structure of the book aims to take these difficulties into account. But for any reader this should only be a starting point and further reading will be highlighted throughout the text (see advice on how to use this book below).

The next two chapters are intended to introduce you to the repertoire of responses to the *why* question in contemporary

ethical theory that are pertinent to the Global Ethics literature discussed in later chapters. Chapters 2 and 3 set out
ethical theories and point out some of the standard ways in
which they have been used and criticized. The aim here is not
only to inform you about moral theories with which you may
not be acquainted but also to begin to get you to practise the
assessment of such theories by weighing up their strengths
and weakness. This in turn should help you to reflect on your
own ethical assumptions and the grounds on which you
make judgements about moral rights and wrongs. Having
set out traditions of response to the *why* question in ethics,
the remaining chapters of the book explore how different
responses to this question have been brought together with
arguments about *what*, *who* and *how* in contributions to
debates in Global Ethics.

Chapters 4 and 5 will both focus on ethical issues arising
out of global socio-economic relations. Chapter 4 will focus
on the ethics of development and chapter 5 on theories of
global distributive justice. Chapters 6 and 7 will focus on the
ethics of war and the ethical challenges posed by 'peace'
respectively. As we will see, there are interconnections and
commonalities between what is ethically at stake in the arguments explored in chapters 4–7. In particular, I will suggest
that five issues emerge as of particular significance for Global
Ethics:

- the nature and basis of the ethical status of the individual
  human being;
- the relative ethical significance of the human individual as
  opposed to community or culture;
- the ethical significance of past interactions in determining
  moral entitlements and obligations for individual and collective actors;
- the relative ethical importance of procedure or process
  as opposed to outcome in responding to global ethical
  problems.

The ethical theories we will be considering in this book
provide different answers and arguments in relation to the
above issues. Adjudicating between these different answers
brings us to the fifth issue, which is fundamental to all of the
others:

- the question of whether and how ethical claims made by theorists of Global Ethics can be authoritative for a global audience. In other words, why should anyone accept one account rather than another of the moral status of human beings, the relative moral significance of community as opposed to individual, the moral significance of past inter-actions, and the ethical importance of procedure in rela-tion to outcome?

In chapter 8, I will argue that the fifth issue, the ongoing problem of formulating and addressing ethical questions in a way that is authoritative for a genuinely global audience, is fundamental to the future of Global Ethics as a branch of ethical inquiry. In order to explore this problem, I will focus on the phenomenon of clashes of ethical value between dif-ferent populations that have become particularly obvious and acute in conditions of globalization. I will suggest that mean-ingful debate within Global Ethics requires, above all, *ethical* ways of responding to such actual and potential clashes of ethical value. This leads me to argue that ethical perspectives that enable us to pay close attention to *who* and *how* ques-tions of Global Ethics make a particularly important contri-bution to the field. Global Ethics will only flourish in the longer term if it is genuinely open to all of the earth's human population to be participants in its debates, regardless of our particular identities and values.

How to use this book

This book is designed as an aid to teaching and learning. You will get the most out of it if you treat it as a starting point for further thinking, reading and discussion. The book is written as a continuous argument, with each chapter building on the previous one. In particular, chapters 4–8 all assume that you have read and understood the material in chapters 2 and 3. Each chapter makes suggestions for further reading and provides a brief comment on what each piece of further reading covers. The references are at the end of each chapter and include further introductory material as well as more advanced reading. You will only get a thorough understanding of the material covered in each chapter if you follow up on further reading. Each chapter also includes a series of reflective exercises. These exercises help you to check your comprehension of material covered and to develop your thinking about the issues explored in the book. Although many of the exercises can be done individually, they will often be most useful when used as the basis of discussion with others, inside or outside of the classroom. Where exercises refer to particular authors or theoretical perspectives, it will normally be helpful to do some further reading before you attempt them. The main point to bear in mind throughout the book is that to get a grasp of the complex ideas and issues that form the subject matter of *Global Ethics*, you need time to think and reflect. *Global Ethics* explores many difficult questions and a range of complex and fascinating ways of answering them. The purpose of this book is to guide you towards making up your own mind about the best way to respond to the ethical dilemmas of a global age.

References and further reading

Appiah, K. A. (2007) *Cosmopolitanism: Ethics in a World of Strangers*, London: Penguin Books. Argues that we need new modes of ethical thinking to respond properly to the changing nature of our ethical existence in a globalized world.

Boonin, D. and Oddie, G. (eds) (2005) *What's Wrong? Applied Ethicists and Their Critics*, Oxford: Oxford University Press. A Reader that includes a variety of examples of arguments in applied ethics putting the case for and against particular ethical positions on issues such as abortion, pacifism, euthanasia and so on.

Brown, C. J. (1992) *International Relations Theory: New Normative Approaches*, Hemel Hempstead: Harvester Wheatsheaf. Sets up the cosmopolitan/communitarian classification as a way of demarcating approaches to normative judgement in international politics.

Browning, D. (ed.) (2006) *Universalism versus Relativism: Making Moral Judgments in a Changing, Pluralistic and Threatening World*, Lanham: Rowman and Littlefield. A useful set of essays that looks specifically at the question of whether moral judgements can claim universal validity.

Cochran, M. (1999) *Normative Theory in International Relations*, Cambridge: Cambridge University Press. Argues for a way beyond the cosmopolitan/communitarian debate drawing on aspects of Rorty's and Dewey's pragmatism.

Copp, D. (ed.) (2006) *The Oxford Handbook of Ethical Theory*, Oxford: Oxford University Press. A collection of essays covering the ground of Meta-Ethics and Normative Ethics; it includes a useful introductory essay by Copp explaining the distinction between Meta-Ethics and Normative Ethics.

Dower, N. (2007) *World Ethics: The New Agenda*, 2nd edn, Edinburgh: Edinburgh University Press. Explores the field of global ethics using the cosmopolitan/communitarian distinction as an organizing principle. The book argues for a 'solidarist–pluralist' cosmopolitanism in which there are universal values and responsibilities but these are compatible with sensitivity to cultural diversity.

Erskine, T. (2008) *Embedded Cosmopolitanism: Duties to Strangers and Enemies in a World of 'Dislocated Communities'*, Oxford: Oxford University Press. Argues for a form of cosmopolitan ethical theory based on the extension of connections between communities rather than abstract universal principles, thereby creating a middle way between cosmopolitan (Pogge, Singer) and communitarian (Frost) alternatives.

Frost, M. (2009) *Global Ethics: Anarchy, Freedom and International Relations*, London: Routledge. Offers an account of global ethics in which global ethical values and principles follow from the 'rules of the game' of the current world order which, for Frost, is comprised of an inter-state society, governed by norms of (conditional) sovereignty and a global civil society governed by norms of human rights.

Gehring, V. V. (ed.) (2007) *The Ethical Dimensions of Global Development*, Lanham: Rowman and Littlefield. A collection of articles covering a range of issues in global ethics.

Held, D. (2004) *Global Covenant: The Social Democratic Alternative to the Washington Consensus*, Cambridge: Polity. Gives an overview of the problematic implications of economic and political globalization and an account of how they should be dealt with.

Held, D. and McGrew, A. (eds) (2003) *The Global Transformations Reader*, 2nd edn, Cambridge: Polity. A series of specialist essays about different sectors of globalization.

Held, D., McGrew, A., Goldblatt, D. and Perraton, J. (1999) *Global Transformations*, Cambridge: Polity. A useful early attempt to examine the meaning of globalization processes and to look critically at how advanced they were in practice.

Hirst, P. and Thompson, G. (1996) *Globalization in Question*, Cambridge: Polity. A critique of globalization theory which argued that globalization was much less advanced than some of its proponents were claiming.

Hutchings, K. (1999) *International Political Theory: Rethinking Ethics in a Global Era*, London: Sage. Argues for a new approach to international and global ethics based on Hegel and Foucault, and as with Cochran, seeks to get beyond the cosmopolitan/communitarian alternatives.

Küng, H. (1990) *Global Responsibility: In Search of a New World Ethic*, Eugene, OR: Wipf and Stock. This is one of the earliest arguments for an explicitly *global* ethic.

Lafollette, H. (ed.) (2000) *The Blackwell Guide to Ethical Theory*, Oxford: Blackwell. A useful compendium of introductory articles on different ethical theories.

Lechner, F. J. and Boli, J. (eds) (2004) *The Globalization Reader*, 2nd edn, Oxford: Blackwell. Puts together a range of readings from a variety of theoretical perspectives on globalization, from those that see globalization as highly advanced to much more sceptical accounts.

Mathews, J. T. (2004) 'Power Shift', in Lechner and Boli (eds), *The Globalization Reader*, pp. 270–6; excerpted from *Foreign Affairs* 76(1) (1997): 50–66. A discussion of the rise of global civil society and its growing importance in relation to the relative decline of state power.

McGinn, C. (1992) *Moral Literacy or How to Do the Right Thing*, London: Duckworth. A short and readable example of a moral philosopher putting the moral arguments for and against particular positions on abortion, euthanasia, animal rights and the use of violence.

Nardin, T. and Mapel, D. (eds) (1992) *Traditions of International Ethics*, Cambridge: Cambridge University Press. This is an account of moral traditions for thinking about international politics that covers Christian and secular positions.

Ohmae, K. (2004) 'The End of the Nation-State', in Lechner and Boli (eds), *The Globalization Reader*, pp. 214–18; excerpted from *The End of the Nation State: The Rise of Regional Economies* (1995), New York: Harper Collins, Free Press. Argues that in the economic sector the nation-state has lost its power in conditions of globalization.

Parekh, B. (2005) 'Principles of a Global Ethic', in J. Eade and D. O'Byrne (eds), *Global Ethics and Civil Society*, Aldershot:

Ashgate. An argument for a global ethic based on difference and dialogue.

Pogge, T. (2008) *World Poverty and Human Rights*, 2nd edn, Cambridge: Polity. This is an argument in which universal ethical principles are applied to questions of global distributive justice.

Robertson, R. and White, K. E. (2003) (eds) *Globalization: Critical Concepts in Sociology*, London: Routledge. A collection of essays on different theoretical approaches to globalization within sociology.

Robinson, F. (1999) *Globalizing Care: Ethics, Feminist Theory and International Relations*, Boulder, CO: Westview Press. An argument that challenges much standard work in international and global ethics and puts the case for a feminist alternative based on the feminist ethic of care.

Rosecrance, R. N. and Stein, A. A. (eds) (2006) *No More States? Globalization, National Self-Determination, and Terrorism*, Lanham: Rowman and Littlefield. Examines the impact of globalization on state power and on movements for national self-determination.

Singer, P. (ed.) (1993) *A Companion to Ethics*, Oxford: Blackwell. A comprehensive collection of introductory articles on Ethics, including essays on the history of ethics, Meta-Ethics, Normative and Applied Ethics.

Singer, P. (2004) *One World: The Ethics of Globalization*, 2nd edn, New Haven and London: Yale University Press. This is an argument that globalization processes necessitate the recognition of universal ethical responsibilities that have always existed.

Sullivan, W. M. and Kymlicka, W. (eds) (2007) *The Globalization of Ethics*, Cambridge: Cambridge University Press. A set of essays that examine a variety of secular and religious perspectives on global ethics, including Christianity, Islam, Confucianism, Buddhism and Judaism. This book includes as appendices the following documents, which can also be located on the web.

Asian Human Rights Charter (1998): http://material.ahrchk.net/charter/mainfile.php/eng_charter/

Bangkok Declaration (1993): http://law.hku.hk/lawgovtsociety/Bangkok%20Declaration.htm

Cairo Declaration on Human Rights in Islam (1990): www.religlaw.org/interdocs/docs/cairohrislam1990.htm

Declaration Towards a Global Ethic (1993): www.weltethos.org/pdf__decl/Decl_english.pdf

International Covenant on Civil and Political Rights (1966): www.hrweb.org/legal/undocs.html

International Covenant on Social, Economic and Cultural Rights (1966): www.hrweb.org/legal/undocs.html

Universal Declaration of Human Rights (1948): www.un.org/Overview/rights.html

Universal Islamic Declaration of Human Rights (1980): www.alhewar.com/ISLAMDECL.html

Watson, J. L. (2004) 'McDonalds in Hong Kong', in Lechner and Boli (eds), *The Globalization Reader*, pp. 125–32. Excerpted from *Golden Arches East: McDonalds in East Asia* (1997), Stanford, CA: Stanford University Press. An influential argument about cultural globalization that claims that different cultures adopt and adapt global brands in their own way, using the example of the way McDonalds operates in Hong Kong.

Wiarda, H. J. (ed.) (2007) *Globalization: Universal Trends, Regional Implications*, Boston, MA: Northeastern University Press. Examines the differential impact of globalization in a variety of countries and regions.

2
Rationalist Ethical Theories

Introduction

Most work on Global Ethics builds on the insights and arguments of existing ethical theories. In this chapter and the following one, the aim is to offer an introductory outline of ways of thinking about ethics and morality that have been influential within the Global Ethics literature. Before we begin our examination of ethical theories, readers should note that any attempt to classify and group moral theories is open to contestation. In other textbooks and overviews you will find a different listing of relevant ethical perspectives. Moreover, just because two theories both come under the same heading in my listing, that doesn't mean that they agree on all points; there are strong disagreements *within* as well as *between* ethical approaches, and they are not always as clearly distinguishable from one another as classification schemes would suggest.

This chapter focuses on rationalist ethical perspectives that first rose to prominence in Europe in the seventeenth and eighteenth centuries (Schneewind 1993), and which have helped shape debates in Global Ethics. The examples we will examine are: utilitarianism, contractualism, deontology and discourse ethics. These are all rationalist theories in two senses: firstly, for all of them different forms of rationality play an important part in providing the basis for the authority of ethical claims, and for differentiating ethical claims from the claims of pure self-interest or subjective feeling; secondly, for all of them, the foundations of ethics can be discovered and explained through the exercise of reason by the ethical theorist, in abstraction from the contexts and concerns of actual ethical debates. The aim of the chapter is to introduce you to the basic assumptions of these rationalist ethical perspectives. In later chapters we will see how a variety of thinkers use these perspectives to address particular global ethical issues. To help you make the connection between the rather abstract discussion below and the concerns of Global Ethics, each of the reflective exercises asks you to think about the implications of each ethical theory for a particular global issue that is discussed later in the book.

Utilitarian ethics

Consequentialist ethical theories argue that the moral worth of particular ethical values and principles depends on the goodness or badness of the outcomes of adopting those principles for individual human beings and aggregates of individual human beings. These kinds of theories are based on assumptions about the nature and motivations of human beings and claim to be derived from material truths about the human condition. In this sense, they run counter to the religiously based approaches to ethics that had dominated in European thought until the seventeenth century. *Utilitarianism* is the most well known and influential form of consequentialist ethics (Pettit 1993; Shaw 2006).

As we will see, most ethical theories draw a qualitative distinction between what motivates ethics or morality on the one hand and the gratification of our individual, selfish desires on the other. Utilitarianism questions this distinction and redraws it in quantitative rather than qualitative terms. Bentham (1748–1832), the founder of utilitarianism, based his arguments on a view of human beings as naturally driven towards pleasure (happiness) and away from pain (unhappiness) and therefore having an interest in pursuing the former and avoiding the latter. On this basis, he built up an ethical theory that had one founding principle, the principle of utility: 'Always act so as to maximize the greatest happiness of the greatest number of people.' He therefore does away with the distinction between moral and non-moral motivation. To act morally, for Bentham, is to act *impartially* so as to promote the fulfilment of as many desires for individual happiness as possible. This clearly doesn't mean that Bentham was promoting selfishness at an individual level; he was insistent that in our moral calculations every individual counted equally, so there could be no *moral* justification for putting one's own interests ahead of anyone else's.

Bentham's version of utilitarianism has been subject to major criticisms and has been modified by later utilitarian thinkers. In particular, his attempts to reduce moral judgement to a *felicific calculus*, in which one could somehow compute the relative weight of happiness or unhappiness to be caused by particular actions, has been subject to ridicule. There are all sorts of problems about how you can foresee outcomes in enough specificity, whether you count only immediate or also medium- and long-term outcomes, and, even more fundamentally, how you measure happiness or unhappiness in the first place. Subsequent utilitarian thinkers, such as J. S. Mill (1806–1873), complicated things further by introducing qualitative distinctions between different sorts of 'happiness', arguing that ethical judgement required differentiation between the lower pleasures to be derived from acts such as eating a sandwich as opposed to those higher pleasures to be derived from acts such as solving a complex mathematical equation (see Frey 2000 for a more detailed introduction to utilitarianism).

In addition to the difficulties involved in working out happiness/unhappiness implications, a further criticism of utilitarianism related to the fact that the principle of utility is an aggregate, majoritarian principle. Critics have pointed out that this meant that it could justify the misery of a small number of people to promote the happiness of many. In twentieth-century debates over the merits of utilitarianism as a moral philosophy, scenarios abound in which the death or torture of a few innocents may be justified in the light of the achievement of the happiness of many. At a more mundane level, if every act were to be subject to a fresh utility calculation, then it would seem that utilitarianism was quite compatible with lying, stealing and cheating, as long as these actions promoted the happiness of the greatest number of people. In response to these kinds of criticisms, utilitarian thinkers introduced the idea of 'rule' utilitarianism as opposed to 'act utilitarianism'. In the case of rule utilitarianism, rather than looking at every act in isolation, instead moral rules should be assessed for their overall contribution to utility for everyone. On these grounds, it has been argued, established ethical principles that outlaw murder, stealing, lying and so on are justified because they work, in general, to promote utility. To act contrary to those principles, even if that may seem to promote utility in a given instance, would actually diminish general utility over time. Even with rule utilitarianism, however, the moral touchstone remains the principle of utility – if it could be shown that killing or lying worked for the maximization of the greatest happiness of the greatest number over time, then the utility principle necessarily trumps our attachment to the worth of moral values, virtues or principles in themselves (see Tännsjö 2002: 25–40 for a useful summary of critiques of utilitarianism; see also Glover 1990; Smart and Williams 1973; Vallentyne 2006 for more thorough critiques of utilitarian and consequentialist thinking).

Bentham was deeply committed to social reform, and it is clear that the principle of utility has a radical cutting edge. For a start, utilitarianism is uncompromisingly universal in both its grounding and its application. According to utilitarianism, every human being is essentially the same (a being driven by the desire for pleasure and the fear of pain) and is of equal significance to every other. The principle of utility calls for all implications of an action to be considered on an impartial basis. From the utilitarian point of view, everyone's happiness is as important as everyone else's and there is no logical reason why the boundaries of moral obligation should be drawn at the borders of the city-state or the nation. More controversially, it could, contrary to its claims to being an egalitarian moral theory, allow for trade-offs in favour of majorities, permitting the suffering of the few in pursuit of the happiness of the many.

For Bentham, utilitarianism follows from rationally apprehensible facts about what people are like and can therefore be applied to any and all individuals. From the utilitarian point of view, we can only give ethical weight to our attachment to specific moral principles or our culturally ingrained values and practices insofar as they contribute to general utility. This differentiates utilitarianism both from theories that want to treat certain values or principles as of absolute ethical value (such as deontological theories discussed below) and from theories that give ethical priority to norms and values embedded in practices and ways of life (see discussion of virtue ethics in chapter 3). For utilitarianism, then, it is possible to make a clear distinction between 'ethics' and 'morality' (see discussion in chapter 1 above). Utilitarian morality operates as a higher-order way of judging the relative merits of the values and principles embedded in particular ways of life.

Reflective exercise

Utilitarianism has had an important influence on ethical debates about global poverty and war (discussed in chapters 4, 5 and 6 below). Consider the following questions:

- Do you think that a utilitarian would see global economic inequality as morally wrong? Give reasons for your answer.
- How might the moral rightness of the use of weapons of mass destruction in war be defended on utilitarian grounds?

Contractualist ethics

Bentham and Mill were writing in the eighteenth and nineteenth centuries, but the utilitarian model of human nature, as driven by desire for pleasure and fear of pain, owed a lot to the work of the earlier, seventeenth-century thinker, Thomas Hobbes (1588–1679). In Hobbes's case, however, different implications were drawn from the account of human nature for how we make distinctions between ethical rights and wrongs. Hobbes built his argument about human morality on the basis of a rigorous procedure, which worked from premises about human nature to a fully-fledged account of the origins and nature of morality and politics. In order to do this, he famously made use of the analytic fiction of a 'state of nature', in which individuals existed without any form of social, legal or political authority and organization. In such a context, Hobbes argues, there is no meaningful distinction between just and unjust. According to Hobbes's materialist account, human individuals are 'matter in motion', each of them a self-contained machine driven by negative (fear) and positive (desire) energy, but with the capacity for instrumental reason, so that they can calculate how to attain or avoid outcomes. Fear and desire, on Hobbes's account, may manifest themselves in all sorts of passions, but there is one fundamental fear/desire that is common across all human beings: the fear of death and the concomitant desire for self-preservation. When Hobbesian individuals are put in a state of nature, in which there is no external regulation of their activities, Hobbes argues that there will be a condition of war of 'all against all'. This is not necessarily because individuals are inherently nasty and evil, but because, without any guarantees of their own security, they are obliged, by their overwhelming fear of death/desire for self-preservation, to accumulate as much power to themselves as possible in order to pre-empt the possibility of attack from others. This grasping of 'power after power', in a situation that, we infer, is not one of abundance of material goods, renders clashes between people inevitable. But because of conditions of rough equality of abilities that Hobbes builds into his model of the state of nature, a settled outcome to conflict within that state is rendered unlikely, except perhaps through external conquest.

Hobbes's story of the state of nature, therefore, puts individuals in an impossible situation in which they are forced by their insecurity into behaviour that renders them even more insecure. As Hobbes puts it, life in the state of nature is 'solitary, poor, nasty, brutish and *short*', and the shortness in particular runs entirely contrary to people's most fundamental desire, the desire to live. This contradictory position, in conjunction with individuals' capacity for instrumental reason, provides a self-interested motive for getting out of the state of nature for each person. Because of the entire absence of trust between human beings in their natural state, they can't just decide to stop killing each other; there needs to be something else that can ground the possibility of them living in peace. The answer, Hobbes argues, can be found in the idea of an agreement, something that he terms a 'covenant' and that has become known as the idea of a 'social contract'. In Hobbes's argument, individuals in the state of nature contract with each other to trade off their individual natural rights to pursue their own self-preservation by all available means. Because there is no inherent reason to trust each other's agreement to this trade-off, the agreement is secured through the creation of an overarching authority (sovereign) with the power to coerce individuals into keeping their word. In effect, the sovereign is authorized by the parties to the contract giving up their natural rights to this new, overarching power. Only at this point, Hobbes argues, does it become meaningful to make distinctions between justice and injustice. Because only now do we have a reliable ground of justification for such distinctions. This ground can be found in the fact that those distinctions have been authorized by an agreed, mutual transfer of power.

Hobbes's argument exemplifies a contractualist approach to ethics because it grounds claims about right and wrong ultimately in the authority of the voluntary consent of individuals, conceived as having certain fundamental characteristics. For many subsequent thinkers, the apparent amoralism of Hobbes's account of human nature and the behaviour of individuals in a state of nature constituted a problem. The idea that notions of 'justice' could only make sense *after* the contract was particularly contentious. It seemed that, for Hobbes, it wasn't possible to draw lines between the domains of morality and politics or law in terms of distinct principles of legitimation. Later contractualist arguments, such as that of Locke (1632–1704), built more elaborate assumptions into their account of the natural rights of individuals in the state of nature, so that one could differentiate between what grounded *moral* rights and wrongs from what grounded *legal* or *political* rights and wrongs (see discussion of natural law below). Nevertheless, the idea that the authority of ethical claims derived from voluntary consent was a tremendously powerful one. It reflected the view that came to predominate in modern western thought, and which was also essential to Bentham's utilitarianism, that the individual was in some sense ethically primary, the source and not simply the object or agent of ethical concern.

Unlike in utilitarianism, however, contractualist thought, precisely because of the reliance on voluntary agreement, put certain limits on the kinds of trade-offs that could be acceptable between human beings. Even Hobbes found it inconsistent with his own argument that individuals should consent to be killed by sovereign authority, since this would defeat the purpose for which the contract had been instituted. He therefore acknowledged the possibility and permissibility of a lapse back into natural right in the post-contract society, in which individuals retained the right to avoid harm by fleeing judicial punishment, and the right to buy themselves out of the obligation to fight on behalf of the sovereign. Other contractualist thinkers found that institutions such as slavery could not be legitimate according to the contractual principle of consent, since slavery contradicted the natural right of the person to dispose of their own bodily skills and capabilities. Underlying contractualist argument, therefore, is always a particular conception of the rational individual, and that conception is crucial for the implications of any given contractualist ethical theory (see Kymlicka 1993; Sayre-McCord 2000; Tännsjö 2002: 47–55 for overviews of contractualism and the different forms it can take in ethical theory).

In addition to a conception of the individual, contractualist argument always also relies on an account of the situation that gives rise to contract. The circumstances that generate contract and that, along with the conception of the individual, generate the contract's authority, are differently articulated by different thinkers. Substantively, accounts of the circumstances necessitating contract vary from the lethal insecurity of Hobbes's state of nature to the much more socialized and regulated accounts of our natural condition in Locke's work. In addition, in Hobbes's case the state of nature is posited as a hypothetical thought experiment, whereas in Locke it is identified with actual, historical circumstances.

Recent contractualist arguments in moral and political theory treat contract hypothetically. Most famously, in *A Theory of Justice* (1971), Rawls drew on the inspiration of the social contract tradition to formulate an account of the meaning and requirements of justice. The principles of justice that he articulated were legitimated by reference to the choices rational individuals would have made if deliberating on principles of justice appropriate to people in a situation in which mutual cooperation is required, behind what he called a 'veil of ignorance'.

As with all contractualist arguments, the crucial elements of Rawls's account were his assumptions about pre-contractual individuals, and his assumptions about the circumstances of the contract. His assumptions about individuals were that they were rational in the sense, like Hobbes's individuals, of being able to work out what it is in their own interests to do. Unlike Hobbes, however, although Rawls saw his pre-contractual individuals as self-interested, they were not essentially driven by a primal desire for self-preservation. This is because Rawls's individuals do not know any specifics about *who* they are; they deliberate under what Rawls called a 'veil of ignorance'. This means that they know general things about human nature and behaviour, about history, social institutions, different ways of organizing political communities and so on. And they are also aware that in the society they are engaged in setting up they could be *anyone*, both personally (greedy or unselfish) and socially (rich or poor). However, they therefore don't know what their particular desires and interests will be and need to choose principles of justice which will maximize their chances of pursuing those desires and interests *whoever* they may be. On the basis of these assumptions, Rawls argued that the principles of justice that would follow from the 'original position' of individuals behind the 'veil of ignorance' would include a list of fundamental individual rights and freedoms, which would be guaranteed to all. In addition, however, he argued that in terms of economic or distributive justice, people in the original position would agree first to a principle of equality of opportunity, and secondly to what he calls the 'difference principle'. The latter, which has been the subject of extensive debate, is the principle that any inequality in wealth could only be justifiable if it also worked to the advantage of the worst-off in society.

In *A Theory of Justice*, Rawls's argument is directed, in particular, against utilitarian accounts of justice. In contrast to utilitarianism, Rawls's reworking of the contractualist tradition embeds a fundamental respect for the rights of each individual by basing itself in the consent of individuals who, because they *could be anyone*, effectively represent the interests of *everyone*. No one would want to be the innocent person sacrificed to save the lives of twenty others, so fundamental rights that cannot be traded off are built into Rawls's account of justice. Both substantively and procedurally, Rawls's contractualism echoes that of earlier examples of the social contract tradition. Substantively, the grounding of ethical principles in consent ensures the non-negotiability, however minimal, of certain fundamental individual rights. Procedurally, the legitimacy of the claims made is argued to lie in a set of premises which, if not entirely self-evident, are nevertheless presented as straightforwardly intelligible and plausible to any rational reader. As with utilitarianism, contractualism claims to be universally salient as a way of making sense of the authority and nature of moral claims. As such it acts, like the principle of utility, as a critical standard against which ethical values and principles can be judged.

Much of the debate around contractualism in ethics centres on the foundational assumptions contractualist theories make about individuals and their circumstances, and on the ethical weight to be carried by individual consent. Critics routinely point out that contractualist assumptions are not as neutral or universal as is claimed. For instance, Rawls has been argued to smuggle both masculinist and western assumptions into his account of the individual in the original position (see Okin's and Walzer's critiques of Rawls discussed in chapters 3 and 5 below). There are also a variety of problems with the role of consent in contractualist theory, both because of problems of identifying what is meant by consent (active agreement, tacit agreement, hypothetical agreement) and because of the ways this apparently limits moral obligations to relations of reciprocity that can be construed as having been entered into voluntarily. Unlike utilitarianism, which embraces all of humanity equally in its scope of application, contractualism justifies making distinctions between those people with whom one is in contractual community and those who are outside the contract (see Freeman 2006 and Pettit 2006 for a debate about the pros and cons of contractualist approaches in moral theory. For a recent contractualist moral theory building on Rawls's work, see Scanlon 1998).

Reflective exercise

- Contractualism requires foundational assumptions about human individuals. Do you think there is such a thing as human nature? And, if so, what do you think it is like?
- Contractualism has played a particularly important role in debates in Global Ethics about the nature and extent of moral obligations to those who are not members of the same political community. Do you think the *moral* arguments for using income from taxation to fund health and education provision for fellow citizens are different to the *moral* arguments for using such taxation income to support poverty relief abroad?

Deontological ethics

Both utilitarian and contractualist ethical theories rely on the idea that human beings are instrumentally rational in the sense of having the capacity to calculate how to maximize their interests. Deontological moral theories argue for a rule-based approach to ethics in which moral principles have an absolute and categorical prescriptive status. As we saw in the previous chapter, some religiously based ethics are deontological in character, in particular those that ground moral claims in divine, and therefore unquestionable, authority. On such accounts, moral claims have the status of truths. Within the Christian tradition in medieval times, knowledge of moral truth was understood to be available through the revelation of the scriptures, but it was also accessible through natural reason, which could know the principles of what was called natural law even without the benefit of scripture. Natural law was a code embedded in all human beings that reflected the true ends of human existence, and thus provided the basis for working out what it was right or wrong for humans to do. In the seventeenth and eighteenth centuries in Europe, the idea that natural law was in some sense innate in human beings, and accessible through reason, was an important counter to the kinds of philosophical anthropology we find in Hobbes. However, in the Enlightenment period, western moral philosophers increasingly moved away from relying on explicitly Christian assumptions. Instead versions of utilitarian or contract theory arguments, which relied on supposedly demonstrable accounts of human nature, became increasingly important. Nevertheless, the idea, originating in Christian thought, that the prescriptions of moral law were somehow inherent in humanity, and could be grasped rationally, independently of the realm of passions and interests, did not disappear. Most famously, it was revived in the moral theory of Kant (1724–1804).

Kant's moral philosophy was part of a broader philosophical project, critical philosophy, in which he sought to settle ongoing philosophical disputes about how to ground knowledge claims about the nature of things, moral claims about what is right or wrong and aesthetic claims about what is beautiful or ugly. At the heart of Kant's critical philosophy was a set of arguments about how human capacities are limited and conditioned. In the context of morality, we were, on Kant's account, limited and conditioned by our susceptibility to being swayed by natural passions and desires (as in Hobbes's view of human nature). At the same time, however, according to Kant, we were also possessed of a faculty of self-legislating (pure practical) reason which, if we so chose, gave us the possibility of transcending and overriding motivation by the passions and acting on the basis of pure practical reason instead. Reason in this context was not contextual judgement on the basis of experience nor an instrumental capacity that helped us get from A to B. Rather, it was the distinctive capacity of being able to discern and act on what the moral law required. To act on the basis of pure practical reason meant to act according to the requirements of the moral law, which also meant that acting morally was ultimately equivalent to acting rationally in this special sense. Kant's argument is clearly reminiscent of natural law arguments that see natural law as somehow inscribed within each human individual, but in Kant's case, however, the recognition of what is rational and moral relies neither on the invocation of God as the author of the moral law, nor on a generalized account of human nature. If we were angels, Kant argues, we would automatically know and do what is right. Because we are not, we need some way of working out what the moral law requires. His answer to how this can be done relies on an unpacking of the formal character of deontological moral principles.

Kant's account of moral principles stressed two factors: first that they are universally prescriptive in form, and secondly that our moral rightness depends not simply on acting *according to* those moral principles but crucially on acting *because* of those moral principles. To do the right thing for the wrong reasons is not to act morally on Kant's account because it is to fail to ground one's actions in the self-legislating power (autonomy) of pure practical reason. For Kant, then, there are two elements in doing what is right. First, one must work out what is the right thing to do, which means identifying the requirements of the universal moral law, and second, one must act on that basis, rather than because it happens to be in one's interest or one happens to feel like doing the right thing at that moment (see O'Neill 1993 and Hill 2006 for more thorough introductions to Kantian ethics).

The criterion of universality is central to how Kant argues that a non-angelic human being can work out the right thing to do. In his famous 'universalization test', he claims that you can work out whether a proposed action is morally right by examining the prescriptive principle (maxim) underlying the action and working out what would happen if that maxim were universally applied as a moral principle. So, if one were contemplating telling a lie in order to protect someone's feelings, then one would need to think about what the implications would be if the principle 'always lie to protect someone's feelings' were to be a universally applicable prescription. In Kant's view, as soon as this maxim was universalized we would be faced with the absurdity of never being able to trust what people say. We therefore know that lying is wrong and one *ought to* act on this basis, regardless of either our own feelings or those of others.

Kant summarized the requirements of morality or pure practical reason in what he called the 'categorical imperative'. There are several formulations of this imperative in his work but two are of particular significance still in contemporary ethical debate. The first formulation states that one should 'act only on maxims that one can consistently will to become universal laws'. This clearly reflects the universalization test idea and is supposed to help us to detach what is morally right from contamination by our particular feelings, identities and interests. A later formulation, which is somewhat different, states that one should 'never treat others solely as means but always also as ends-in-themselves'. The meaning of this may seem a little obscure, but when unpacked it follows from Kant's view that morality is grounded in a faculty of autonomous pure practical reason which all humans possess and which sets them apart from other living creatures. In treating others as 'ends-in-themselves', we are acknowledging and respecting the source of humanity's unique worth which is that it is capable of transcending the determination of nature. To treat a human being solely as a means, for instance by enslaving him or her, is to violate what makes humanity special and reduces not the enslaved but rather the enslaver to the condition of an animal incapable of respecting the self-determining moral law. To the extent that a person capable of knowing the moral law acts in violation of it, then he or she is guilty of immorality and should be held responsible for what he or she has done.

Kant's moral theory is often used as the counter to Bentham's utilitarian ethics. Where Bentham stresses the importance of utility as an outcome, Kant stresses the significance of moral principles regardless of their consequences in specific contexts. Where Bentham allows for a trade-off of the rights of some in pursuit of the maximization of utility, Kant insists on the necessity of respecting every individual as an end in him- or herself. Nevertheless, Kant's arguments, like Bentham's, have been subject to major criticisms, in particular the idea of the universalization test which many have argued doesn't actually provide any self-evident guidance for what can and cannot be consistently universalized (Tännsjö 2002: 56–72 for an overview of Kantian deontology; see Davis 1993 and Kerstein 2006 for the pros and cons of deontology in contemporary moral philosophy).

The most common objection to Kant's moral theory, however, made by utilitarians and contractualist thinkers alike, is that it is too abstracted from context and too demanding as a set of moral prescriptions (Davis 1993: 217–18; Tännsjö 2002: 60–73). As with utilitarianism and contractualism, Kantian moral theory draws a distinction between morality and ethics but in the case of Kantian moral theory this line is drawn in such a way as to rule out the moral salience of contractual relations, interests, emotion and desire altogether. Kant's universalism is not bound by conceptions of human nature; his claim is that the moral law stands for all rational beings, human or non-human. The difference between humans and angels is not to do with different moral standards, but with human imperfection that means that we experience moral rules as a constraint on our non-rational drives and desires.

Reflective exercise

Deontological ethics endows all human beings with an absolute moral status. This has significant implications for thinking about killing and punishment within Global Ethics (see chapters 6 and 7 below). Think about the following questions:

- How might a deontologist object to utilitarian defences of the use of weapons of mass destruction in war?
- How might a utilitarian object to a deontological argument that, in the aftermath of war, war criminals must be hunted down and punished?

Discourse ethics

Utilitarianism, contractualism and Kantian deontology locate the foundations of ethics in the individual, as utility maximizer, as a bearer of natural rights or as a being capable of moral self-legislation. Discourse ethics, in its different forms, criticizes the individualist and rationalist assumptions of the first three types of moral theory, but in a way that seeks to hold onto the idea of the rational foundations and universal scope of ethical claims. The most influential proponent of discourse ethics is Habermas.

The starting point of Habermas's moral theory is Kantian deontology, and the kind of distinction that it draws between morality and ethics. For Habermas, Kant is right that moral claims have a universal form and provide a critical standard that can be applied across different contexts. Without the possibility of such claims, for Habermas, there could be no criteria by which to judge entrenched cultural practices as morally wrong, such as happened historically in the cases of slavery and torture, which used to be considered acceptable and are now seen as morally abhorrent. For this reason, Habermas sees ethical theories that embed ethics in social and cultural contexts as inherently conservative and incapable of accounting for moral progress. In addition to this, however, Habermas also argues that in *modern* societies there is a strong movement towards recognizing that certain principles are and *ought to be* universalizable. Habermas allows for the possibility that there may be a whole range of values that can orient and inform the way we live our lives, but argues that we need to distinguish the 'good' in this latter sense, which is always context specific and may take a plurality of forms, from the 'right', which must take the form of universalizable principles. The right helps us to determine what kinds of versions of the good life are morally permissible.

The form and substance of Habermas's moral theory follows Kantian lines, but it departs radically from Kant in terms of its response to the *why* question. For Habermas, the foundations of Kant's argument are untenable. They involve undemonstrable claims about the moral subject, including the invocation of a notion of pure, transcendental reason, and therefore essentially collapse into metaphysical assertions about the human condition. For Habermas, this is the hallmark of what he terms 'monological' theorizing, in which the philosopher is somehow supposed to be able to work out moral truth through contemplation of the individual moral agent. Utilitarian and contractarian groundings of ethics fall into the same problem; in both cases they entail assumptions about human beings that are claimed to be self-evidently reasonable but that cannot be rationally demonstrated. Habermas, therefore, looks for an alternative way of grounding moral claims, one that could securely underpin a distinction between morality and ethics, the good and the right. And he finds this alternative in discourse – dialogue rather than monologue (see Edgar 2006: 44–6; Habermas 1990, 1993; Outhwaite 1994: 38–57; Rehg 1994).

Habermas's discourse ethics is embedded in a broader theory of communicative action and reason, to which it is impossible to do justice here. The key point to bear in mind, however, is that this broader theory involves shifting the grounding of all kinds of claims about the world, scientific as well as normative, from an extra-linguistic foundation (empirical, logical or metaphysical) to the procedure of communication itself. From this point of view, claims are valid or invalid, not because of their mirroring of an external truth, but because they are agreed to under conditions of fair argumentation. The conditions of fair argumentation themselves are inherent in the presuppositions of communication, for instance the fact that there can be no successful communication if people lie consistently, or if certain people are consistently silenced or misrepresented. In taking part in an argument, according to Habermas, participants necessarily rely on certain rules and assumptions that make that argument possible, and if they breach these rules and assumptions they are enacting what he calls a 'performative contradiction' by denying that on which they simultaneously rely (for example, the claim 'I am lying' is a performative contradiction in this sense). An argument can only actually be an argument if proper communication is possible. Proper communication relies on the absence of coercion and manipulation, neutralizing, as Habermas puts it, 'all motives other than that of the cooperative search for the truth' (Habermas 1990: 86).

In the context of moral theory, Habermas uses this idea of performative contradiction to demonstrate that sceptical claims that universal moral principles are impossible to justify are undermined by assumptions sceptics themselves make in putting their argument forward (they rely for instance on the universal value of truth-telling: Edgar 2006: 104–5). He goes on to argue that, following simply from the explication of the presuppositions of a process of argumentation about a contested norm, consent to that norm could only follow if 'the consequences and the side-effects which the *general* observance of a controversial norm can be expected to have for the satisfaction of the interests of *each individual* can be *freely* accepted by all' (Habermas 1990: 90). He calls this a principle of universalization and clearly sees it as fulfilling the same function as Kant's universalization test, something that must hold if any norm is to count as genuinely moral. What follows from this is a principle of discourse ethics, which is effectively the Habermasian categorical imperative: 'only those norms can claim to be valid that meet (or could meet) with the approval of all concerned in their capacity as participants in a practical discourse' (Habermas 1990: 90; Moon 1995).

Habermas makes a very strong claim that his principle of discourse ethics is formal and does not prejudge the substance of moral norms. The latter need to be decided through actual discourses in which the moral theorist does not have a privileged position, unlike in the monological moral theories of which he is critical. Nevertheless, the parenthetical 'or could meet' in the discourse ethics principle above suggests that it might be possible to identify (or rule out) moral norms in principle, even without an actual moral debate taking place. Habermas himself explicitly rules out what he calls 'evaluative' claims as potential moral norms. These are values that express conceptions of the good life inherently tied up with culture and identity and therefore *in principle*, he claims, are incapable of being decided rationally. In addition, the presuppositions of argumentation themselves, which involve the protection of the right of all to participate, and the absence of coercion or exclusion of those concerned, suggest principles of equality, freedom and individual right that are out of keeping with, for instance, hierarchical assumptions about humanity.

Habermas argues that, although communicative reasoning is universally present in all human societies, some kinds of society are more conducive to recognizing and institutionalizing its critical possibilities than others. For Habermas there is a process of collective 'moral learning' that occurs historically. Modern societies are morally superior to previous social forms because they explicitly embed the principle of universalization inherent in communication, the principle that, as he puts it, 'cuts like a knife' between evaluative claims about the good life and normative claims about the universally right (Outhwaite 1994: 58–67). For Habermas, the presuppositions of successful communication provide a way of detaching moral reasoning from particular ways of life without relying on metaphysical assumptions, accounts of human nature, or presuming the rightness or wrongness of any particular moral principle in advance (Warnke 1995).

Habermas's discourse ethics appears to *democratize* moral theory by grounding moral authority in that which could be inter-subjectively agreed. Critics of his argument fall into two camps. There are those that see his project as failing entirely, either because it collapses into the Kantian assumptions that it claims to transcend, or because it is premised on mistaken views about the nature of communication or of ethics (such critics include virtue, feminist and postmodernist ethical theorists, discussed in chapter 3 below). However, there are also many critics who see the communicative justification of the universality of moral principles as a promising route forward but argue that Habermas's version of communicative ethics needs to be reformulated (for instance, Benhabib, discussed in chapters 5 and 8 below: Benhabib 1990, 1992). In both cases, criticisms tend to cluster around the account that Habermas gives of the presuppositions of communication and argumentation, and the extent to which they are practicable and plausible. In terms of practicability, as Habermas himself admits, the idea of an argument in which all affected had an equally respected voice, and in which there was a complete absence of external coercion and internal prejudice, is an ideal which could never be realized in practice. This tends to undermine his claim to have escaped from the abstraction of traditional moral theory. In terms of plausibility, a common criticism is that Habermas's account of what makes communication possible is overly narrow and rationalistic, too much influenced by cognitivist models of communicative practice, in which a particular model of the rational subject and of moral truth is assumed in a way that can only be justified by reference back to the kinds of substantive assumptions that he claims to reject (Benhabib 1992: 182–5).

Discourse ethics aims to avoid being committed to a strong account of human nature or transcendental reason. Nevertheless, there are clearly elements of discourse ethics that correspond quite closely to the role of consent in contractualism, as well as to the Kantian deontological requirement that moral principles are universal in form. However, from the discourse ethicists' point of view, there is something different going on here, most importantly that the *why* question in moral theory is not being answered in terms of assumptions about individuals as rational utility maximizers or as having the capacity to identify the demands of pure practical reason. Instead, the authority of ethical claims is grounded in communicative rationality, which is necessarily embedded in inter-subjective processes. This means that the approach to thinking about moral questions is, for the first time, linked to what we could reasonably expect others to accept in an actual interaction, as opposed to what follows from maximizing our own interests in the hypothetical abstraction of the state of nature or original position, or independently submitting our maxims to a universalization test.

Reflective exercise

Imagine a debate under fair conditions of argumentation between citizens of rich states and citizens of poor states about the justifiability of current global economic inequality. Would such an argument necessarily result in an agreement to redistribute wealth from the rich to the poor? Is it a performative contradiction to claim that moral values are purely subjective?

Conclusion

Although all of the ethical theories discussed above are rationalist, they are clearly not rationalist in the same way, and this leads to differences as well as commonalities in their procedural and substantive implications. We will conclude with a brief account of these differences and commonalities, and then move on to point to how the ethical theories discussed here are applied in the Global Ethics literature. In the next chapter we will turn to recent arguments that take issue with all of the theories discussed so far and to the comparative assessment of the full range of theoretical perspectives.

Utilitarian and contractualist ethics share the assumption that ethics is derivable from a set of claims about the human nature of individuals. In both cases the idea of the individual as naturally a desiring creature, possessed of instrumental reason and the capacity to choose, is essential. For utilitarians, however, there is no particular ethical weight attached to the idea of consent; the emphasis instead is on the outcomes that all individuals are argued to desire or fear. In contrast, contractualists see consent as the crucial basis for the legitimacy of ethical principles, although they differ between themselves in their views about what human beings would or could consent to accept. Both utilitarians and contractualists enshrine principles of individualism and of equality in their theories, but do so differently. With utilitarians, individual equality means that the happiness of any human being counts as the same as the happiness of any other, but it is the aggregation of happinesses that counts in the end – there are no non-negotiable trade-offs according to the principle of utility. For contractualists, in contrast, individual equality is captured in terms of natural individual freedom which puts certain constraints on the kinds of relations and practices to which humans could consent. This attaches contractualist ethical theories to the idea of non-negotiable individual *rights*. In both cases, however, ethics relies on the calculation of individual interest in a context in which human beings are obliged to cooperate with each other. There is no pre-existing, inherent link between the individual and a broader humanity.

In the case of Kantian deontological ethics, human beings are conceived of as torn between natural passion and transcendental reason, with the capacity to act according to either. Here we find a form of reason at work that has more in common with religious conceptions of natural law implanted in humanity by God than with the calculative reason of utilitarianism and contractarianism. We also find a different understanding of freedom than the negative freedom characteristic of the contractualist tradition and its conception of humans as choosers. Kantian moral agents are also choosers, but they are not choosing between a set of desires; they are choosing whether to follow the requirements of self-legislating reason, or to act on the basis of desires and preferences. Kantian ethics is a rule-based ethics. It shares, though for different reasons, with contractualist ethics the idea that there is a non-negotiable ethical worth inherent in the human individual, which means that Kantian ethics can also lend itself to the idea of a moral language of rights. In this respect, both Kantian and contractualist arguments line up against the potential utilitarian willingness to trade off the rights of some against the gains of others. However, the Kantian emphasis is, ultimately, more on the absoluteness of the *obligations* inherent in the moral law than on the inalienability of our *rights*.

Discourse ethics can be seen as combining aspects of contractualism, with its emphasis on agreement, and Kantian deontology, with its emphasis on the categorical and universal status of certain moral principles. In this respect, as with contractualism and deontology, discourse ethics is lined up against utilitarianism, the focus on aggregative outcomes and the possibility of ethical trade-offs. Having said this, however, there is also a sense in which discourse ethics takes us into a different kind of world of ethical theory. This is a world in which the ability of the philosopher, sitting in his or her armchair, to derive substantive ethical principles is challenged. In this respect, discourse ethics provides something of a bridge between the rationalist theories discussed in this chapter and the theories that we will be discussing in the following chapter which also criticize the idea that moral principles can be derived from abstract philosophical reasoning.

All of the above theories, individually and in combination, are influential in contemporary debates in Global Ethics. Singer, for example, builds on the insights of utilitarianism to make a moral argument for the global redistribution of wealth (see chapter 4). In contrast, Rawls extends his contractualist account of justice within the state to argue for a theory of international justice in which the requirements for economic redistribution are limited (see chapter 5). Pogge, in the meantime, drawing on elements of both contractualist and deontological thinking, argues for compulsory schemes of global distributive justice (see chapter 5) and Forst, drawing on discourse ethics, argues for global democratization as the prerequisite for global justice (see chapter 5). Norman provides a deontological argument for pacifism, and Anscombe a deontological argument for the justification of war (see chapter 6), and utilitarians and deontologists clash over the moral centrality of bringing war criminals to justice (see discussion of Orend and Bellamy in chapter 7). Benhabib builds on discourse ethics as the basis for resolving moral dilemmas of immigration (chapter 5) and clashes of cultural values in a globalized world (chapter 8). In all of the above cases, which will be explained and explored below, you will only be able to understand and assess the argument being made for a particular global outcome if you have a grasp of the ethical perspective that underlies that argument.

References and further reading

Benhabib, S. (1990) 'Afterword: Communicative Ethics and Current Controversies in Practical Philosophy', in S. Benhabib and F. Dallmayr (eds), *The Communicative Ethics Controversy*, Cambridge, MA: MIT Press, pp. 330–69.

Benhabib, S. (1992) *Situating the Self: Gender, Community and Postmodernism in Contemporary Ethics*, Cambridge: Polity. A series of essays in which Benhabib argues for a moderated version of Habermasian communicative ethics.

Bentham, J. (1982 [1789]) *An Introduction to the Principles of Morals and Legislation*, ed. J. H. Burns and H. L. A. Hart, London: Methuen.

Copp, D. (ed.) (2006) *The Oxford Handbook of Ethical Theory*, Oxford: Oxford University Press.

Davis, N. A. (1993) 'Contemporary Deontology', in Singer (ed.), *A Companion*, pp. 205–18. A critical discussion of the limitations of deontological ethical theories.

Dreier, J. (ed.) (2006) *Contemporary Debates in Moral Theory*, Oxford: Blackwell.

Edgar, A. (2006) *Habermas: The Key Concepts*, London: Routledge. Includes entries for all of Habermas's main concepts including 'discourse ethics' and 'performative contradiction'.

Freeman, S. (2006) 'Moral Contractarianism as a Foundation for Interpersonal Morality', in Dreier (ed.), *Contemporary Debates*, pp. 55–75. An argument in favour of contractualism that claims that it forms a middle way between a purely egoistic position and the pure impartiality of act utilitarianism.

Frey, R. G. (2000) 'Act-Utilitarianism', in Lafollette (ed.), *Blackwell Guide*, pp. 165–82. An introductory overview of act utilitarianism.

Glover, J. (ed.) (1990) *Utilitarianism and Its Critics*, New York: Macmillan. A collection of essays dealing with the pros and cons of utilitarianism.

Habermas, J. (1990) 'Discourse Ethics: Notes on a Program of Philosophical Justification', trans. S. Weber Nicholsen and C. Lenhardt, in F. Dallmayr and S. Benhabib (eds), *The Communicative Ethics Controversy*, Cambridge, MA: MIT Press, pp. 60–110.

Habermas, J. (1993) 'Remarks on Discourse Ethics', in *Justification and Application*, trans. C. Cronin, Cambridge: Polity, pp. 19–111.

Hill, T. E. (2006) 'Kantian Normative Ethics', in Copp (ed.), *Oxford Handbook*, pp. 480–514. An introductory overview of Kantian ethics.

Hobbes, T. (1991 [1651]) *Leviathan*, ed. R. Tuck, Cambridge: Cambridge University Press.

Kant, I. (1981 [1785]) *Grounding for the Metaphysics of Morals*, trans. J. W. Ellington, Indianapolis: Hackett.

Kerstein, S. J. (2006) 'Reason, Sentiment, and Categorical Imperatives', in Dreier (ed.), *Contemporary Debates*, pp. 129–43. An argument for a deontological rationalist approach to ethics against perspectives that ground ethics in feeling or sentiment.

Kymlicka, W. (1993) 'The Social Contract Tradition', in Singer (ed.), *A Companion*, pp. 186–96. Introductory overview of contractualism as an ethical perspective.

Lafollete, H. (ed.) (2000) *The Blackwell Guide to Ethical Theory*, Oxford: Blackwell.

Locke, J. (1988 [1690]) *Two Treatises of Government*, ed. P. Laslett, Cambridge: Cambridge University Press.

MacIntyre, A. (1967) *A Short History of Ethics: A History of Moral Philosophy from the Homeric Age to the Twentieth Century*, London: Routledge and Kegan Paul. See chapters 10, 14 and 17 for coverage of Hobbes, Kant, Bentham and Mill.

Mill, J. S. (1962 [1861]) *Utilitarianism*, ed. M. Warnock, London: Fontana.

Moon, J. D. (1995) 'Practical Discourse and Communicative Ethics', in White (ed.), *Cambridge Companion to Habermas*, pp. 143–64. An in-depth account of Habermas's discourse ethics.

Norman, R. (1983) *The Moral Philosophers: An Introduction to Ethics*, Oxford: Clarendon Press. See chapters 6 and 7 for coverage of Kant and Mill.

O'Neill, O. (1993) 'Kantian Ethics', in Singer (ed.), *A Companion*, pp. 175–85. An introductory account of Kantian ethics which includes a consideration of standard criticisms and potential responses.

Outhwaite, W. (1994) *Habermas: A Critical Introduction*, Cambridge: Polity. A useful introduction to Habermas's work as a whole and the link between his ethical and social theory.

Pettit, P. (1993) 'Consequentialism', in Singer (ed.), *A Companion*, pp. 230–48. An introductory overview of ethical consequentialism, including utilitarianism.

Pettit, P. (2006) 'Can Contract Theory Ground Morality?' in Dreier (ed.), *Contemporary Debates*, pp. 76–96. A critical response to contractualist moral theory.

Rawls, J. (1971) *A Theory of Justice*, Oxford: Oxford University Press.

Rehg, W. (1994) *Insight and Solidarity: A Study of the Discourse Ethics of Jürgen Habermas*, Berkeley: University of California Press. One of the few English language books devoted to Habermas's ethics, it is useful in particular for how it situates Habermas's discourse ethics in relation to other ethical perspectives.

Sayre-McCord. (2000) 'Contractarianism', in Lafollette (ed.), *The Blackwell Guide*, pp. 247–67. A useful overview of different types of contractualist argument.

Scanlon, T. (1998) *What Do We Owe to Each Other?* Cambridge, MA: Harvard University Press. A contractualist moral theory that builds on some of Rawls's work.

Schneewind, J. B. (1993) 'Modern Moral Philosophy', in Singer (ed.), *A Companion*, pp. 147–57. A brief introduction to the history of modern moral philosophy in European thought from the sixteenth century.

Shaw, W. (2006) 'The Consequentialist Perspective', in Dreier (ed.), *Contemporary Debates*, pp. 5–20. A defence of ethical consequentialism.

Singer, P. (ed.) (1993) *A Companion to Ethics*, Oxford: Blackwell.

Smart, J. J. C. and Williams, B. (1973) *Utilitarianism: For and Against*, Cambridge: Cambridge University Press. A classic version of the debate for and against utilitarianism as a moral theory.

Tännsjö, T. (2002) *Understanding Ethics: An Introduction to Moral Theory*, Edinburgh: Edinburgh University Press. A useful introduction to ethical theory, it includes chapters on utilitarianism, contractualism and deontology.

Vallentyne, P. (2006) 'Against Maximising Act Consequentialism', in Dreier (ed.), *Contemporary Debates*, pp. 21–37. A critique of full-blown act-utilitarian arguments.

Warnke, G. (1995) 'Communicative Rationality and Cultural Values', in White (ed.), *Cambridge Companion to Habermas*, pp. 120–42. A discussion of the way Habermas draws his distinction between morality and ethics that relates Habermas's argument to the work of Walzer, amongst others.

White, S. K. (ed.) (1995) *The Cambridge Companion to Habermas*, Cambridge: Cambridge University Press. A collection of essays covering the full range of Habermas's philosophical work.

3
Alternatives to Ethical Rationalism

Introduction

In the past thirty years there have been a variety of critiques of the answers to the *why* question embedded in rationalist moral theories. These critiques themselves take different forms and some are more radical than others in their criticism of particular strands of the kinds of moral theory discussed in the previous chapter. For our purposes, these critiques are significant because they have also inspired ways of thinking within Global Ethics and are part of ongoing debates within the field. As with the theories considered before, however, these critical perspectives were not originally formulated with Global Ethics in mind. The aim of this chapter is to offer an introductory exposition of these alternative theories of ethics so as to enable you to reflect on their assumptions and implications for the nature of moral judgement and action in general. In what follows I outline three broad perspectives in ethical theory that take issue with ethical rationalism: virtue ethics; feminist ethics; and postmodernist ethics. The reflective exercises will, as in the previous chapter, help you to begin to think about the implications of these perspectives for issues in Global Ethics to be discussed later in the book. Readers should bear in mind the point made in the previous chapter, that any attempt to classify theories in a particular terminology is always contentious and never exhaustive.

Virtue ethics

Traditions of virtue ethics base ethical values in traits of character. In other words, virtue ethics takes its starting point from what kinds of people are morally good or bad, as opposed to from moral rules or principles. Versions of virtue ethics can be found in many religious traditions and it is often claimed to be the way of thinking about right and wrong that is most common historically across different cultures. In western philosophy, virtue ethics is usually traced back to the classical Greek thought of Aristotle (384–322 BCE) (Rowe 1993). As a philosophical account of ethics, it was also tremendously important in medieval Christian thought, which drew directly on Aristotle's work, and it has a more recent history within modern, secular moral and political philosophy. In the last thirty years, virtue ethics has been explicitly revived as an alternative to the rationalist ethical theories of utilitarianism, contractualism and deontology (Annas 2006; Tännsjö 2002: 91–103).

Aristotle had a highly differentiated understanding of the nature of different kinds of human lives (for instance making very strong, hierarchical distinctions between the souls of free men, slaves and women). But he argued that, depending on which kind of human you were, it was possible to differentiate between being that kind of human in better or worse ways. The standards for 'better or worse' were inherent in the purposes (or *telos*) that the natures of different kinds of human being were designed to serve. Aristotle was particularly concerned with what it meant to live the best kind of life as a free male citizen. And he described how flourishing as a free man involved cultivating virtues of temperance, justice, prudence and courage. In describing the meaning of these virtues, Aristotle saw them as embedded in the way of life that, to him, expressed the highest excellence of which men were capable. The particular excellences of each of the virtues were tied up with ideas about what was necessary to sustain a stable and wealthy city-state, in which men (some men) were responsible for the proper government, defence and enrichment of that city-state. It's in this context that Aristotle's idea of the 'golden mean' of virtue makes sense.

For him, virtue was often about finding a middle way between excess and lack. For example, someone who was recklessly brave to the point of foolhardiness and someone who was completely cowardly were, for Aristotle, both less worthy than the person who had courage but was able to make judgements about when and how to take risks. Temperance and prudence are crucial virtues precisely because they help to moderate extremes and encourage men to tread the proper middle path (MacIntyre 1967: 57–83; Norman 1983: 37–55).

It's clear from the above account that Aristotle's ethical philosophy was contextual, in the sense that it was embedded in a particular way of life and reflected, amongst other things, the social hierarchies of his day. However, it would be misleading to assume on this basis that Aristotle did not see his account of the virtues as having implications beyond his context. On the contrary, Aristotle saw the Greek city-state as embodying the highest ideals for human life and human well-being, at the individual as well as the collective level. This was therefore a model of human flourishing with general application. Moreover, his ethical philosophy also includes another element that transcends specific context, the notion of *phronesis* (usually translated as 'practical reasoning'). One of Aristotle's quarrels with his predecessor Plato, and Plato's account of his own mentor, Socrates, was that the latter both argued that we could arrive at ethical truths in the same way as mathematical or metaphysical truths. Aristotle, on the contrary, made a clear distinction between intellectual reasoning, such as we might use in mathematics, and the kind of reasoning we engage in when confronted with ethical choices. As Aristotle noted, it was not uncommon for young people to have well-advanced skills of intellectual reasoning that went beyond those of their teachers. However, it was very rare indeed for young people to demonstrate the ability to make good judgements about right and wrong independently of what they had been taught (in Ancient Greece, as now, there were infant prodigies when it came to mathematics but not many infant moral sages). As Aristotle saw it, this was evidence for there being a separate faculty of *phronesis* that emerged out of education and experience and that was linked to the development of people's character over time.

Phronesis is clearly distinguishable from the instrumental rationality of utilitarian and contractualist thinking, but also from 'pure practical reason' in Kantian deontology. *Phronesis* cannot be reduced either to chains of deductive inference from self-evident premises or to empirical claims about what is or is not the case. Neither is it a faculty that can be developed through individual contemplation alone; it is an inherently social capability, arising from, and contributing to, human community (see Annas 2006: 516–19 for a discussion of practical reasoning).

We find versions of virtue ethics being revived in seventeenth- and eighteenth-century Europe as counters to utilitarian and contractarian ethical theories. Where Aristotle put his emphasis on a capacity for *phronesis*, which was inseparable from the cultivation of the virtues for enabling us to distinguish right from wrong, Hutcheson (1694–1746) and a range of other ethical philosophers grounded morality in a 'moral sense' that connected each person to humanity in general and made us value both our own virtue and that of others. Although the basis of the argument is different, thinkers such as Hutcheson shared ground with Aristotle both in the emphasis on virtue rather than utility as being at the centre of ethics, and in the connection he made between the ethical individual and the community of which she is a part. For Hutcheson, the four cardinal virtues of temperance, courage, prudence and justice were at the centre of ethics because they were universally necessary to promote the public good. The public good, in principle, was as wide as the scope of humanity itself so there was no hard and fast distinction between our moral identities as members of a specific community and our moral identities as members of the human race. This theme was continued in Hume's (1711–1776) moral theory, which also grounded ethics in our feeling for virtue, though in a modified version in which our moral feeling is nurtured and cultivated through what Aristotle would have termed intellectual reason.

In the later eighteenth century until the latter part of the twentieth century, debates in moral philosophy turned away from thinking about ethics in terms of character, and the idea of moral feeling or moral sense was largely discredited. Nevertheless, insights from the virtue ethics tradition remained important in the critique of utilitarianism, contractualism and deontology in both ethics and politics. Hegel (1770–1831) drew on the Aristotelian tradition in his critique of Kant's moral theory, which he argued abstracted the individual from the social and cultural contexts that made moral judgement and action meaningful. Marx's (1818–1883) account of the alienation of humanity under capitalism was influenced by an Aristotelian notion of human flourishing. And he used this idea to criticize the atomic, instrumentally rational, rights-bearing conception of the individual that was central to contractualism. In place of the prevailing focus on rights in moral philosophy, Marx argued for the ethical centrality of the concept of human *need* (MacIntyre 1967: 199–214; Norman 1983: 145–201).

The kind of critique of rationalist moral theories made by thinkers such as Hegel and Marx was revived in moral theory in the latter part of the twentieth century. Most well known amongst contemporary versions of virtue ethics has been the work of MacIntyre whose book, *After Virtue* (1981), criticized alternative modern deontological, contractarian and consequentialist ethical traditions from the point of view of a version of Aristotelianism (see Nussbaum 1986 for another example of a contemporary revival of Aristotelian ethics). MacIntyre's work has inspired a massive secondary literature and has developed in various ways since the publication of *After Virtue*. But at the heart of his initial argument was the claim that virtues were a better guide to distinguishing right from wrong than basing moral argument in supposedly universally valid principles derived from decontextualized accounts of human reason or desire (which is what he argued dominant deontological and utilitarian theories did). The reason that virtues were a better guide was that they were already embedded in a variety of social contexts and practices, as well as in broader traditions of moral thought. Within these contexts, the criteria for what counted as 'excellences' were already built in, in the same way as what it means to play chess well is already implicit in the rules of the game. For MacIntyre, therefore, the link between individual and community already noted in previous examples of virtue ethics is very much emphasized, to the extent that ethics is presented as always a contextual matter. However, the term 'context' should not be interpreted too narrowly. In his recent work, MacIntyre develops a vision of the virtues that is tied to a general account of the human condition.

> The virtues that we need, if we are to develop from our initial animal condition into that of independent rational agents, and the virtues that we need, if we are to confront and respond to vulnerability and disability both in ourselves and others, belong to one and the same set of virtues, the distinctive virtues of dependent rational animals, whose dependence, rationality and animality have to be understood in relationship to each other. (MacIntyre 1999: 5)

As is evident in the above quotation, MacIntyre makes the conception of *need* foundational to ethics, as opposed to a conception of right. The meaning of need and the responsibility to respond to it is engrained in an account of human flourishing, something that MacIntyre sees as only possible within particular communities. In profound contrast to the model of the human being as a rational 'chooser', MacIntyre stresses the importance of affect, vulnerability and dependency in human life. In keeping with the traditions of virtue ethics, he rejects instrumental reason or Kantian self-legislation as the key to acting rightly, instead reintroducing Aristotelian *phronesis*. *Phronesis* has to be cultivated in relation with others; it enables independence of judgement and action but always within a context in which the limits on what it would be reasonable and right to do are already implicit. There is room for criticism of the status quo in MacIntyre's ethical theory, but it is far removed from the radicalism of the kind of cutting edge that thinkers such as Bentham or Habermas identified with genuine morality (Tännsjö 2002: 91–105).

Virtue ethics is at odds with utilitarianism, contractualism and deontology in its fundamentally social assumptions about humanity and in its understanding of *phronesis* (Annas 2006; Pence 1993; Slote 2000). For virtue ethicists it isn't possible to separate the individual from the broader community and ethics is always already inherent in the institutionalized relations between human beings, although different virtue ethicists have different views about what these links involve, and how much they restrict the scope of ethics to particular communities (see, for instance the contrast between Nussbaum and Walzer, both discussed below and in chapters 4 and 5). The idea of the atomistic individual as the basic building block for ethical argument makes no sense from a virtue perspective. Moral reasoning is neither purely instrumental nor somehow self-legislating; it is a capacity that relies on experience and character, and is therefore inseparable from *who* you are. Ethics, for virtue theorists, therefore, is about the cultivation of character, or of the good life, rather than the maximization of a particular value or obedience to a moral law expressed in terms of prescriptive rules.

Critics are particularly concerned with the implications of virtue ethics for moral judgement. From the virtue ethics point of view, moral judgement is always contextual and there are no impartial or transhistorical criteria that can be identified through which decisions about the right or wrong response to moral dilemmas could be determined. From utilitarian and deontological points of view, virtue ethics has a place when it comes to the moral education of human beings, but it fails to confront the question of how it is possible to determine rights and wrongs when it is ways of life themselves that are in question. In other words, what criteria can we find in virtue ethics for the moral condemnation of practices inherent in certain ways of life, such as slavery (a practice that Aristotle accepted without question)? As we will see, the charge of ethical conservatism or complacency is also one made against virtue ethics by feminist critics (see debate between Hursthouse 2006 and Driver 2006 for an argument about the pros and cons of virtue ethics).

Reflective exercise

The planet is threatened with destruction because of global warming and the rapid using up of the earth's resources. What would be an appropriate ethical response to this situation? How do you think the response of a virtue theorist to this question would differ from that of a utilitarian or a deontologist?

Feminist ethics

Feminist ethics is a branch of feminist philosophy. Feminist philosophy originated in a critique of the assumptions of traditions of western philosophy in general because, feminists claim, they reflect a systematic privileging of male over female, masculine over feminine and men over women. This critique extends from the classical thought of Plato and Aristotle to the modern philosophy of Descartes and Kant (Fricker and Hornsby 2000). Feminist ethics, like virtue ethics, is critical of answers to the *why* question given in rationalist ethical theories. In addition, however, feminists are also suspicious of virtue ethics in contemporary as well as classical versions. Feminist ethics takes a variety of forms but it has been most influential in the version known as the 'ethic of care'. In what follows I will first of all outline the feminist critique of different mainstream ethical theories and then move on to examine the feminist ethic of care in more detail and its relation to other strands of feminist ethical thought.

In our examination of Aristotelian virtue ethics above, we saw that Aristotle incorporated a hierarchical understanding of humanity into his vision of the good life. On Aristotle's account, women were naturally inferior to men and played very little part in the account of the virtues and human flourishing that he offered. Modern virtue ethics does not share Aristotle's explicit attachment to the idea of women's inferiority but, from a feminist point of view, virtue ethics has, on the whole, continued to valorize accounts of the good life in which there is little recognition of women's moral agency and value, and in which gendered hierarchies of power remain unquestioned. At the heart of feminists' discomfort with virtue ethics is its dependence on the embeddedness of the virtues in existing practices and ways of life. The problem, for feminists, is that this makes it difficult to identify criteria on which those existing practices and ways of life could be challenged. This problem becomes particularly acute when the 'way of life' in question is identified with dominant cultures since, in so many cases, dominant cultures repress women and devalue their contribution to the good life in general. In spite of this, however, we will see below that feminist and virtue ethics do have quite a lot in common as critics of utilitarian, contractualist and deontological ethics. In the case of care ethics there are also more substantive areas of agreement with virtue ethics.

Feminism is a modern ideology; its origins are bound up with the same historical processes that underpinned the emergence of utilitarianism and contractualism in which the individual became the reference point for both moral value and the validation of moral claims. From the feminist point of view, however, the model of the individual as a rational 'chooser' is highly problematic. On both utilitarian and contractualist accounts, the moral agent is presented as independent and instrumentally rational, with complete discretion over his or her own body and capabilities. In contractualist accounts, in addition, the individual is often explicitly or implicitly assumed to be a property-owning citizen and head of household. Feminists argued that this view of the individual was clearly premised on the specific identity of adult men or of a subset of adult men (white, able-bodied, middle class). This was because it was only adult men that approximated to the model of an embodied human being that was never pregnant, never physically dependent and had the legal and political status of a property-owning citizen at the time in which these ethical theories were formulated. What became screened out by these accounts were not just women, children and other categories of men, but whole aspects of human life to which patterns of dependency and internal physical connection were central. In modern market societies, these aspects were relegated to the *private sphere* of family and household and either entirely taken for granted or valued only insofar as they supported the realm of independence, the *public sphere* of civil society, market and state. Feminists argued that this resulted in a distorted account of moral agency and of the nature and scope of moral values and moral judgement (Cole and Coultrap-McQuin 1992; Tronto 1993). The feminist critique of contractualism is exemplified in Okin's criticism of Rawls's theory of justice. Okin argued that Rawls's gendered assumptions about individuals in the original position, behind the veil of ignorance, enabled the justice of existing family structures in western societies to be taken for granted (Okin 1989).

Feminist critiques of deontological and discourse ethics also point to the paucity of the assumptions about humanity that underlie these theories. Here it is the disembodied rationalism of the answers to the *why* question that is seen to be at fault. For feminists, both Kant and Habermas perpetuate the western tradition of a fixed and hierarchical distinction between reason and emotion in which the former is linked to masculinity and the latter to femininity. On investigation, feminists argue, this binary hierarchy is untenable and sets up moral claims to fail by identifying what is right with a series of impossibilities. In Kant's case, the impossibility of moral judgement wholly unaffected by either feeling or consequences, and in Habermas's case the impossibility of consensus arising out of debate under conditions of fair argumentation for all affected. This linking of morality to an abstract and unattainable 'ought-to-be', feminists argue, dematerializes ethics even further than theories that rely on conceptions of human nature and confirms the exclusion of supposedly 'emotional' and 'fleshy' women from the parameters of ethics (Tännsjö 2002: 106–10).

It's clear from the above that feminist discomfort with mainstream ethical theories stems from the latter's implication in systems of thought that sustain the oppression of women, but also from the idea that mainstream theories exclude ethically significant aspects of human life and sources of moral value. We can see both of these elements at work in the study that kick-started research in contemporary feminist ethics, Gilligan's *In A Different Voice: Psychological Theory and Women's Development* (1993). As the title suggests, Gilligan's book is not a work of moral philosophy as such but of social psychology. In it, Gilligan used evidence from the actual moral reasoning of women to argue against the prevailing model of human moral development which, in the work of Kohlberg, identified moral maturity with deontological ethics. According to Kohlberg, human beings reached moral maturity when, as in Kantian and Habermasian arguments, they acquired the ability to detach themselves from circumstances and act according to universal moral principles. As long as they continued to take their cue from the specificities of their situation, then individuals remained morally immature. Whilst agreeing that deontological moral reasoning was a mark of moral maturity, Gilligan argued, on the basis of her research, that there were also forms of contextual moral reasoning that were equally mature. The women in her study, in response to moral dilemmas, rather than abstracting themselves out of the situation and seeking a universal rule to govern conduct, made decisions on the basis of embedded relations of care and responsibility between relevant moral actors (Tännsjö 2002: 110–13). Famously, Gilligan referred to deontological reasoning as expressing an 'ethic of justice' and contextual reasoning as expressing an 'ethic of care'. Feminist philosophers took up the idea of an ethic of care as an alternative approach to ethics that would avoid the masculinism and exclusions of mainstream ethical theories (see Held 1993, 2006a, 2006b).

The ethic of care is, like virtue ethics, a contextual and relational ethics. In place of the cardinal virtues of classical virtue ethics and their link to the flourishing of men in the public sphere, however, the ethic of care locates the source of moral value in the practices, relationships and responsibilities of care on which the public sphere depends. Care is thus able to provide a critical perspective on the values that govern public life as well as providing the model for virtue in the private sphere. An example of care ethics can be found in the work of Ruddick who bases her argument on the virtues inherent in the relation between mother and child (Ruddick 1990). Ruddick's argument exemplifies care ethics in two respects: firstly, she locates the source of moral value and moral judgement in the virtues inherent in caring work, in which neither responsibility nor power is equally distributed. In place of the equal situation of 'individuals' in a state of nature, we are presented with dependencies and inequalities, and in place of the flourishing citizen as our ethical end, we are given the flourishing human being who will themselves be able to recognize and act appropriately on the responsibilities of care. Secondly, there is no clear distinction between 'reason' and 'feeling' in Ruddick's argument; rather there is an idea of emotional intelligence in which feelings are a crucial part of what it means to be a morally functioning human being. Ruddick outlines a set of values and virtues that follow from the practice of maternal care, what she terms 'maternal thinking', and argues that these values and virtues should also orient our behaviour towards more remote others in the public sphere as well as the private sphere, applying her ethics, in particular, to issues of war and peace. What follows is an ethics in which needs and responsibility, as well as sensitive contextual judgement, are central as opposed to an emphasis on rights and duties coupled with abstract reasoning.

Criticisms of care ethics, both feminist and otherwise, have predominantly come from two directions: deontological or postmodernist (see Grimshaw 1993 and Jaggar 2000 for examples of feminists making these objections to care ethics). From the deontological point of view, the contextualism of care ethics collapses the distinction between morality and ethics and thereby makes the same mistake as traditional virtue ethics in identifying the right with the good, thus contradicting the inherent universalism of certain moral claims. For example, the ethic of care has been criticized for drawing the boundaries of moral obligation at the limit of those to whom one has caring responsibilities. It has also been argued that the valorization of care risks removing the ground of critique of the existing sexual division of labour and thereby risks reinforcing a distinction between private and public spheres that operates to maintain gendered relations of power. For this reason, many feminists have upheld an 'ethic of justice' against Gilligan's 'ethic of care', as with Okin, who criticizes Rawls's contractualist argument from a feminist perspective, but then extends the Rawlsian argument to cover the private sphere. In particular 'justice' feminists have taken issue with any suggestion that the fact that women give birth confers on them some kind of moral privilege (Okin 1989).

The latter criticism is common too from postmodernist critics, who complain that the ethic of care is in danger of universalizing what is in fact a highly particular socio-historical model of family relations, peculiar to modern western societies. Rather than accusing care ethics of being too particular, such critics see it as being too general because of the way in which it generalizes about the nature and experience of women and women's values (see below). In spite of these criticisms, however, care ethics has acquired a stronger profile than other feminist ethical arguments within debates over moral theory. From the perspective of virtue ethics, in particular, it has been identified as a potentially compatible approach. MacIntyre, in his later work *Dependent Rational Animals* (1999), praises care ethics for grasping the moral significance of human vulnerability and dependency and identifies maternal care as a practice which is key to the development of virtue in general.

Reflective exercise

Do contractualists, utilitarians and deontologists identify *human* with *man*? Imagine a debate between a deontologist and a feminist about the rights and wrongs of imposing economic sanctions on an aggressive state. To what extent do you think they would agree or disagree in their ethical assessment of this kind of international action?

Postmodernist ethics

Virtue ethics and feminist ethics depart from ethical rationalism in the ways in which they ground their ethical theories. Nevertheless, they both retain two features that are also inherent in the theories discussed in the previous chapter. Firstly, both argue that it is possible to ground claims about ethics in general and also to establish grounds for distinguishing between what is ethically right or wrong, better or worse. Secondly, both assume an understanding of moral agency in which the moral subject is a coherent, unified entity with the capacity to know and to do what is right. It is these two features, shared by all of the ethical theories considered so far, that are the object of radical critique from a postmodernist perspective.

The term 'postmodernist' is a highly contentious one and I am using it here in a specific and stipulative way. The term 'postmodern' originally described an architectural form that drew eclectically on a variety of styles and challenged the uniform rationalism of 'modernist' building. It was later used to describe features of late-twentieth century industrial, market societies, which had moved from the centralized, large-scale patterns of social and economic organization to more fragmented and decentralized forms. In addition it has become used to signify arguments in philosophy and social theory that reject the idea that there are universally valid criteria for determining truths about the world (Lyotard 1984). For the purposes of this book, I am using the term to cover a body of thought about ethics that challenges foundationalism of all kinds. Ethical foundationalism encompasses any ethical theory that argues that there is a fundamental ground for moral judgements, for instance, in truths about human nature or human reason. One of the founders of postmodernism as the critique of foundationalism is the philosopher Nietzsche (1844–1900). In his book *On the Genealogy of Morality*, Nietzsche argued that utilitarian and deontological foundationalist moral claims disguised the instinctive (as opposed to rational) origins of morality in the resentment of the weak and poor against the powerful and rich (Nietzsche 1994). Contemporary postmodernist critics of foundationalism include poststructuralist thinkers such as Derrida (Critchley 1992; Derrida 1992, 1997) and Butler (Butler 2004a, 2004b, 2009; Loizidou 2007: 45–86) and pragmatist thinkers such as Rorty (1989, 1993).

In the case of all of the above thinkers there is a complex political and philosophical history underlying their critique of mainstream philosophy and ethics, which can only be touched on here (Schroeder 2000). All of them criticize the idea that ethics can be given a rational grounding, that moral claims can have the status of truths, and that there are certain fixed, essential properties associated with being 'human'. They argue against all of the above not only because of the philosophical difficulties they entail, but also because these kinds of assumptions are claimed to be inherently *dangerous*. For postmodernists these ideas have actively contributed to the ills of modernity, including world war, technologies of mass destruction, colonization, genocide and imminent ecological disaster. Utilitarianism and deontological ethics are, in particular, singled out as exemplifying the misleading and dangerous character of modernist ethics. In the case of utilitarianism, this is because of its willingness to trade off the happiness of the few in favour of the greater good and, in the case of deontology, because of its formalism and universalism. We will look first at the reasons why postmodernists reject ethical foundationalism, and secondly at where this leaves postmodernist ethics in terms of its positive implications.

Postmodernists argue that any answer to the *why* question in ethical theory is always open to deconstruction. This is because all such answers make assumptions that cannot be accounted for in terms of procedural reason, empirical evidence or an appeal to the self-evidence of particular theories of human nature or the good life. In other words, there is always an ungrounded assumption at work that violates the claim to secure foundations. Foundationalist theories therefore, it is argued, either contradict themselves or get caught in a logic of infinite regress in which appeal is always necessary to a higher ground of authority in order to validate the foundational claim that is being made. This kind of critique isn't particularly new. As we have seen, critics of specific ethical theories often attack the foundational premises of those arguments. For example, Kant's universalization test was criticized almost from the outset for relying on reference to particular situations and outcomes that belied the claim to abstract universality made on behalf of the moral law. The difference with postmodernist critiques is that they do not see the failure of particular foundations as the problem, but the failure of foundations in general. Rorty argues that for existing moral theories, the aspiration is to be able to treat moral claims in the same way as we treat other claims about the world, that is, as demonstrably true or false. But he argues that this aspiration is based on a mistaken understanding of how any kind of truth claim is in practice demonstrable or otherwise.

For Rorty, both truth claims about what *is* the case and moral claims about what *ought to be* the case actually have meaning only as part of specific socially constructed 'languages' or ways of making sense of the world. To attempt to convince someone of your moral point of view by rational argumentation or pointing to empirical evidence or self-evident first principles is, for Rorty, a fundamental mistake

(Rorty 1989, 1993). In order to share your moral views, others have to share your universe of meaning, and universes of meaning are not subject to external validation. Rorty's is just one example of a postmodernist argument about language and sources of meaning. Derrida's theory of language and meaning is very different but it shares with Rorty the argument that any resting place of authority for our claims about the world is always illusory. This account of language is clearly in fundamental contradiction to the Habermasian understanding of communication in which ethical universals are presupposed (Borradori 2003; Critchley 1992; Hill 2007).

One aspect of the foundations of modern ethical theories that postmodernists target in particular is the accounts of the human subject on which they rely. As with feminist critics, postmodernist critics have pointed out that the supposedly 'natural' man of utilitarian and contractarian ethics in fact reflects substantive assumptions about human beings that are derived from particular historical circumstances, and therefore reflect some interests and identities rather than others. This not only results in false universalization but also always fails to do justice to the complexity of the human subject and the bases of human agency. The postmodernist critique of the moral subject seeks to unravel mainstream accounts from two directions. On the one hand, and in line with the claims of virtue and feminist ethics, it is pointed out that individuals cannot actually be defined in isolation, not just from each other but also from the social and linguistic systems of meaning into which they are born and in which they operate. From the postmodernist point of view, the idea that the moral subject is 'a rational chooser' or 'autonomous' is a fantasy that vastly overestimates the extent to which anyone is the author of his or her own judgement, speech and actions. On the other hand, postmodernism (in particular poststructuralist theories) also take psychoanalysis seriously. This means that the moral subject is understood to be internally complex, contradictory and fragmented. From the point of view of Hobbes or Bentham, desire is a simple thing, a drive of which we can be conscious and which we can rationally manage and direct. The postmodernist subject has a subconscious, and does not have full self-knowledge, let alone the capacity to be fully self-directed (Bauman 1993: 62–81).

The postmodernist critique of ethical theory, however, extends beyond the critique of foundationalism. The problem is not just that ethical theorists can't actually demonstrate the authority of their response to the *why* question; it's the implications of the presumption that they *can* demonstrate that authority. As we have seen, in particular for the modern moral theories of utilitarianism, contractarianism and deontology, the point of being able to ground ethics in rationally grounded first principles was to be able to provide a ground for the critical assessment of actual moral values and rules. In general, ethical theories, including discourse and feminist ethics, have sought to establish ways of making judgements between different moral orientations or courses of action. From the postmodernist point of view, it is this project that is the fundamental problem because, they argue, it is a project that seeks, ultimately, to legitimate power and control on the grounds of moral certainty. This tendency is, on the postmodernist account, compounded in utilitarian, contractarian and deontological arguments in which the moral subject is figured as an autonomous actor who is able to know his or her own ends, to know their rightness or wrongness and to act accordingly. From the postmodernist perspective, rationalist moral theories and the fiction of human autonomy between them have contributed significantly to the ills of modernity by feeding an illusion of the possibility of control through knowledge (Bauman 1993: 16–36).

Postmodernist theorists who want to think about ethics are therefore faced with the challenge of constructing an anti-foundationalist argument which eschews both procedural and substantive grounds of validation. Postmodernist theorists have responded to this challenge by taking the *impossibility* of establishing the grounds of ethical judgement as the starting point for thinking about ethics. The implications of this impossibility have been unpacked in different ways. One important reference point for many postmodern ethical theories is the philosophy of Levinas (1906–1995) that makes the ethical relation – an absolute and impossible obligation to do justice to the other – the centre of his moral thinking (Bauman 1993; Critchley 1992; Schroeder 2000: 391–3). For some theorists, for example Butler, the impossibility of grounding ethics has led to a focus on how the ethics of agency and judgement shift when the status of moral claims is recognized to be necessarily unstable and revisable; for others, for example Rorty, the impossibility of rational ethical grounding directs attention to the significance of sentiment as an anchor for moral beliefs. In both cases these arguments involve a reassertion of the significance of communication for ethics, but are underpinned by a very different account of communication than we find in discourse ethics.

Butler exemplifies the first kind of response in her argument that any claim to ethical universality, because it can only be expressed and understood in particular terms, always turns out to depend on certain exclusions and therefore fails to live up to its universal promise. She applies this argument to the idea of universal human rights, pointing out how what are claimed to be universal rights always presume particular models of what it means to be 'human'. In the case, for instance, of the universal right to marriage and family written into the *Universal Declaration of Human Rights*, the assumption is that humans are heterosexual. But of course not all humans identify themselves as heterosexual, which means that a right that claims universality actually excludes whole categories of human beings, often with grave consequences for how that category of human beings may be treated. In unpacking the implications of this argument for ethics, she argues that it means that the moral judge and actor should always start from an orientation towards moral humility, that is to say, from a willingness to treat his or her own moral convictions as open to question.

This suggests that ethics is less about the views that you hold and more about the way that you hold them and what this implies for your interaction with others with whom you may disagree. Butler argues that the recognition of the necessary failure of universal ethical claims necessitates paying attention to the different, always inadequate, ways in which the universal is expressed and understood by different categories of people. In this respect, she argues for an ethics of 'cultural translation' through which the differences as well as the commonalities between different ethical viewpoints may be recognized and negotiated. In contrast to the discourse ethics account of communication, however, cultural translation is not about reaching agreement in conditions of fair

argumentation but about expanding the range of understandings of the universal and constructing new, always revisable,
understandings in the light of interaction with other points
of view (Butler 2004a: 17–39).

For Rorty, the impossibility of grounding ethical claims
rationally leads him to a focus on the question of why, given
this impossibility, people nevertheless hold their ethical beliefs
as if they were true. Again using the example of universal
human rights, Rorty asks how it is that the category of the
'human' as such can make sense if we aren't able to make
reference to a demonstrable set of claims about human nature
or reason. The answer, he argues, is that the notion of the
'human' in human rights is entrenched within the historically
particular *liberal* way of life where, for a variety of contingent
historical reasons, the notion of individual rights has become
embedded and a basis of solidarity within those societies. It
just happens to be the case that in liberal societies humans
feel solidarity with other humans on grounds of their being
human, not just on grounds of their being particular types of
human. In order to get non-liberals also to embrace that
notion of the 'human', Rorty argues, it would be necessary
to expand non-liberals' universe of felt solidarity from particular tribe, gender or nation to the category of human
beings as such. Reason cannot ground such a shift but, Rorty
argues, it is possible to expand the range of human solidarity
by using stories to encourage people to empathize with others
who are understood to be 'not like them', and thus lessen the
difference between them. In an odd kind of way, therefore,
Rorty is returning to the idea of moral sentiment that we
found in eighteenth-century virtue ethics but in this case it is
a constructed feeling of connection rather than some kind of
inbuilt faculty that connects the individual person to humanity in general (Rorty 1993).

Critics of postmodernist accounts of ethics tend to take
two forms. Either postmodernists are accused of smuggling
foundational answers to the *why* question back in or they are
accused of simply undermining the possibility of ethics altogether and thereby legitimizing an 'anything goes' approach
to ethics in which it is impossible to discriminate between
moral rights and wrongs at all and we end up in a situation
of ethical nihilism. In terms of the latter critique, it is certainly

the case that postmodernism undermines the notion that there can be reliable criteria for discrimination but this doesn't imply that discrimination is either impossible or undesirable. Most postmodernist theorists clearly see themselves as engaged in *rescuing* the 'ethical' from the mistakes of modern rationalist approaches. This suggests that the first line of criticism has rather more purchase, although it's not clear that, even if it is true, postmodernists' answers to the *why* question take quite the same form as we have seen those answers take before. Nevertheless, it is worth noting that postmodernist ethics does echo themes that we have encountered before in discourse ethics, virtue ethics and feminist ethics. There is a lot of common ground in the critiques all of these approaches make of mainstream utilitarianism, contractualism and deontology. Moreover, as with virtue and feminist ethics, postmodernist ethics focuses attention on context and on the *way* in which ethical judgements are made as much as on their specific content, suggesting that ethics is about situation, character and attitude more than it is about rules or outcomes. In addition, the postmodernist rejection of 'monological' moral reasoning follows discourse ethics in bringing communication, albeit differently understood, to the fore as the way in which the exclusiveness of supposedly universal ethical judgements can be addressed.

Reflective exercise

- Are postmodernists right to see the assumptions made about individual rationality in utilitarian and contractualist ethics as dangerous?
- Deontologists argue that individuals must be held responsible for actions such as war crimes. Do you think this idea makes ethical sense from a postmodernist point of view?

Conclusion

As with the rationalist ethical theories discussed in chapter 2, the perspectives discussed above have been influential in debates within Global Ethics. This is especially the case with virtue ethics which, in particular in versions that stress the link between ethics and virtues embedded in specific communities, has been the most prominent source of critique of rationalist arguments in Global Ethics. Feminist and postmodernist ethics have been more recent entrants into the field, but have also become increasingly significant as counters to rationalism. In the chapters that follow, Walzer and Nussbaum, in different ways, build on the insights of virtue ethics to critique utilitarian and deontological accounts of global justice and offer alternatives (chapters 4 and 5). In chapter 4, Robinson will argue for an ethical approach to policies of aid and development based on a feminist ethic of care, and Edkins will draw on both care and postmodernist ethics in her critique of the ethics of humanitarianism. In chapter 5, Rorty will use postmodernist arguments to undermine the idea that global distributive justice is possible at all. In chapter 6, Campbell will draw on an approach to the ethics of war based on postmodernist insights; and Sjoberg will argue for a new theory of just war derived from feminist ethics. In chapter 7, we will encounter virtue, feminist and postmodernist arguments for the importance of *post bellum* justice. And, in chapter 8, Benhabib will draw on a combination of insights from virtue and feminist, as well as discourse ethics to argue for an ethical approach to the clash of ethical values in a globalized world. Before we move on to explore these arguments, however, it will be useful to pause to take stock of what we have learned so far.

In this and the previous chapter we have surveyed the grounds of ethical theory and, briefly, the grounds and implications of alternative ways of thinking about ethics. In the chapters that follow we will re-encounter these perspectives, sometimes in combination with each other (see below), applied to global ethical issues. All of the perspectives considered here involve a philosophical hinterland to which it has not been possible to do justice. In conclusion, however, it's worth reminding ourselves of some of the key debates arising out of differences between the theories on questions about the foundations, procedures and substantive content of ethics.

Questions about foundations

Q: Are there any foundational truths about human beings as such that we can use to ground our ethical theories?

A: In different ways, utilitarianism, contractualism, deontology and virtue ethics all suggest that there are, whereas feminists and postmodernists reject the idea and argue that what/who we are is gendered and fragmented.

Q: Is ethics grounded in reason and, if so, what kind of reason is this?

A: Utilitarians and contractualists give instrumental reason a crucial role in ethics, which contrasts with the 'pure practical reason' of Kantian deontology and the communicative reason of Habermas. *Phronesis* in virtue ethics is another version of reasoning but this time one that is entangled with relations with others and linked to feelings of solidarity. For thinkers such as Rorty, it is sentiment rather than reason that enables moral claims to be held as if they were true.

Q: Is ethics grounded in the individual or in the social?

A: On this point utilitarianism, contractualism and Kantian deontology are clearly lined up against discourse, virtue, feminist and postmodernist ethics. For the former, the individual is ethically primitive – the building block from which everything else follows. For the latter, individuals have no moral existence outside of their interrelation with others. Although there are differences in how this sociality is understood. Habermas stresses the inter-subjectivity of communication and Ruddick relations of care; virtue ethics often refers back to communities such as the city-state or the ideal socialist society, and postmodernists invoke multiple possible relations of solidarity.

Questions about procedures

Q: What is the right way to approach working out what it is morally right to do?

A: The rationalist moral theories all give us a procedure that involves abstraction and universalization as a way of testing the validity of moral judgements. In all cases, moral judges are asked to detach themselves from their particular self and situation and to reason on behalf of everyone. In the case of contractualist and deontological theories, this involves a complex set of hypothetical moves in which one imagines oneself in a state of nature, or that one's maxim has become a universal moral law. In contrast, discourse ethics (at least in theory) and virtue, feminist and postmodernist ethical theories emphasize either *phronesis*, which is the capacity to tease out the appropriate judgement by reference to the way of life of one's community, or actual communication with others.

Questions about substance

Q: Should we think about ethics in terms of principles, rules, utility (satisfaction of desire) or virtues?

A: This question drives a wedge between utilitarians and the other rationalist theories on the one hand, and between rationalists and anti-rationalists on the other. For utilitarians ethics is the maximization of a particular value (happiness – which is assumed to be a universal value), whereas contractualists and deontologists (Kantian and Habermasian) insist on the priority of certain principles, such as consent or respect for the rights of others. Virtue, feminist and postmodernist ethical theories are all much more attached to the idea that particular virtues or ways of being are fundamental to ethics. Unlike utility, virtues are not ethically valuable because they are what human beings desire but because they are good in themselves.

Q: Is ethics about needs, rights or duties?

A: In terms of rights versus needs, the most obvious disagreement is between contractualist arguments which treat rights as central, and virtue and care arguments that claim the same about need. The crux of this division is the account of the human condition with which these theories start. For contractualists, the starting point is the free, instrumentally rational, desiring individual who is of equal significance and equal capacity to everyone else. For virtue and care ethicists, the starting point is a human being enmeshed in relations of inequality, dependency and responsibility who requires certain things in order to flourish. This means that virtue and care ethics are also centrally concerned with the duties inherent in those relations but in a different way to Kant who sets an absolute duty to obey the moral law at the heart of his moral theory.

Q: Can we distinguish between 'ethics' and 'morality'?

A: This question points to a fundamental split between the theories discussed in the previous chapter and in this one. For the rationalist theories, the definition of morality is tied up with universality and with the idea of a standpoint outside of particular practices, languages and ways of life, from which the latter can be critically interrogated. Rationalist theories accuse those who refuse to make the morality/ethics distinction of an inherent conservatism which, as we have seen, is one reason for feminist concerns about virtue ethics and feminist splits over the ethic of care. Countering this position, however, virtue, care and postmodernist ethical theories maintain that the ideas of universality and of the 'standpoint outside' are an illusion. And moreover that this is a dangerous illusion because it enables what are actually parochial, historically specific values and principles to masquerade as universally meaningful.

All of the questions raised above recur in the debates in Global Ethics to which we will turn in the following chapters. As we move on to look at these debates, we need to bear in mind the following points: firstly, ethical arguments often reflect deep and antithetical assumptions about human beings and human reason embedded in ethical theories. We will see examples of this in discussing global distributive justice and the ethics of war, for instance in the different views taken by utilitarian as opposed to deontological theorists (Singer versus O'Neill in chapter 4 on the ethics of aid; Bellamy versus Orend in chapter 7 on the requirements of *post bellum* justice). Secondly, more confusingly, it can sometimes be the case that ethical theorists come to the *same* conclusions for *different* reasons. For example, Nussbaum and Pogge (discussed in chapter 5) come to very similar conclusions about the wrongs of global poverty and the need to address them, but whereas Nussbaum bases her argument on a notion, drawn from virtue ethics, of the human good, Pogge bases his argument on a commitment to universal human rights that is derived from a combination of deontological and contractualist reasoning. Thirdly, because ethical traditions are contested and open to different interpretations, it can also be the case that ethical theorists are drawing on the *same* broad ethical perspective but in *different* ways. For example, as already mentioned, Walzer (discussed in chapters 5 and 6) draws on virtue ethics but in a way that emphasizes the relatively exclusive nature of moral community, practices and values; whereas Nussbaum (discussed in chapters 4 and 5) draws on a much more universalist version of virtue ethics, which has important implications for the conclusions both draw about global distributive justice. Finally, it is important to note that ethical theorists often *combine* different ethical theories within a *single* argument. For example, in arguments concerning global distributive justice discussed in chapter 5, we find a combination of contractualist- and virtue-based arguments used to sustain the idea that there are special obligations of justice to fellow citizens (Miller, Walzer), and a combination of contractualist and deontological thinking in rights-based arguments in favour of global redistribution (Pogge).

As our argument proceeds, you will need to reflect on your own deep assumptions about human beings and human reason and how they shape and influence your views about particular ethical questions arising from globalization. Your views about 'what should be done' about global poverty, global warming or political violence are the tip of the iceberg in thinking about issues in Global Ethics. The rest of the iceberg is made up of the reasons underlying those views, how they are grounded and how they relate to one or more of the available ethical theories that frame scholarship within the field. If you do believe in the global redistribution of wealth, then is this on utilitarian, deontological, virtue or feminist grounds? Are the ethical assumptions underlying your substantive ethical claims consistent with one another; can you be a utilitarian one day and a postmodernist the next? Are your ethical views about distributive justice consistent with your ethical views about war? Are the prescriptive implications of your ethical views acceptable to you? If your principles tell you that you should give away all luxury goods, then is this something you would act on? If not, does this mean you need to revisit your principles? All of these are questions that you will need to keep asking yourself during the course of this book.

References and further reading

Annas, J. (2006) 'Virtue Ethics', in Copp (ed.), *Oxford Handbook*, pp. 515–36. An overview of virtue ethics.

Bauman, Z. (1993) *Postmodern Ethics*, Oxford: Blackwell. This is an example of a postmodernist ethical argument in which Bauman builds on Levinas's ethics to argue for the possibility of moral responsibility in the absence of moral foundationalism.

Borradori, G. (2003) *Philosophy in a Time of Terror: Dialogues with Jürgen Habermas and Jacques Derrida*, Chicago: University of Chicago Press. This illustrates the contrast between the ways in which Habermas and Derrida think about ethics and politics.

Butler, J. (2004a) *Undoing Gender*, London: Routledge. Develops postmodernist ethical arguments that build on the critique of the exclusivity of universal moral claims about humanity, focusing on issues of gender and sexuality.

Butler, J. (2004b) *Precarious Life: The Powers of Mourning and Violence*, London: Verso. Essays that focus on ethical questions to do with war and violence and the ways in which some lives (and deaths) are recognized as worthy of being counted and some not. The essay of the title 'Precarious Life' engages with Levinas's thought.

Butler, J. (2009) *Frames of War*, London: Verso. A further development of the arguments in *Precarious Life*.

Cole, E. B. and Coultrap-McQuin, S. (eds) (1992) *Explorations in Feminist Ethics*, Bloomington: Indiana University Press. A useful early collection of essays on feminist ethics, including discussion of the ethics of care versus ethics of justice debate.

Copp, D. (ed.) (2006) *The Oxford Handbook of Ethical Theory*, Oxford: Oxford University Press.

Critchley, S. (1992) *The Ethics of Deconstruction*, Oxford: Blackwell. This is an examination of the ethical implications of Derrida's thinking and his debt to the arguments of Levinas.

Darwell, S. (ed.) (2003) *Virtue Ethics*, Oxford: Blackwell. Contains extracts from Aristotle, Hutcheson, Hume, MacIntyre.

Derrida, J. (1992) 'Force of Law: The "Mystical Foundations of Authority" ', in D. Cornell, M. Rosenfeld and D. G. Carlson (eds), *Deconstruction and the Possibility of Justice*, New York: Routledge, pp. 3–67. This is a difficult essay to read. In it Derrida criticizes foundationalism in ethics, politics and law, arguing that there is no claim to ethical authority without a violent interruption of what would otherwise be an infinite regress.

Derrida, J. (1997) *On Cosmopolitanism and Forgiveness*, London: Routledge. A rather more accessible example of Derrida's work in which he argues for the ethical importance of striving for an unconditional commitment to the claims of others detached from any foundation in sovereign authority.

Dreier, J. (ed.) (2006) *Contemporary Debates in Moral Theory*, Oxford: Blackwell.

Driver, J. (2006) 'Virtue Theory', in Dreier (ed.), *Contemporary Debates*, pp. 113–23. A critique of virtue theory.

Fricker, M. and Hornsby, J. (eds) (2000) *The Cambridge Companion to Feminism in Philosophy*, Cambridge: Cambridge University Press. A collection of essays covering a range of work in feminist philosophy.

Gilligan, C. (1993) *In a Different Voice: Psychological Theory and Women's Development*, 2nd edn, Cambridge, MA: Harvard University Press. The book that launched feminist ethics as a distinctive branch of moral philosophy.

Grimshaw, J. (1993) 'The Idea of a Female Ethic', in Singer (ed.), *A Companion*, pp. 491–9. A feminist critique of care ethics.

Held, V. (1993) *Feminist Morality: Transforming Culture, Society and Politics*, Chicago: University of Chicago Press. A useful example of the argument for care ethics in feminist moral theory.

Held, V. (2006a) *The Ethics of Care: Personal, Political, and Global*, Oxford: Oxford University Press. An example of the feminist ethic of care applied to a variety of aspects of social and political life.

Held, V. (2006b) 'The Ethics of Care', in Copp (ed.), *Oxford Handbook*, pp. 537–66. Introductory overview of feminist care ethics.

Hill, L. (2007) *The Cambridge Introduction to Jacques Derrida*, Cambridge: Cambridge University Press. An accessible, basic introduction to Derrida's work.

Hursthouse, R. (2006) 'Are Virtues the Proper Starting Point for Ethical Theory?' in Dreier (ed.), *Contemporary Debates*, pp. 97–112. A defence of virtue theory.

Jaggar, A. (2000) 'Feminist Ethics', in Lafollette (ed.), *Blackwell Guide*, pp. 348–74. Introductory overview of feminist ethics.

Lafollette, H. (ed.) (2000) *The Blackwell Guide to Ethical Theory*, Oxford: Blackwell.

Levinas, E. (1985) *Ethics and Infinity*, trans. R. A. Cohen, Pittsburgh: Duquesne University Press. This text and the one below are examples of Levinas's ethics of absolute responsibility to and for the other which have been significant for a variety of postmodern ethical theorists.

Levinas, E. (1999) *Alterity and Transcendence*, New York: Columbia University Press.

Loizidou, E. (2007) *Judith Butler: Ethics, Law, Politics*, Abingdon: Routledge Cavendish. An interpretation of Butler's thought with a particular focus on her ethical perspective.

Lyotard, J.-F. (1984) *The Postmodern Condition: A Report on Knowledge*, Manchester: Manchester University Press. The definitive statement of the meanings of postmodernism, this became crucial to the identification of postmodernism as a distinctive way of thinking.

MacIntyre, A. (1967) *A Short History of Ethics: A History of Moral Philosophy from the Homeric Age to the Twentieth Century*, London: Routledge & Kegan Paul. See chapters 7 and 15 for coverage of Aristotle and Hegel and Marx.

MacIntyre, A. (1981) *After Virtue: A Study in Moral Theory*, London: Duckworth. This book revived virtue ethics in contemporary moral philosophy.

MacIntyre, A. (1999) *Dependent Rational Animals: Why Human Beings Need the Virtues*, London: Duckworth. One of the arguments made in this book is for similarities between MacIntyre's virtue ethics and the feminist ethic of care.

Nietzsche, F. (1994) *On the Genealogy of Morality*, Cambridge: Cambridge University Press. An important influence on postmodernist ethical thinking, Nietzsche argues for the origins of morality in the resentment of the oppressed against the powerful and criticizes the idea of moral truth.

Norman, R. (1983) *The Moral Philosophers: An Introduction to Ethics*, Oxford: Clarendon Press. See chapters 3, 5, 8 and 10 for coverage of Aristotle, Hume, Hegel and Marx.

Nussbaum, M. (1986) *The Fragility of Goodness*, Cambridge: Cambridge University Press. An alternative example to MacIntyre of a contemporary moral theorist building on an Aristotelian account of ethics.

Okin, S. M. (1989) *Justice, Gender and the Family*, New York: Basic Books. Critical engagement with Rawls's *A Theory of Justice* that points to its gender-blindness.

Pence, G. (1993) 'Virtue Theory', in Singer (ed.), *A Companion*, pp. 249–58. An overview of virtue ethics.

Rorty, R. (1989) *Contingency, Irony and Solidarity*, Cambridge: Cambridge University Press. A series of essays that spells out the implications of Rorty's anti-foundationalism for ethical and political thought.

Rorty, R. (1993) 'Human Rights, Rationality and Sentimentality', in S. Shute and S. Hurley (eds), *On Human Rights: The Oxford Amnesty Lectures 1993*, New York: Basic Books. The text in which Rorty revises Humean ideas about moral sentiment as a way of thinking about the universalization of human rights in the absence of rationalist foundations.

Rowe, C. (1993) 'Ethics in Ancient Greece', in Singer (ed.), *A Companion*, pp. 121–32. Overview of Ancient Greek ethics that includes a brief account of Aristotle.

Ruddick, S. (1990) *Maternal Thinking: Towards a Politics of Peace*, London: Women's Press. An example of feminist ethics that builds on the ethics of care specifically in relation to questions about war and peace.

Schroeder, W. R. (2000) 'Continental Ethics', in Lafollette (ed.), *Blackwell Guide*, pp. 375–99. Examines the roots of ethical thinking outside of the Anglo-American canon of moral theory, including brief introductions to Nietzsche and Levinas on ethics.

Singer, P. (ed.) (1993) *A Companion to Ethics*, Oxford: Blackwell.

Slote, M. (2000) 'Virtue Ethics', in Lafollette (ed.), *Blackwell Guide*, pp. 325–47. Overview of contemporary virtue ethics.

Tännsjö, T. (2002) *Understanding Ethics: An Introduction to Moral Theory*, Edinburgh: Edinburgh University Press. A useful introduction to ethical theory that includes chapters on virtue and feminist ethics.

Tronto, J. (1993) *Moral Boundaries: The Political Argument for an Ethic of Care*. New York: Routledge. An argument for the significance of the ethic of care for politics.

4
Ethics of International Aid and Development

Introduction

Historically, most ethical systems, religious and philosophical, have acknowledged poverty and deprivation to
be bad things in themselves. But they have also accepted
them as an inevitable part of the human condition and offered moral justifications for them, often on the grounds of
the moral failings of the poor themselves, or as part of the
workings of an inscrutable providence. Modern ethical perspectives are less inclined to take poverty and deprivation
morally for granted. In contemporary debates, if poverty and
deprivation are to be morally acceptable, then this requires
explicit justification. In this chapter we will be concerned
with ethical arguments surrounding two kinds of responses
to global poverty and deprivation: *humanitarianism* and
development. Humanitarian aid is intended to address immediate and extreme situations of need, such as famine or the
consequences of natural or man-made disasters. Development
aid is intended to address ongoing, systemic poverty.

International humanitarian relief, in the form of charitable
giving to threatened populations by both state and non-state
actors, has a longer history than international development
aid (the former is often dated back to the foundation of the
Red Cross in 1863). This is partly because it is only in the

modern era, following the tremendous economic development of certain industrialized states, that systemic poverty has been seen as something that could, potentially, be overcome. In both cases, however, humanitarian and development policies have become a systematic part of global politics and global governance since 1945 and the setting up of the UN (Barnett and Weiss 2008b; Thomas 2008). As we will see, the practices of both kinds of aid are bound up with controversies over the causes of humanitarian crisis and of global poverty, and also about how the latter are related to each other (see the first two sections below). Over the past forty years, as a result of revolutions in communications technology, people have been increasingly exposed to the consequences of humanitarian disasters and poverty for other people in other parts of the world. In addition to journalistic coverage of crises, there has also been a tremendous growth in the number of humanitarian INGOs lobbying states, IGOs and individuals in support of their cause and becoming more closely involved in cooperating with states and IGOs in the delivery of relief and longer-term development aid (Fearon 2008). In this context, since the 1970s, a significant literature has grown up on ethical issues to do with emergency aid across borders, the nature of 'development' and the kinds of transnational obligations it involves (Crocker 2008).

This chapter will begin by looking at ethical debates surrounding emergency aid, such as famine relief. We will move on to the ethics of development and, finally, consider the ethical issues raised by ecological constraints on global economic development and the idea of 'sustainable development'. We will conclude by considering arguments surrounding the nature of the ethical obligations for individuals and institutions involved in international aid and development. Is the fulfilment of such obligations morally desirable or morally required? If it is morally required, then what are the reasons for this? This will take us into the question of 'justice' that is the explicit focus of the following chapter. Readers should read chapters 4 and 5 in relation to each other, since they both deal with ethical questions of distribution and redistribution of global wealth and between them enable you to address the question of whether redistribution of global wealth is a matter of charity or a matter of justice.

Humanitarian aid

Humanitarian aid is distinguished from development aid because it aims to address a specific, temporary set of needs, rather than to build up the capacity of a community to relieve poverty and deprivation over time. As we will see, this distinction is not necessarily as robust as it initially appears but for the moment we will treat it as unproblematic. Charity is identified as a virtue in most ethical traditions, religious and philosophical, and the traditional assumption has been that international humanitarian aid is a species of charity. Ethical traditions differ, however, over whether charity is a requirement or a work of 'supererogation' (morally commendable but not obligatory), and even where charity is seen as morally required it is normally expected to operate under certain limits and at the discretion of the giver. For example, religious traditions that require charity of their adherents, such as the giving of a tithe of income to the poor, both limit the amount *required* (you can obviously opt to give more) and leave it up to you which particular 'poor' you decide will be the recipients of your gift. In the early 1970s, in response to the ongoing and appalling famine in East Bengal, the utilitarian thinker Peter Singer challenged the idea that giving aid could be seen as either optional or limited in the way that most people assumed.

Singer's argument was simple and proceeded as follows:

1   Suffering and death from lack of food and medical care are bad.
2   If it is in our power to prevent something bad from happening, without thereby sacrificing anything of comparable (or in a weaker version, significant) moral importance, then we ought, morally, to do it.
3   It is in our power to prevent the suffering and death in East Bengal from happening without such a sacrifice.
4   Therefore we are morally required to give to famine relief at least up to the amount we currently spend on consumer 'trivia' and potentially up to the point of 'marginal utility', at which the utility of the victims of famine and the givers of relief has been roughly equalized. (Singer 2008)

Singer argued that in a world in which the practical limitations that might have affected the effectiveness of transnational aid had disappeared it made no sense to limit the range of utilitarian calculation to the context of the state. He also argued that there was no reason not to understand the obligation to give aid as being both categorical (morally required) and incumbent on each individual, not simply on collective entities such as states. This obligation on individuals, he argued, was analogous to the obligation of any able adult to rescue a child drowning in a puddle. His argument precipitated a plethora of philosophical ethical debates about famine and emergency aid more generally.

Perhaps the most notorious response to Singer's argument came in Hardin's 'Lifeboat Ethics: The Case against Helping the Poor', in which Hardin, who also based his argument on utilitarian premises regarding the maximizing of utility, argued that helping the starving would not improve the position of the starving and would also radically worsen the position of the affluent (Hardin 2008). Rather than being like the adult passing the drowning child, according to Hardin, the affluent were like the people in a lifeboat who would all drown along with the shipwrecked if they took any of the shipwrecked people in the water on board. The contrast between Singer's and Hardin's arguments was taken by many to illustrate the weaknesses of utilitarianism that were noted in chapter 2, in particular concerning the difficulty of calculating aggregate utility and the ever-present possibility of trade-offs. But it also focused attention on the *who* and *how* questions in relation to the ethics of emergency aid. Were individual affluent actors those morally responsible for delivering aid, and how was the ethical status of the recipients of aid being conceptualized on the utilitarian account (*who*)? Was giving emergency aid of this kind the appropriate way to address the problem of famine (*how*)?

In Singer's argument, the famine is, in ethical terms, treated as a given. Although Singer acknowledges that famines arise out of man-made as well as natural causes, he sees this as morally irrelevant to the requirement to ameliorate the famine. For other thinkers, however, the fact that famines are not 'acts of God' is of considerable moral significance. Sen, one of the major contributors to the philosophical literature on hunger, argues that famines are not so much about lack of food as about failure of entitlement, that is to say, a situation in which some people cease to be able to get access to food in the normal way. This is a result of failures in economic systems, which may happen for a variety of reasons, but it is neither 'natural' nor inevitable. In this context, Sen argues that the appropriate moral vocabulary is one of 'rights' and 'metarights' rather than the utilitarian language of minimizing suffering. For Sen, rights may be of various kinds, including embodying moral claims that may not yet be able to be met. In this sense, there is a human right not to be hungry (Crocker 2008: 255–93; Sen 1984). To the extent that the right is unclaimable in the actual world, however, he invokes the idea of 'metarights' which are rights to work towards establishing institutional arrangements in which the moral right not to be hungry could be met. The idea that the ethical requirement to do something about famine relates to basic human rights, rather than to the moral significance of suffering as such, is also taken up by Shue who argues for a limited package of fundamental human rights that include the right to subsistence (Shue 1980; see further discussion of Shue's argument in chapter 5 below). Because the idea of a right implies the idea of a correlative duty, in contrast to Singer, rights-based accounts tend to put more emphasis on the need for institutions to be set up to fulfil the moral obligation to prevent hunger.

Since the work of Sen and Shue, a variety of thinkers have formulated ethical arguments around emergency aid in terms of human rights and the correlative obligation to fulfil them. If we examine these arguments, they justify the rights-based approach in rather different ways. For thinkers such as Sen and Shue, the argument for rights relates fundamentally to 'needs'. In Sen's case, this is linked to a concept of human flourishing that owes something to virtue ethics (see the discussion of human development in the following section). For other thinkers, however, the morality of basic rights can be grounded in deontological claims about the unique moral significance of each individual, or in arguments reminiscent of both utilitarian and contractarian traditions that base rights on fundamental human desires or interests. Either way, as Sen's notion of 'metarights' acknowledges, one of the objections to rights-based arguments is that rights are essentially entitlement claims but that claims to entitlement don't make sense unless it is clear from whom those entitlements can be claimed. O'Neill has argued that this is a fundamental flaw with rights-based responses to the problem of hunger. 'When the poor are powerless, it is the powerful who must be convinced that they have certain obligations – whether or not the beneficiaries claim the performance of these obligations as their right. The first concern of an ethical theory that focuses on action should be obligations, rather than rights' (O'Neill 2008b: 150). Drawing on a Kantian deontological argument in which the categorical nature of moral obligations is primary, O'Neill formulates an argument for the strict obligation of state and transnational institutions to address human needs. This is an argument that makes collective, institutional actors of central moral salience in the provision of emergency aid and of more long-term development assistance.

Utilitarian and deontological arguments about famine relief, such as those of Singer and O'Neill respectively, set up strong moral obligations on capable actors (individual or collective) to address the problem of famine. In doing this, however, they situate the potential recipient of famine relief as an essentially passive victim. The assumption seems to be that those affected by famine are powerless and that they must depend on external agents, acting according to what is morally right, for their plight to be addressed. In *Whose Hunger? Concepts of Famine, Practices of Aid* (2000), Edkins argues that this whole ethical debate tells us more about the desire of those witnessing famine to attain (an impossible) self-certainty and control in the presence of incomprehensible trauma than it does about the ethical predicament of the starving. Drawing on a poststructuralist ethics, Edkins argues that there are two international discourses of response to famine: the first is a technical, scientific discourse that sees famine as a problem amenable to expert solution; the second is a moral humanitarian discourse that claims to be grounded in universal truths (Barnett and Weiss 2008b; Calhoun 2008; MacGinty and Williams 2009: 153–74). In both cases, according to Edkins, the claim to knowledge of what should be done is bogus. This is because there is no *general* answer to the ethically appropriate response to famine. She challenges the views both that those affected by famine are powerless and that aid will necessarily address the problem. As contemporary research into complex emergencies has shown, famines are constructed in a variety of ways. Some people in famine-affected areas as well as outsiders *profit* from famine, and international aid sometimes exacerbates rather than resolves the problem (Barnett and Weiss 2008a).

'Rather than seeing famines, conflicts, and poverty as problems that call for technical solutions from experts, or codes of practice and principles of action, what is needed is political and ethical engagement that produces a climate where responsibility for decisions about intervention and aid is inescapable' (Edkins 2000: 30). In place of the universalist ethical positions described above, Edkins argues that we need to abandon the search for a moral truth about the *who* and *how* of famine relief and instead approach the issue contextually, in terms of the complex web of relations that connect the actors involved and the causal and constitutive role of a range of local and global political and economic factors. We can't know in advance what the right thing to do is, and we can't assume that we know who the appropriate agents to do the right thing might be, but we still are responsible for acting. She argues that this kind of ethical approach echoes that recommended in the feminist ethic of care (Edkins 2000: 150).

As Edkins acknowledges, her argument to some extent follows up on Sen's insight that famines are not natural disasters but are economically and politically constituted phenomena. And in much of the literature relating to the ethics of emergency aid there is a recognition that crises don't come out of nowhere and that the potential for famine is embedded in broader conditions of poverty that keep a large percentage of the world's population living at not much more than subsistence level. The discussion of the ethics of famine relief therefore tends to merge into the discussion of the ethics of development aid in general, that is to say, aid that is directed towards the long-term relief of poverty and promotion of affluence. In the following section, we will move on to consider the broader terrain of the ethics of development aid.

Reflective exercise

How convincing is Singer's argument that *individuals* are morally required, on utilitarian grounds, to give up luxuries to contribute to famine relief?

In 2008, a major natural disaster caused a humanitarian emergency in the sovereign state of Burma/ Myanmar but the ruling regime was reluctant to allow international agencies to intervene to deliver aid. What do you think the ethical responsibilities/obligations of the international community should be in a case like this?

Is Edkins right to suggest that the discourses of humanitarian aid are themselves ethically problematic?

Development aid

As already mentioned, the practice of international humanitarian aid, aimed at emergency relief, has a history going back to the nineteenth century and the formation of the International Red Cross in 1863. The policy of international development aid, on the part of both states and international organizations, took shape in the post-1945, Cold War period. In the early part of this period (1950s and 1960s), the predominant view was that the key to eradicating poverty was economic modernization. According to this view, the process of modernization that industrialized economies had already gone through was an evolutionary process that all economies would (or at least could) follow over time. Economic modernization was identified as historically inevitable as well as desirable. All that was needed was for the right kind of help to be given to enable evolution towards affluence across the globe. Although this viewpoint remained influential throughout the Cold War period and beyond, it has also been contested in a variety of ways.

An early critique, underpinned by the dependency theory pioneered by Latin American-based economists such as

Prebisch, argued that the poverty of most postcolonial states was actually the *product* of the modernization of 'developed' economies. It had only been possible for rich states to industrialize and maintain their levels of affluence on the basis of their exploitation of dependent state economies (often ex-imperial possessions) that produced cheap raw materials and labour. Development for 'underdeveloped' economies was therefore not something that could happen without a radical breaking away from their economic ties with so-called 'developed' economies. This counter-discourse to standard modernization accounts of development, though politically significant for mobilizing development strategies for so-called 'third world' countries, was to a large extent subsumed by the world economic problems of the 1970s which caused a major debt crisis in developing economies and prompted the rise of neo-liberalism. In the 1980s, the prerequisites of economic development were identified with conditions of trade liberalization, privatization and deregulation and, although there have been modifications to the extremes of 'structural adjustment' policies of that era, neo-liberalism has continued to be the most influential economic doctrine in the global political economy since the end of the Cold War (Thomas 2008; Woods 2008).

In the wake of neo-liberalism and its mixed effects on levels of poverty in different parts of the world, another alternative discourse of development has emerged. Dependency critiques of modernization theories did not actually question the value of economic development itself. In the 1990s, however, debates about international development aid have increasingly not only been about the *means* through which development could be possible but about the *ends* of development themselves. Traditionally, poverty in development discourse was defined as lack of the resources to pay for basic material needs. This definition was tied to a modernization view that the way out of poverty was the transformation of subsistence, agrarian economies into industrialized ones that would produce surpluses and increase the income at the disposal of the poor. Development could therefore be measured by economic growth, for instance by looking at changes in Gross Domestic Product (GDP). Alternative discourses of development start from a different definition of poverty, to include not just the lack of ability to fulfil material needs but also non-material needs. On this account, development is not about growth in income but about 'human development', which involves growth in a range of capabilities that ensure a certain level of quality of life for each individual. The idea of human development is not necessarily linked to the development of an ever-expanding industrialized market economy. Measurement of development in this sense does not only look at levels of disposable income (where relevant) but also at the extent to which a range of material and non-material needs are met, including for instance in terms of education and health care, but also in terms of people's ability to participate in decisions affecting their own well-being (Thomas 2008). The UN Millennium Development Goals (MDGs) reflect this, less economistic, view of the meaning of development. The goals are to:

1   eradicate extreme poverty and hunger;
2   achieve universal primary education;
3   promote gender equality and empower women;
4   reduce child mortality;
5   improve maternal health;
6   combat HIV/AIDS, malaria and other diseases. (Thomas 2008: 478)

As with humanitarian aid, the debates surrounding the ethics of development aid are necessarily linked to views about the accuracy of the economic and historical arguments underpinning the idea of development, as well as by views on the desirability of all national economies coming to resemble those of affluent, industrialized states. We'll begin by looking at ethical arguments surrounding whether development aid is morally justifiable in the first place, and then at arguments that agree on aid as an ethical requirement but differ about what 'development' should mean and about the grounds of the justification of aid (see Crocker 2008, Goulet 1995 and Gasper 2004 for a more comprehensive view of debates in development ethics).

Ethical arguments *against* the provision of development aid come, I suggest, in two versions. First, there are those that claim that such aid is ineffective or even counter-productive. Secondly, there are those that claim that even if such aid may be a morally good thing for the recipients, there is no ethical obligation for inhabitants of rich states to help out inhabitants of poor states. There are a variety of rationales for the first claim, including the Hardin-type utilitarian argument discussed above in which aid is claimed to exacerbate rather than resolve problems of scarce resources over time. A different type of rationale comes from those who see aid as effectively propping up an essentially unjust system of global inequality and/or as endorsing it as a desirable end (Bauman 2001; Nielsen 1998). Marxist critiques of aid provision exemplify this sort of rationale which is rooted in the virtue ethics tradition. From the Marxist point of view, capitalism is not conducive to human flourishing so an aid policy that sustains and promotes capitalist development must be morally suspect (Nielsen 1998).

The second anti-development aid claim, unsurprisingly, is most often justified on contractualist and virtue ethics grounds. The contractualist arguments most likely to object to international aid programmes are those that build the most minimal assumptions about natural right into the actual or hypothetical contract and, for that reason, tend also to be strongly opposed to welfare provision within the state. These *libertarian* versions of contractualist ethical thought, in giving priority to individual liberty, also give priority to those human liberties that can be enjoyed with the least amount of encroachment on the liberties of others. Redistributing wealth via taxation within the state, let alone via aid programmes beyond the state, requires the active encroachment on individuals' property rights and must therefore be morally wrong, unless there is some problem with their property entitlement in the first place (e.g. that it was stolen) (see Nozick 1974 for a well-known example of this kind of libertarian argument). Even for non-libertarian contractualists, however, it is often argued that people would only consent to a strong obligation to aiding others within the community of contractors; obligations to outsiders would be much more minimal, perhaps extending to emergency aid but going no further (Rawls 1999; Rawls's argument is discussed in detail in chapter 5).

From a virtue ethics perspective, human flourishing is always contextual and is actively nourished through special relations with those who share a way of life. Again, this does not necessarily preclude aid to outsiders but it does preclude the imposition of the values inherent in one way of life onto that of another, which pushes against the universalist discourse of development, especially in those versions that rely on a modernization discourse (Gasper 2004: 191–220). Versions of virtue ethics that locate human flourishing within self-determining, democratic political communities may similarly see development aid as undercutting the self-determination of both donors and recipients (see discussions of Walzer and Miller in chapter 5 as examples of this kind of position).

Arguments that development aid to the global poor is an ethical requirement for the global rich include ones already familiar from the discussion of humanitarian aid above. Utilitarian (Singer), human rights (Shue) and duty-based (O'Neill) arguments apply in much the same way to the project of eradicating global poverty as they do to addressing situations of humanitarian crisis. Indeed, as was pointed out by O'Neill and others, the two problems are related to each other. All we need to do to see this is to compare the effects of an emergency, such as an earthquake or hurricane, on rich states as opposed to poor ones. We therefore also find similar arguments surrounding the *who* and *how* questions. Utilitarian arguments continue to point to individual responsibilities to give aid, whereas thinkers such as O'Neill put emphasis on the role of a variety of collective agents, not only states but also international governmental and non-governmental organizations. Beyond the issues of where moral responsibility lies for addressing development needs, however, is an ethical debate about what we should understand development needs to mean. In this respect debates over the ethics of development aid are intertwined with the debates over development policy referred to above. Amongst the challengers to economistic understandings of development as reducible in meaning to growth in income have been thinkers such as Sen and Nussbaum. They have argued that rethinking the idea of development in terms of 'human development' is not only more ethically defensible in general but also undermines the critique of aid that we find in certain forms of virtue ethics and has the potential to bring rights-based and needs-based arguments for aid together.

For Sen and Nussbaum, the aim of development should not be identified with the maximization of wealth as such but with the outcomes that are enabled by the means of wealth, that is, the ability to live flourishing lives. A flourishing life involves the achievement of certain levels of functioning (such as being well-nourished, healthy, mobile) but also and crucially the capability to choose between different priorities. 'Two persons who have identical achievements of *other* functionings may still not be seen as enjoying the same level of well-being if one of the two has no option to choose any other bundle of functionings, whereas the second person has significant options' (Sen 2008: 166). Sen's argument, in giving ethical priority to human flourishing, takes its inspiration from virtue ethics, but links this also to the idea that there are certain necessary conditions for any human being to flourish and that these universal conditions should be what development aid aims for. Sen does not think that there can be a general specification of these conditions of human flourishing but Nussbaum builds on his argument to do so in her book, *Women and Human Development* (2000). In the book she uses the human capabilities approach to establish a kind of yardstick against which to judge levels of development for women. This renders the goals of development both more complex and more demanding than the mere maximization of wealth, since it also draws attention to the importance of social and cultural practice and institutions for establishing the conditions for human flourishing. Nussbaum sets out ten capabilities that she argues are necessary for a flourishing human life:

1 Life – ability to live out a natural life span
2 Bodily health – ability to have good health including reproductive health, adequate nourishment, shelter
3 Bodily integrity – freedom of movement, security from physical violation, sexual and reproductive autonomy
4 Senses, imagination, thought – ability to use all of these fully in an educated way
5 Emotions – ability to be attached to others, to have a capacity for love and affection
6 Practical reason – to be able to reflect rationally, identify one's own conception of the good life and plan for it

7   Affiliation – ability to live with others in personal rela-
     tionships and social communities
8   Other species – ability to live in relation to nature
9   Play – ability to enjoy recreation
10 Control over one's material and political environment
     – ability to participate in political choices, ability to hold
     property, to work on equal terms with others (Nussbaum
     2000: 78–81)

On Nussbaum's account, the above list constitutes the
threshold conditions for a meaningful ethical life but she
argues that it allows for variation in the kinds of ethical life
that flourishing human beings construct, and is thus compatible with the emphasis of virtue ethics on the importance of
context and culture. In addition, she argues that human capabilities, as grounds to entitlement, bring together rights-based
and needs-based arguments from both contractarian and
deontological traditions and therefore provide a unifying
ground for an ethics of development. Unsurprisingly, however,
it has been argued that her list is less universal and culturally
uncontentious than she claims it to be. In particular the
requirements under 3 and 10 appear to reflect a liberal,
western set of assumptions about human nature and to
presume a liberal economic structure of property rights and
market relations. Critics have argued that this exemplifies the
false universalization of parochial moral assumptions, but
also a tendency to attribute the reasons for underdevelopment
to culture rather than to the workings of the global political
economy. This takes us back to one of the fundamental criticisms of development aid mentioned at the beginning of this
section, that is, that it relies too much on the view of both
the moral desirability and the historical inevitability of the
kind of development that certain liberal capitalist states have
enjoyed. And that it pays too little attention to the extent to
which the contemporary global economy constructs inequality and maintains global poverty, simultaneously making the
rich richer and the poor poorer (Jaggar 2008).

In this respect, one of the ethical issues raised by international aid policies relates not just to *what* such policies seek
to achieve but also to *how* they should be carried out.

Contrary to the impression given by the term 'aid', most development aid is not a simple gift on the part of the rich to the poor. It is bound up with long-standing bilateral and multilateral relationships between states and is often 'tied' in a variety of ways. Aid is one of the instruments of state foreign policy and is used to cement mutually advantageous relations between states, or between the state elites. So, for instance, aid may be given towards the construction of a dam in the recipient country but the engineering work on the dam will be required to be carried out by the donor country. Patterns of bilateral aid often reflect past colonial ties between states. And aid is often also tied to a set of economic or political conditions, most notoriously in the 'structural adjustment' policies of the 1980s when recipient states were obliged to liberalize their economies as a condition of receiving aid.

Moreover, the management and accountability mechanisms of aid budgets and projects are often in the hands of expert outsiders rather than of local people. From a utilitarian point of view, the *means* through which aid is delivered is a moral problem insofar as it fails to maximize the outcome of development. And there is considerable evidence to suggest that aid policies have not fulfilled this purpose, too often enriching local elites, or being applied by outsiders according to a model that doesn't take account of local conditions. From the point of view of Sen or Nussbaum, with their emphasis on human development, aid policies that are essentially paternalistic cut against the value that they put on autonomy as a human capability. This poses problems for aid projects that are top-down, even when they may work to improve other aspects of people's quality of life. Though, as we have seen in Nussbaum's case, the respect for autonomy as a key human capability could also justify political conditionality, in which aid is conditional on democratization processes, paradoxically imposing from above the possibility of choices from below.

In response to the critique of the technocratic, paternalistic view of aid, different approaches to the practice of aid have been developed, notably approaches that, in line with the concerns of the human development theorists, put emphasis on participation and empowerment for the recipients of aid

(Crocker 2008; Goulet 1995). Increasingly, the delivery of aid has been devolved to international non-governmental organizations which are then actively required to involve local groups on the ground and incorporate aims of recipient participation and project 'ownership', as well as poverty alleviation. Arguing from the perspective of a feminist ethic of care, Robinson welcomes these kinds of changes and sees them as a move away from the abstract universalism of traditional ethical positions on aid (Robinson 1999). In her view, the focus on grass-roots involvement in the construction as well as the implementation of aid projects recognizes the ethical value of concrete attachments between people. These projects build, extend and consolidate relations of care and responsibility not just between the local people but also between local people and international aid workers. This enables a relation between affluent and poor that is ethical and dialogical rather than technocratic and paternalistic. Moreover, it creates a context in which needs are more effectively met than when economic needs are separated out as a distinct category.

> These approaches are guided explicitly by *an ethics*, which is more than just a recognition of a problem that, for instance, 'it is morally wrong that people live in poverty' – a problem about which it is often assumed that we can address and solve using economic strategies. By contrast, these approaches reject the separation of economics, politics and morality by recognizing the transformatory potential of so-called intangible resources such as 'social networks, organizational strength, solidarity and a sense of *not being alone*'. (Robinson 1999: 162)

Human development and feminist ethical positions converge on the importance of properly recognizing the recipients of development as moral agents, in contrast to the focus on their 'powerlessness' in utilitarian, rights- and duty-based arguments. This shift in emphasis in terms of the answer to the *who* question has significant implications for the *how* question, so that, from this point of view, the ethical value of aid inheres as much in the process of delivery as in the amount that is given or the purely economic outcomes that may follow.

Reflective exercise

- Consider Nussbaum's list of human capabilities How definitive is this list? What would you add or subtract?
- Do outcomes matter more than processes when it comes to the delivery of development aid?

Sustainable development

When the notion of 'development' was first used, it was assumed not only that development would follow the particular pathway of existing 'developed' economies, but also that there was no problem in practice or principle with the idea of all economies becoming developed over time. From the 1970s onwards, however, it became increasingly recognized that the universalization of economic development was going to run into a variety of what Dower terms 'finiteness' problems (Dower 2007: 171). These problems included the finiteness of global non-renewable resources (such as coal and oil), the finiteness of the capacity of the planet to absorb the effects of development (global warming) and the finiteness of areas of the world producing renewable resources (food, timber). Some commentators and policymakers denied the importance of 'finiteness', either by challenging the scientific basis of claims about global warming and so on or because they were convinced that ways of tackling these problems would be discovered before they had done irreparable damage. However, by the 1980s a widespread consensus had emerged that environmental problems had to be taken into account in development policies. In the face of these problems, therefore, a new set of ethical issues emerged in relation to development which both put the old model of development into question and raised new questions about the appropriate ethical response to poverty in a global situation that was not only profoundly unequal but also unsustainable over time (Goulet 1995: 119–35; Low 1999).

At the most fundamental level, environmental issues put the anthropocentrism of standard debates about the ethics of development into question. Arguably, the root of pending ecological disaster is the move away from ways of living as humans that were compatible with the survival of other species and of the ecosystem more broadly. If this is the case, then the levels of affluence associated with industrialized processes of mass production and mass consumption are achieved at the expense of planetary destruction. This also implies that the 'speciesism' of ethical arguments in favour of development aid, premised on giving priority to *human* wants and needs, may be part of the problem rather than of the solution although, of course, this depends to some extent on how human wants and needs are understood (Gasper 2004: 49–83; see also Singer 1999 for a critique of speciesism in ethics). Biocentric ethics argues for the moral significance of all species, ecocentric ethics sees ecosystems and biospheres as having their own moral value, aside from the species of which they are made up (Attfield 1999: 27; Benson 2000; Schmidz and Willott 2002; Wenz 2001). At the most radical end of the spectrum, therefore, environmental ethics calls for a complete rethinking of moral traditions that put human beings at the centre. A less radical position calls for the recognition that without taking more account of the environmental costs of industrial levels of production and consumption, human wants and needs will be incapable of satisfaction at all. This view fits to some extent with the critique of economism in development already put forward by proponents of the idea of 'human development'. In terms of development policy, this has led to the view that the appropriate response to problems raised by environmental degradation is not to abandon the idea of development but to think in terms of 'sustainable development' (Stenmark 2002: 1). From this point of view, human development, including economic growth, can be reconciled with environmental stewardship and with obligations to future generations. In this context a variety of arguments about the ethics of sustainable development have emerged (Stenmark 2002).

Determining the ethics of approaches to sustainable development raises a series of issues to do with features specific to environmental problems. One such feature is the manifestly *global* impact of *local* practices when it comes to the environment. As we have seen, both contractualist and virtue ethics arguments can be made against the idea of a strong obligation for one state to give development aid to another. But in both cases, this is on the presumption that the line between what belongs to one state as opposed to another can be straightforwardly identified. The effects of phenomena such as climate change are not contained within sets of territorial borders and make the local practices of one state necessarily the business of all. Whether they like it or not, developed and developing states find themselves in relations to outsiders of actual and potential 'ecological debt', that is to say, of benefiting (at least in the short term) from ecological harms inflicted on others as well as themselves. Deep ecological interdependence fits badly with the delimitation of the scope of sustainable development to the boundaries of state authority or cultural community (Bullard 1999).

A second feature of environmental problems is that they have arisen largely as unintended consequences of actions undertaken for other reasons, and their immediate and medium-term effects are unequally distributed. Nineteenth-century industrialists (and contemporary British car drivers) did not deliberately set out to cause the climate change that is leading to all kinds of deleterious consequences in terms of weather patterns and desertification for many people in (mostly) poorer parts of the world. Nevertheless, the effects of these actions amount, in Singer's terms, to 'bizarre new ways of killing people' (Singer 2004: 19). This raises particular problems for the question of who owes what to whom when it comes to sustainable development. Should the polluter pay, even if they cannot afford to invest in clean energy? Should the most affluent pay, even if this means a reduction in the standard of living of their populations? From a utilitarian point of view, what matters morally is the outcome of actions rather than the motives that underlie them. According to Singer, this commitment to maximizing utility normally aligns utilitarian views about resource distribution with the Rawlsian principle of giving priority to the worst off. This is because the less you have, the more your utility will be increased even by a very small amount of additional goods, whereas for the rich the opposite applies: when you have a great deal already, then additional goods increase your marginal utility very little. In Singer's view, this means that the utilitarian response to climate change would indicate that the rich nations should pay much more, perhaps even all, of the burden of reducing emission of greenhouse gases (Singer 2004: 42–3).

Versions of contractualist and deontological arguments come to similar conclusions, though for somewhat different reasons. The contractualist case for rich countries bearing the burden of reducing global emissions rests on the 'ecological debt' argument. Because the rich nations have historically expropriated common environmental resources, and continue to be primary polluters of the global atmosphere, then they are under an obligation to make some kind of restitution to the poor nations by taking on the major share of costs of reducing emissions. Shue makes a somewhat different deontological spin on this argument, which involves squaring the task of tackling problems posed by global warming with a basic respect for human needs. For Shue, 'it is not equitable to ask some people to surrender necessities so that other people can retain luxuries' (Shue 2008: 228). He suggests, therefore, that poor countries should be given autonomy over a certain amount of environmental damage, in the interests of meeting basic human needs, and that it is the rich countries' capacity to pay, rather than their responsibility for the state of the environment, that underpins their moral obligation to bear the cost of reducing greenhouse gases. In a rather different vein, Hayward argues that the way forward is to institutionalize the universal human right to an adequate environment at the level of the state. This, he suggests will both push affluent states into more ecologically sound domestic policies, strengthen international law and regulation of environmental policy, and allow poorer states protection from the ongoing expropriative effects of global markets (Hayward 2005).

The above ideas about how to handle the 'finiteness' problems created by human action focus on establishing ethical principles for state action. However, Shue's emphasis on basic needs, and Hayward's on the human right to an adequate environment, that is to say one adequate for human health and well-being (first articulated in the Brundtland Report in

1987, discussed in Stenmark 2002), take us back to the deeper problem of the tension between economic development and environmental sustainability. It has been estimated that, if all countries developed to the extent of the richest nations, 'four planet earths would be required to provide the necessary ecological space' (Hayward 2005: 195). If this is the case, then it's clear that even if rich nations subsidize poor nations when it comes to allowances for economic growth and environmental damage, this isn't going to enable anything like the levels of development currently enjoyed by the rich.

From the point of view of virtue, feminist and postmodernist ethics, this points to a problem with individualist and rationalist ethical responses to environmental problems. Utilitarian, contractualist and deontological arguments still treat the environment essentially as a resource to be drawn on for the purposes of human goods, rather than as integral to human life as such. And they share rather than challenge the individualist and rationalist assumptions that are also inherent in the discourses of economic development. Here human development and care arguments, already encountered in relation to international development aid in general, suggest a different way of approaching the 'finiteness' problem by asking *how* lives might be lived ethically in a way that integrates our immanent connection with the environment, rather than focusing on the fairest way to manage environmental scarcity.

Ecological feminists, in particular, have argued that there are deep, long-standing links in western thought between the exploitation of the natural world and the exploitation of women, non-western men and animals. On this view, a radical transformation of our ethical values, which moves away from nature being understood and treated solely as a resource, is what is needed (Plumwood 1999; Warren 1999, 2000; Wenz 2001: 188–209). Other work seeking to develop an ecological global ethic has been inspired by postmodernist insights. Rose, for example, draws on Levinas's ethics and the idea of unconditional commitment to the other, to build links and learn from the indigenous ecologies of Australian Aboriginal peoples (Rose 1999). For Rose, ecological ethics is not about determining outcomes so much as it is about enabling dialogue between different understandings of the relation of humans to their environment (Rose 1999: 184). In a different, but equally postmodernist, vein, Harvey points to the impossibility of arriving at a universal consensus on environmental ethics to underpin environmental activism. He argues instead that the ethical task is to identify potential alliances between different viewpoints in order to pursue environmental justice politically, even in the (necessary) absence of agreement as to what it means (Harvey 1999). These arguments shift the ethical agenda away from determining an ethical solution to the problem of sustainable development (*what*) to the question of *how* to live ethically, without the assumption that any such solution is possible.

Reflective exercise

- Is it possible to have an adequate environmental ethics that is anthropocentric?
- How do you assess the relative ethical weight of development for poor countries as opposed to sustainability for the planet as a whole?
- Do you have a responsibility to change your lifestyle in response to the problem of global 'finiteness'?

Conclusion

Just as the discussion of the ethics of emergency relief is difficult to disentangle from the ethics of aid aimed at long-term solutions to the problem of world poverty, so the discussion of the ethics of development aid is inseparable from bigger questions about the way the global economy works as a whole, and the role and responsibility of different actors within it. The problem of environmental sustainability reinforces, as well as complicates, the requirement to look at aid and trade at a global level. When the idea of international development was originally formulated, it was assumed that economic growth and free trade could solve problems of scarcity. In the meantime, it seemed, all that was needed was for richer states and individuals to provide help for the poor while they were catching up. In the contemporary world, international development is understood to be a contributor to certain crucial forms of environmental scarcity and it's clear that rich states and individual lifestyles have had, and continue to have, an actively damaging effect on the world's poor, and that catching up may not even be a possibility.

As we have seen in this chapter, some of the arguments surrounding aid suggest that obligations of humanity or charity are discretionary, whereas others see them as categorical, but in either case the aid relation remains one-sided. Barry offers a useful summary of the difference between obligations of humanity and obligations of justice in relation to international aid. If aid is an obligation of humanity, he argues, then what matters is that it brings about the *outcome* of humanitarian relief. If this means interfering in the recipient state to make sure that the relief is properly distributed, then this is perfectly ethically acceptable and the recipient has no right to object. However, if aid is an obligation of justice, then it is a matter of *entitlement* on the part of the recipient; the donor is obliged to give the aid and has no right to interfere further (Barry 2008). For utilitarian approaches to the ethics of aid, this distinction between humanity and justice does not make sense. In general for utilitarianism, the means through which good outcomes are achieved are not ethically significant in comparison to the ends. A good outcome is what matters, whether that outcome was brought about by coercion or consent. However, in somewhat different ways, all of the other perspectives considered above put the paternalism of the aid relation into question and suggest that what is needed is a much more holistic understanding of the ethical requirements embedded in relations between rich and poor. In this respect, thinking about the ethics of aid and of sustainable development is a starting point for thinking about questions of global distributive justice in general, and it is to these questions that we turn in the following chapter.

References and further reading

Attfield, R. (1999) *The Ethics of the Global Environment*, Edinburgh: Edinburgh University Press. Provides an overview of key arguments in environmental ethics from the perspective of biocentric utilitarianism, that is to say the overall utility of the ecosystem, not just the well-being of the human species.

Barnett, M. and Weiss, T. G. (eds) (2008a) *Humanitarianism in Question*, Ithaca and London: Cornell University Press. A very good collection of essays that looks critically at contemporary international humanitarianism, especially since the end of the Cold War.

Barnett, M. and Weiss, T. G. (2008b) 'Humanitarianism: A Brief History of the Present', in Barnett and Weiss (eds), *Humanitarianism*, pp. 1–48. A brief history of contemporary trends in humanitarianism.

Barry, B. (2008) 'Humanity and Justice in Global Perspective', in Pogge and Moellendorf, *Global Justice*, pp. 179–209. First published in J. R. Pennock and J. W. Chapman (eds) (1982), *Nomos XXIV: Ethics, Economics and the Law*, New York, New York University Press, pp. 219–52. Establishes the distinction between obligations of humanity and obligations of justice.

Bauman, Z. (2001) 'Whatever Happened to Compassion?' in T. Bentley and D. Stedman Jones (eds), *The Moral Universe, Demos Collection* 16, pp. 51–6. A critique of contemporary attitudes to global poverty.

Baylis, J., Smith, S. and Owens, P. (eds) (2008) *The Globalization of World Politics: An Introduction to International Relations*, 4th edn, Oxford: Oxford University Press. A comprehensive set of introductory essays on all aspects of global politics.

Benson, J. (ed.) (2000) *Environmental Ethics: An Introduction with Readings*, London: Routledge.

Brender, N. (2001) 'Political Care and Humanitarian Response', in P. DesAutels and J. Waugh (eds), *Feminists Doing Ethics*, Lanham: Rowman and Littlefield, pp. 203–18. A critical examination of the application of an ethic of care to international humanitarianism.

Bullard, R. (1999) 'Environmental Justice Challenges at Home and Abroad', in Low (ed.), *Global Ethics and Environment*, pp. 33–44. Looks at the global costs of local practices for the global environment.

Calhoun, C. (2008) 'The Imperative to Reduce Suffering: Charity, Progress and Emergencies in the Field of Humanitarian

Action', in Barnett and Weiss (eds), *Humanitarianism*, pp. 73–97. A critical examination of the ethics of contemporary humanitarianism.

Crocker, D. (2008) *Ethics of Global Development*, Cambridge: Cambridge University Press. An argument in favour of the capabilities approach to development, bringing out its implications for the participation and empowerment of recipients of aid.

Dower, N. (2007) 'The Environment', chapter 8 of *World Ethics: The New Agenda*, 2nd edn, Edinburgh: Edinburgh University Press, pp. 170–90. A useful overview of global environmental ethics.

Edkins, J. (2000) *Whose Hunger?: Concepts of Famine, Practices of Aid*, Minneapolis: University of Minnesota Press. A postmodernist critique of the ethical assumptions at work in contemporary emergency aid and development practices.

Fearon, T. (2008) 'The Rise of Emergency Relief Aid', in Barnett and Weiss (eds), *Humanitarianism*, pp. 49–72. An analysis of contemporary trends in the provision of emergency aid.

Gasper, D. (2004) *The Ethics of Development*, Edinburgh: Edinburgh University Press. A good overview of debates in development ethics, including the tension between more economistic and more 'human development' approaches.

Goulet, D. (1995) *Development Ethics: A Guide to Theory and Practice*, London: Zed Books. This is written from the point of view of one of the proponents of a 'human development' approach.

Hardin, G. (2008) 'Lifeboat Ethics: The Case Against Helping the Poor', in Pogge and Horton (eds), *Global Ethics: Seminal Essays*, pp. 15–27. First published in *Psychology Today* 8(4) (1974): 38, 40–3, 123–4, 126. Famous utilitarian case *against* helping the world's poor.

Harvey, D. (1999) 'Consideration on the Environment of Justice', in Low (ed.), *Global Ethics and Environment*, pp. 109–30. A postmodernist argument for the impossibility of deciding what environmental justice is and the necessity of pursuing it.

Hayward, T. (2005) *Constitutional Environmental Rights*, Oxford: Oxford University Press. A systematic argument for the institutionalization of the human right to an adequate environment within state constitutions.

Jaggar, A. (2008) ' "Saving Amina": Global Justice for Women and Intercultural Dialogue', in Pogge and Horton (eds), *Global Ethics: Seminal Essays*, pp. 565–603. Originally published in A. Follesdal and T. Pogge (eds), *Real World Justice*, Dordrecht: Springer, pp. 37–63. A critique of the arguments of Okin and Nussbaum which put the emphasis on 'culture' as the key cause of women's oppression.

Low, N. (ed.) (1999) *Global Ethics and Environment*, New York: Routledge. A useful collection of essays that put forward different perspectives on the ethics of sustainable development.

MacGinty, R. and Williams, A. (2009) *Conflict and Development*, London: Routledge. An exploration of the ways in which issues of conflict and development are intertwined in contemporary world politics.

Nielsen, K. (1998) 'Is Global Justice Impossible?', *Res Publica* IV(2) 1998: 131–66. A Marxist-influenced critique of the idea of international development.

Nozick, R. (1974) *Anarchy, State and Utopia*, Oxford: Blackwell. A libertarian, contractualist argument against the redistribution of wealth to the poor, mainly targeted against Rawls's (1971) *A Theory of Justice*.

Nussbaum, N. (2000) *Women and Human Development*, Cambridge: Cambridge University Press. Develops a framework based on the ethics of human development for minimal criteria of human flourishing in relation to the position of women in India.

O'Neill, O. (2008a) 'Lifeboat Earth', in Pogge and Moellendorf (eds), *Global Justice: Seminal Essays*, pp. 1–20. First published in *Philosophy and Public Affairs* 4(3) (1975): 273–92. One of the earliest statements of the obligation on the global rich to help the global poor on deontological grounds.

O'Neill, O. (2008b) 'Rights, Obligations and World Hunger', in Pogge and Horton (eds), *Global Ethics: Seminal Essays*, pp. 139–55. First published in F. Jimenez (ed.) (1987), *Poverty and Social Justice*, Tempe, AZ: Bilingual Press, pp. 86–100. Arguing for the limitations of rights discourse as the appropriate way to frame transnational humanitarian moral obligations.

Plumwood, V. (1999) 'Ecological Ethics from Rights to Recognition: Multiple Spheres of Justice for Humans, Animals and Nature', in Low (ed.), *Global Ethics and Environment*, pp. 188–212. An approach to environmental ethics that draws on feminist arguments.

Pogge, T. and Horton, K. (eds) (2008) *Global Ethics: Seminal Essays, Volume II*, St Paul: Paragon House.

Pogge, T. and Moellendorf, D. (eds) (2008) *Global Justice: Seminal Essays, Volume I*, St Paul: Paragon House. This collection and the one above bring together a comprehensive collection of influential essays in Global Ethics. Where I refer to essays in these collections, I have included the original publication details for the article in question.

Rawls, J. (1999) *The Law of Peoples*, Cambridge, MA: Harvard University Press. A contractualist argument that defends limitations on the obligation of rich to poor states, discussed in more detail in chapter 5.

Robinson, F. (1999) 'A Critical Ethics of Care in the Context of International Relations', chapter 7 in *Globalizing Care: Ethics, Feminist Theory and International Relations*, Boulder, CO: Westview, pp. 137–68. Draws out the implications of feminist care ethics for addressing issues of poverty and underdevelopment.

Rose, D. B. (1999) 'Indigenous Ecologies and an Ethic of Connection', in Low (ed.), *Global Ethics and Environment*, pp. 175–87. An argument for dialogue with indigenous peoples based on Levinas's ethics.

Schmidz, D. and Willott, E. (eds) (2002) *Environmental Ethics: What Really Matters, What Really Works*, New York: Oxford University Press. A selection of readings across all aspects of environmental ethics.

Sen, A. (1984) 'The Right Not to Be Hungry', in P. Alston and K. Tomasevski (eds), *The Right to Food*, Boston and Utrecht: M. Nijhoff. Elaborates on the idea of 'metarights' as a way forward for establishing a human right not to be hungry.

Sen, A. (2008) 'The Concept of Development', in Pogge and Horton (eds), *Global Ethics: Seminal Essays*, pp. 157–80. First published in H. Chenery and T. N. Srinivasan (eds), *Handbook of Development Economics, Volume I* (1988), Amsterdam: Elsevier Science Publishers B. V., pp. 9–26. Questions accounts of development that rest on a wholly economistic understanding of the term.

Shue, H. (1980) *Basic Rights: Subsistence, Affluence and US Foreign Policy*, Princeton: Princeton University Press. An influential statement of a needs-based account of basic human rights.

Shue, H. (2008) 'Subsistence Emissions and Luxury Emissions', in T. Pogge and K. Horton (eds), *Global Ethics: Seminal Essays*, pp. 207–32. Originally published in *Law and Policy* 15(1) (1993): 39–59. Argues for the need for international agreements on limiting greenhouse gas emissions to respect the basic human rights of the poorest.

Singer, P. (1999) 'Ethics across the Species Boundary', in Low (ed.), *Global Ethics and Environment*, pp. 146–57. A defence of Singer's inclusion of all sentient beings as having moral status.

Singer, P. (2004) 'One Atmosphere', chapter 3 in *One World: The Ethics of Globalization*, 2nd edn, New Haven: Yale University

Press, pp. 14–50. Offers an argument that the rich nations should pay the bulk of the costs of limiting greenhouse gas emissions.

Singer, P. (2008) 'Famine, Affluence and Morality', in Pogge and Horton (eds), *Global Ethics: Seminal Essays*, pp. 1–14. First published in *Philosophy and Public Affairs* 1(3) (1972): 229–43. A crucial text that provoked an extensive literature on ethical approaches to emergency aid and famine relief in the 1970s and 1980s which continues to be a reference point for contemporary debates.

Stenmark, M. (2002) *Environmental Ethics and Policy Making*, Aldershot: Ashgate. An ethical interrogation of the meaning and implications of sustainable development.

Thomas, C. (2008) 'Poverty, Development and Hunger', in Baylis et al. (eds), *Globalization of World Politics*, pp. 468–87. Introductory overview of international development policy since the end of the Second World War.

Unger, P. (1996) *Living High and Letting Die: Our Illusion of Innocence*, New York: Oxford University Press. Follows through Singer's argument that individuals have an obligation to give to those in extreme need.

Warren, K. (1999) 'Care-Sensitive Ethics and Situated Universalism', in Low (ed.), *Global Ethics and Environment*, pp. 131–45. An argument for a care approach to environmental ethics.

Warren, K. J. (2000) *Ecofeminist Philosophy: A Western Perspective on What It Is and Why It Matters*, Lanham: Rowman and Littlefield. See chapters 5 and 8 for a more in-depth discussion of the ethics of eco-feminism.

Wenz, P. S. (2001) *Environmental Ethics Today*, Oxford: Oxford University Press. A good overview of the range of perspectives within environmental ethics.

Woods, N. (2008) 'International Political Economy in an Age of Globalization', in Baylis et al. (eds), *Globalization of World Politics*, pp. 242–60. An introductory overview of developments in the global economy since the end of the Second World War.

5
Global Distributive Justice

Introduction

In the previous chapter we explored ethical arguments surrounding emergency and development aid and examined questions about the obligations of the rich and the entitlements of the poor in the aid relation. We also examined how the ethics of development is in complicated tension with the dangers posed by unrestricted economic growth to the global environment. The discussion of aid and development, therefore, necessarily opened up questions about the moral evaluation of the distribution of wealth in the current world order, the ways in which the variety of human needs are met and the idea of 'development' as a solution to problems of poverty. In this chapter we will examine some of the attempts to develop a global theory of distributive justice which could then provide a yardstick by which not just the ethics of development projects or humanitarian aid could be assessed but the justice of global economic arrangements in general. As we will see in the course of the discussion, as was the case with the ethics of aid, ethical debates about global distributive justice are always entangled with other kinds of ethical questions, for instance about the intrinsic value of rights to collective political or cultural self-determination, about the relation between economic or welfare rights and other kinds of individual rights, about the ethics of migration and immigration, and about the location of moral responsibility for extremes of poverty in the contemporary world. We will begin with Rawls's two-stage contractualist theory of international distributive justice and a variety of related contractualist and virtue ethics arguments that all support a strong distinction between distributive justice *within* states as opposed to *between* them. In the second section we will explore critiques of the ethical significance of the inside/outside distinction for the requirements of distributive justice and will look briefly at Rorty's argument for the current impossibility of global distributive justice. In conclusion, we will consider the implications of the arguments explored in both this and the previous chapter for the question of 'who owes what to whom and how' and summarize the ethical stakes in those arguments.

Two faces of justice

We have already discussed Rawls's work as an example of contemporary contractualist moral theory in chapter 2. His book, *A Theory of Justice* (1971), was important both for its version of the contractualist method and for the substantive implications that he drew from that method. As we noted earlier, he used the device of a hypothetical 'original position', in which participants possessed rational self-interest and had knowledge of generalities, including the desirability of certain 'primary goods', but did not know precisely who they would be in terms of social position, wealth, character or abilities in the society that would be constructed according to the principles of justice that they were framing. Three key principles of justice followed: a principle of equal liberties, which entrenched familiar liberal civil and political rights; and then two explicitly distributive principles, the principle of equality of opportunity and the 'difference' principle, according to which material inequality would only be permitted if it worked to improve the position of the worst-off. In *A Theory of Justice*, Rawls states that justice only applies where people are involved in a scheme of social cooperation, and he assumes that this kind of scheme applies within states but not between them. When he discusses inter-state relations in *A Theory of Justice*, he confirms minimal principles of non-intervention, obligations to fulfil treaties and respect for the laws of war but does not see distributive principles as having a place. Relations between individual people from different states do not figure as of any relevance to justice at all (Rawls 1971: 377–82). The way in which the argument of *A Theory of Justice* is presented is in keeping with the contractualist tradition. The suggestion is that anyone would find the assumptions built into Rawls's original position uncontentious and that therefore the resultant theory of justice should have universal appeal. However, in his later work, partly in response to critics, Rawls acknowledged that his theory of justice effectively crystallized the nature of justice for liberal societies rather than providing a wholly neutral account of the meaning of justice in general. It was after this shift in his thinking about the status of the claims of *A Theory of Justice* that Rawls turned his attention again to the question of international justice in *The Law of Peoples* (1999).

For Rawls, international justice is also contractually based, but rather than being a hypothetical contract between individuals it is a hypothetical contract between 'peoples'. Peoples are distinct from states since peoples reflect the character of the principles on which their own association is founded, whereas states, on Rawls's account, act independently of peoples in a way more akin to Hobbesian security maximizers in an anarchic state of nature: 'in proposing a principle to regulate the mutual relations between peoples, a people or their representatives must think not only that it is reasonable for them to propose it, but also that it is reasonable for other people to accept it' (Rawls 1999: 57).

Rawls starts from the point of view of liberal peoples and existing principles of international society that he argues would be agreed to by them to regulate their affairs with each other (inter-liberal people justice). He identifies eight principles of justice between peoples, of which the first is a principle of respect for the freedom and equality of other liberal peoples. Following from this he extrapolates a set of requirements, including those previously articulated in *A Theory of Justice*, to do with non-intervention, obeying the laws of war and so on. Two of the principles are relevant to questions of distributive justice between peoples: first, that peoples honour human rights; and second, that 'peoples have a duty to assist other peoples living under unfavourable conditions that prevent their having a just or decent political and social regime' (Rawls 1999: 37). Rawls then moves on to consider non-liberal peoples and their relation to the law of the peoples between liberal states. He distinguishes between different types of non-liberal people, coming up with four ideal-type categories: decent hierarchical peoples; outlaw peoples; societies burdened by unfavourable conditions; and benevolent absolutisms. Of these, it is only 'decent hierarchical peoples' who, Rawls argues, would endorse the inter-liberal law of peoples, essentially because their own internal organization meets certain minimal criteria of justice, including respect for basic human rights. Human rights, in Rawls's view, are a subset of the more extensive individual rights embodied in liberal justice. He identifies them with rights to life, liberty, property and formal equality (Rawls 1999: 65). The right to life includes the right to means of subsistence as well as security.

Rawls calls both liberal and decent hierarchical peoples 'well ordered'. The law of peoples essentially sets out the conditions of toleration between peoples and therefore also its limits. Outlaw states have tyrannical and aggressive governments that violate human rights of their own citizens, in particular those of security, liberty and equality, but also pose a threat to other states. Because outlaw states exist beyond the bound of toleration by either liberal or decent peoples, it is permissible to intervene in their affairs. The aim of such intervention, however, is to enable outlaw states to eventually become well ordered and therefore subscribe to the law of the peoples. 'Burdened societies' are similarly situated from the point of view of well-ordered ones, but with rather different implications:

> Burdened societies, while they are not expansive or aggressive, lack the political and cultural traditions, the human capital and know-how, and, often, the material and technological resources needed to be well ordered. The long-term goal of (relatively) well-ordered societies would be to bring burdened societies, like outlaw states, into the Society of well-ordered

peoples. Well-ordered peoples have a *duty* to assist burdened societies. It does not follow, however, that the only way, or the best way, to carry out this duty of assistance is by following a principle of distributive justice to regulate economic and social inequalities among states. (Rawls 1999: 106)

Rawls give several reasons why a scheme of distributive justice such as he has recommended within liberal states should not apply to the law of peoples. One reason is that he argues there is no necessary connection between a people being wealthy and a people being well ordered. In the law of peoples it is the latter aim that is crucial. A second reason is that he sees the levels of wealth of different peoples as inherently linked to their political culture. To some extent following Sen's argument about famine as a failure of entitlement rather than as following from a lack of resources, Rawls argues that it is more important to address problems with the burdened society's basic structure than to provide direct economic assistance. A third reason he puts forward is the importance of self-determination as a principle and the way this is undermined by paternalistic aid giving. Underlying Rawls's ethical arguments for limiting the requirements of distributive justice between peoples is the assumption that peoples are essentially responsible for their own economy and that the economies of peoples operate relatively discretely (Rawls 1999: 108). The duty of assistance that well-ordered peoples owe to burdened societies is reminiscent of the rationale for development aid discussed in the previous chapter in that it is designed to ensure that those societies become capable of managing themselves, rather than to deliver a particular set of goods to all individuals. In his conclusion to *The Law of Peoples*, Rawls contrasts his view with that of cosmopolitan arguments that would make the individual the reference point for international distributive justice. Rawls is adamant that the law of peoples does not refer to individuals but to collectives.

Rawls is not alone in seeking to make a clear distinction between principles of justice within, as opposed to between, societies. A variety of other thinkers follow a similar path. Typically such arguments rely on versions of contractualism, on the kind of moral contextualism inherent in MacIntyre's virtue ethics, or on some kind of mixture of the two. Nagel, for instance, draws on a Hobbesian version of contractualism in order to argue that justice is dependent on mechanisms of enforcement that are available only within states and not between them. On these grounds he argues that schemes of distributive justice can only be applied within the state. Without a world state, the idea of global distributive justice simply doesn't make sense (Nagel 2005). In a rather different version of a contractualist argument, Miller locates the moral validity of the inside/outside distinction in the principle of national self-determination and the ethical qualities inherent in relations between fellow citizens as opposed to between fellow human beings. For Miller, the justice of distributive schemes within states is grounded in the possibility of democratic agreement which sets up a distinctive set of obligations between citizens that are different in kind from the obligations of humanity that may transcend political borders (Miller 2008). Moreover, he argues that these distinctive obligations are embedded in national solidarities that make it possible for citizens of the same state to recognize the justice of paying taxes to help fellow citizens but which effectively make it very difficult to nurture global solidarities that might have the same effect. On this view, not only does the principle of national self-determination imply that political communities must take responsibility for their own members but also that there is a necessary tension between democratic self-determination and the idea of global principles of justice.

Walzer develops a different kind of argument that builds on a distinction between moral maximalism and moral minimalism (Walzer 1994). Moral maximalism refers to complex, culturally and historically embedded moral traditions; moral minimalism refers to the principles that can be abstracted out from specific maximal moralities to provide a common, universally shared moral vocabulary. Moral minimalism, for Walzer, is only capable of doing quite limited work; at most it enables common recognition of gross injustices perpetrated by others and promotes a principle of tolerance similar to Rawls's first principle in the law of peoples. As far as Walzer is concerned, principles of distributive justice are always maximalist. This is because, on his account, the very recognition of something as a 'good' to be distributed varies between different maximal moralities, reflecting different understandings of what it means to live a good life within specific cultural and historical contexts. Taking as his example the principle of 'equality of opportunity' from Rawls's *A Theory of Justice*, Walzer argues that this principle relies on the understanding of human life as a 'career', which is highly specific to modern liberal societies and would simply not make sense in other sorts of contexts. For somewhat different reasons, then, Nagel, Walzer and Miller argue for a position similar to that of Rawls in *The Law of Peoples*. Schemes of distributive justice apply within societies or states. Beyond them there may be requirements to give aid out of obligations of humanity, or in order to secure justice between states (as opposed to between individuals), but that is all. One of the implications of this position is that distributive justice depends on clear borders between political communities. In Walzer's case, this means that national communities must have a right to control immigration, not only in order to maintain the availability of goods within the state but so that the maximalist understanding of justice within any given national community may be sustained (Walzer 2008).

Reflective exercise

- Should principles of global distributive justice apply only between political communities rather than between individuals?
- How convincing do you find Walzer's claim that conceptions of distributive justice are 'maximal' and therefore always specific to particular ways of life?

Justice is not two-faced

As we might expect, following arguments already encountered in the previous chapter, the idea that schemes of distributive justice should apply only within political communities, rather than between them, has been heavily contested from a variety of ethical perspectives. Broadly speaking, the arguments against the 'two-faced' view of justice fall into two kinds, separately or in combination: first, there are arguments that ground human entitlements to a certain share of economic goods in moral principles or values that are independent of actual economic relations and circumstances (what they are, how they came about, etc.); and secondly, there are arguments that see economic relations and circumstances as morally relevant, but counter that those circumstances are not in practice bounded by political community or cultural commonality in the ways suggested by Rawls or Walzer. Arguments of the first kind include utilitarianism, which as we have already seen undermines the distinction between humanitarian obligations and obligations of justice. 'When subjected to the test of impartial assessment, there are few strong grounds for giving preference to the interests of one's fellow citizens, and none that can override the obligation that arises whenever we can, at little cost to ourselves, make an absolutely crucial difference to the well-being of another person in real need' (Singer 2004: 180).

For Singer, the obligation to promote human welfare is not discretionary. The impartial standard is one in which every individual, as Bentham requires, counts as one, and none as more than one. There is therefore an absolute obligation, bearing on all individuals, to address world poverty, both directly through charitable giving and indirectly through promoting just institutions to govern provision of aid and the management of the world economy.

Traditionally, rights-based theories of justice have lent themselves less obviously to schemes of global redistribution than utilitarian arguments. This was because in the dominant liberal human rights tradition, fundamental rights were identified with so-called 'negative' security and liberty rights as opposed to 'positive' economic rights. Negative rights were seen as more fundamental because they only required others to refrain from certain kinds of actions (not to kill, not to torture, not to steal), whereas positive rights, such as rights to means of subsistence, health care or education, as pointed out in the previous chapter, required both the identification of, and positive action by, correlative duty-bearers. Henry

Shue responds to this issue in his rights-based account of international justice which rejects the negative/positive distinction when it comes to fundamental human rights (Shue 1980). For Shue, we can identify economic rights (such as the right to subsistence) as fundamental human rights, along with liberty and security, firstly, because they presuppose each other: without the means to subsist, then the right to life and liberty doesn't make sense; without life and liberty, then the means to subsist are not worth having. Secondly, he questions the view that liberty and security rights do not require a great deal of positive action on the part of duty-bearers, pointing out how institutions of law and criminal justice are necessary to uphold people's rights not to be murdered, tortured, robbed and so on. On his view, this means that a world in which the human right to subsistence is not guaranteed is fundamentally unjust. Shue includes, in his right to subsistence, rights to adequate food and clothing as well as minimal health care and access to unpolluted air and water. In contrast to Rawls, who also argued that subsistence is a human right, Shue argues that guaranteeing the right to subsistence requires changes in international political and economic institutions. We all share an obligation to construct world institutions with mechanisms for distributive justice that would address the injustice of the violation of the subsistence rights of so many people in the current world, even if global redistributive schemes may be contrary to our own immediate individual interests.

Many theorists have followed Shue's lead in developing rights-based theories of global distributive justice. In some cases, such theories are grounded in the deontological idea of the intrinsic equal moral worth of human beings, whereas others see human rights as grounded more naturalistically in universal human interests or needs. But however they are justified, rights theories make the specific circumstances of people's lives essentially irrelevant to what counts as a legitimate claim to justice. As with other fundamental rights, the point is that you cannot *lose* the right to have enough to eat; it is something you possess purely in virtue of being human, although what you do with it when you have it is up to you. Contrary to utilitarianism, however, rights-based theories hold on to a distinction between obligations of justice and of humanity. Theorists vary as to how to specify economic rights, some giving a more maximalist version than others, but respecting such rights is not the same as furthering the open-ended goal of maximizing human welfare. On a rights-based account such as Shue's, justice is served if your subsistence rights are fulfilled, beyond them you may still be much poorer than others, but the mere fact of economic inequality or comparative poverty is not itself unjust.

Nussbaum's 'human capabilities' account of global justice is strongly outcome-oriented, but also strongly anti-utilitarian. One of the problems that she sees with utilitarianism is that utilitarians premise their moral thinking on an idea of equality that is fundamentally misrepresentative of actual global inequalities between people. This means that utilitarianism cannot take account of the way that preferences are distorted by poverty, deprivation and culture so that, for instance, what it means to be in 'real need' is going to be perceived differently by someone who has always survived at subsistence level, or who is used to being considered of lower status than others, than by someone used to a higher standard of living and personal respect. For Nussbaum, utilitarianism doesn't provide a way of identifying real need. Moreover, as we saw in the previous chapter, she argues that in practice utilitarian approaches to development have been crude and unmindful of people's actual situations.

In *Women and Human Development* (2000), Nussbaum develops a feminist theory of global justice that is critical of both feminist care and postmodernist approaches. Nussbaum's critique of care and postmodernist ethics is linked to her critique of utilitarianism in that she sees them as unable to take account of the ways in which people's expectations and self-worth are distorted by conditions of extreme poverty. In her view, the valorizing of women's work in care ethics is in danger of justifying traditional, unequal, gendered divisions of labour (Nussbaum 2000: 241–97). Meanwhile the deference paid to multiculturalism in post-modernist arguments leads to the danger of losing the capacity to critique the status of women, particularly in non-western cultures. In this respect, Nussbaum clearly embraces a feminist ethic of justice, similar to that also put forward by Okin (Okin 1989, 2008). Okin argues that postmodernist approaches to justice, because they reject the idea that women's situations are similar across cultural boundaries, become uncritical of women's oppression except where it is clearly articulated by women themselves. This fails to deal with cultures that either educate women into accepting their own inferiority or do not allow them the space to speak about their concerns (Okin 2008; see Jaggar 2008 for a critical response to both Nussbaum and Okin, and Robinson 2006 for a defence of a care approach to global distributive justice).

Although more sympathetic to rights-based theories than to utilitarianism or non-universalist feminist ethics, Nussbaum nevertheless suggests that they (rights-based theories) tend to lend themselves to moral minimalism in accounts of global justice. She argues that they draw the line between justice and humanity too low, and get too bogged down in dealing with the problem of correlative duties. For this reason she prefers to base her theory on an account of the human good: 'my main contention will be that we cannot solve the problem of global justice by envisaging international cooperation as a contract for mutual advantage among parties similarly placed in a State of Nature. We can solve [it] only by thinking of what all human beings require to live a richly human life' (Nussbaum 2005: 97–8).

However, even though Nussbaum argues for the superiority of a virtue over a rights-based approach to global justice, there is much in common between her idea of 'human entitlements' grounded in capabilities (discussed in the previous chapter) and those theories of human rights that ground themselves in accounts of fundamental human needs or interests, such as Shue's. As with Shue's argument, Nussbaums's theory is holistic, with the just distribution of economic goods being intrinsically linked to other facets of what makes human life worth living. As with Shue again, on Nussbaum's account, the ethical standards inherent in her account of the human good require an institutional response, including rich nations giving substantial proportions of their GDP to poor nations, and multinational corporations having the responsibility to promote human capabilities in the regions in which they operate (Nussbaum 2005: 215).

Nussbaum derives her account of global justice solely from the moral implications of what it means to be human. She is therefore also highly critical of proceduralist theories of global justice, such as Rawls's two-stage contractualist account. But for other theorists, fundamental human rights or entitlements alone do not sufficiently account for the requirements of global justice. These obligations are also bound up with the specific ways in which humans are, and have been, historically related to each other. Theorists making this kind of claim acknowledge the Rawlsian contractualist point of the special ethical relevance of the kinds of reciprocal relations between people involved in a common scheme of social cooperation but see these relations as going beyond the boundaries of political community.

One of the best-known arguments against the two faces of distributive justice was made by Beitz who, in *Political Theory and International Relations* (1999), directly challenged Rawls's two-stage theory. Using Rawls against himself, Beitz argued that the facts of differential geographical distribution of natural resources and cross-border economic interdependence between individuals meant that global distributive justice would necessarily be of concern to people in the original position. Once this was acknowledged, Beitz argued that Rawls's own conclusions in *A Theory of Justice* would follow, and people in the original position would opt for a global difference principle. Pogge made a similar argument in relation to Rawls (Pogge 2008a) and has gone on to articulate a full-blown theory of global justice that brings together an 'institutionalist' human rights position with a version of the economic interdependence claim (Pogge 2008b). The main aim of his institutionalist account has been to set the bar between justice and humanity higher than other 'interactionist' rights-based theories have done. 'On the interactional understanding of human rights, governments and individuals have a responsibility not to violate human rights. On my institutional understanding, by contrast, their responsibility is to work for an institutional order and public culture that ensure that all members of society have secure access to the objects of their human rights' (Pogge 2008b: 71).

On Pogge's account, just as all human beings have a right not to be murdered and a duty not to murder others, so all human beings have a right not to be extremely impoverished (and therefore hungry, ill and in danger of untimely death) and, correspondingly, all human beings have a duty to refrain from violating this right. In conditions of economic interdependence, in which past colonialism and present dominance of the institutions governing the global political economy mean that certain rich societies control global economic outcomes, Pogge concludes that this means that the rich have a categorical duty, as a matter of justice, to stop actively violating the rights of the poor. Going back to Singer's analogy of the child drowning in the puddle, Pogge argues that this misrepresents the relation of rich to poor in the global economy – the adult in question is not an innocent 'helper' but the one who pushed the child into the puddle in the first place. Pogge's argument takes direct issue with Rawls's claims that economies of peoples are relatively discrete, and that the primary reason for inequalities in living standards between them are to do with domestic political culture. He also pushes the implications of a rights-based theory of justice further by claiming that we are already in an institutional order that has the capacity to address the deep wrongs inherent in current global distributions of wealth. This implies compulsory schemes for the global redistribution of wealth such as a 'global resources dividend', and having rights-based principles of justice underpinning global economic transactions, which would involve major reforms in the regulation of the world economy.

> As affluent people and countries, we surely have positive moral duties to assist persons mired in life-threatening poverty whom we can help at little cost. But the label detracts from the weightier, negative duties that also apply to us: we should reduce severe harms we will have caused; and we should not take advantage of injustice at the expense of its victims. These two negative duties apply to us if we (sometimes together with third world elites) are imposing a global order whose unfairness benefits us while exacerbating severe poverty abroad. (Pogge 2008c: 552)

Pogge's work introduces a new dimension to theories of global justice by his stress not just on the injustice of current global distributions of wealth but also on the moral relevance of how that injustice came about and is sustained in the current world order. For Pogge, justice is global in two senses: firstly because there are universal human rights to which all human beings are entitled; secondly because we live in a globalized economy which has been unjustly structured over a long period of time. A major advantage of this argument, in comparison to other rights-based theories, is that it addresses the problem, to which O'Neill drew attention in the previous chapter, of how to identify the obligation-bearer when it comes to dealing with global poverty immediately rather than in a projected future. As Caney has pointed out, however, Pogge's insistence on negative duties as morally 'weightier' continues to draw a justice/humanity distinction by confining categorical responsibilities to address extreme need to those responsible for the harm involved. In other words, your responsibility to relieve suffering is more acute if you bear some of the responsibility for inflicting that suffering, for instance by being part of a dominant economic elite that sets the rules of the global economic order, than if you do not. This puts the situation of those harmed by, for example, natural disasters such as earthquakes on a different moral footing from those dispossessed by a colonial history. In his insistence on the moral significance of reciprocal relations between people there is, therefore, a continuity between Pogge's argument and theorists such as Rawls and Miller, both of whom are only able to maintain a clear distinction between justice inside and outside the state on the assumption that rich states, and their citizens, *are not* directly responsible for the situation of poor states and their citizens (Caney 2005).

From Singer to Pogge, arguments against the two faces of justice challenge the idea that justice must be different within and between states. Crucial to this challenge is the dismissal of the ethical significance of bounded political communities in themselves on contractual, democratic or cultural grounds, although most global justice theorists agree that the state remains an important instrumental mechanism for the achievement of the goals of justice across the globe. Unsurprisingly, these globalist accounts, particularly in the stronger versions of Nussbaum and Pogge, have been countered in turn by those who insist on the validity of the two-faced argument. Issues that are hotly disputed include the

claim that rich states are in some sense culpable for the position of poor states (Rawls versus Pogge), the question of
whether globalist accounts of justice are politically and culturally imperialist (Okin and Nussbaum versus Jaggar), and
the question of whether allowing unrestricted economic
migration would be one way to fulfil the requirements of
justice (Carens versus Walzer; see Carens 2008; Walzer 2008).

Reflective exercise

- All the thinkers discussed in the second section
  above consider that the current global economic
  order is unjust. Do you agree? If you agree, then
  what reasons would you give for your view?
- What kind of account of individual or collective
  moral responsibility is implied by Pogge's institutional account of a rights-based approach to global
  justice?

Beyond the statist/globalist impasse

In an article, 'Towards a Critical Theory of Transnational
Justice', Rainer Forst attempts to find a way through this
apparent impasse between two-faced ('statist') accounts of
global justice and their 'globalist' critics by drawing on the
resources of discourse ethics (Forst 2001: 170). In doing so,
he follows Pogge in differentiating judgements about justice
from other kinds of moral judgement because such judgements involve allocations of responsibility. However, he
argues that this idea of justice has to be operationalized
across different levels and in different contexts in a way that
connects justice in local, national, international and global
contexts but also allows for justice to mean different things
in different settings. This is possible because discourse ethics
is not solely concerned with specific outcomes but with practices of justification, in which all those affected have a right
to participate. The principle of justification is fundamental

and applies regardless of actual political contexts. However, Forst goes on to point out that *actual* practices of justification necessarily happen within particular political settings and that therefore the institutional specification that follows from the principle of justification is likely to differ between different political communities. To impose a 'thick' globalist account of justice on specific political communities is to violate the rights to political and cultural self-determination that are inherent in the principle of justification. However, in order for those fundamental rights to be respected, global justice is nevertheless required.

> To break the vicious circle of multiple, internal and external domination and to establish *political autonomy both within particular states and within the international system*, a principle of *minimal transnational justice* is called for. According to this principle, members of societies of multiple domination have a legitimate claim to the resources necessary to establish a (minimally) justified democratic order within their political community *and* that this community be a participant of (roughly) equal standing in the global economic and political system. (Forst 2001: 182)

In Forst's view, a discourse ethics approach can be used to reconcile the insights of both statism and globalism. It allows for the complexity of relations of domination in which responsibility for injustice may lie in the global economic system or in local culture or corruption. It also combines respect for the political and cultural autonomy of political communities, in a way that fits with Rawls's, Miller's and Walzer's arguments, with an acknowledgement of the way that global structures effectively undermine that autonomy, as argued by Pogge. In line with all of the above thinkers, it insists on a bottom-line set of human rights, inherent in the (according to Forst culturally neutral) principle of justification, that underpins both national and transnational justice.

Another example of a theorist using discourse ethics to address the statist/globalist impasse in contemporary theories of global distributive justice is Benhabib (Benhabib 2004). One of the issues that split the two sides of the debate relates to the ethical significance of membership of political communities. Statist theories, for example those of Walzer, relate the exclusionary character of membership of political community to the conditions of possibility for robust distributive justice. They therefore are committed to the right of political communities to limit movement of peoples across their borders and to control access to citizenship rights. In contrast, globalist theories, with no investment in the ethical significance of political membership as such, are much more open to the idea that restrictions on economic migration should be lifted. As Carens has pointed out, rights-based and utilitarian positions both make strong cases for open borders (Carens 2008). Benhabib, building on the assumptions of discourse ethics, argues that both of these extreme positions are flawed. The statist position is flawed because it confuses the boundaries of ethical community (those potentially affected by the opening or closing of borders) with those of political community (current members of the community). The globalist position is flawed because it puts the achievement of global justice above the democratic process. Rather than adopting a fixed position on closed or open borders, Benhabib argues for a process of 'democratic iteration', essentially a dialectical engagement between those included and those excluded by particular borders. As with Forst, the answer lies in a particular kind of process rather than a specific set of outcomes.

On reflection, as one might expect given the deontological roots of discourse ethics, the form and substance of Forst's and Benhabib's arguments are more closely allied with globalist than with statist thinkers. In spite of his claims to the contrary, it is difficult to reconcile Forst's '(minimally) justified democratic order' with Rawls's 'decent well-ordered societies', or the requirement for the resources necessary for the achievement of minimal democracy with Rawls's view that being a well-ordered society is not primarily a matter of resources. Moreover, although Forst claims that the human rights inherent in the principle of justification are culturally neutral, and correspond to Walzer's 'thin' morality, this depends on an abstracted account of what meaningful participation in processes of justification implies, which underpins rather than is extrapolated out of 'thick' morality. The deontological aspect of Forst's argument carries more weight than Walzer's 'thin' morality can bear, in particular in its implications for distributive justice. In the case of Benhabib, as she acknowledges, her critique of the globalists depends more in the end on a universalist commitment to democratic process than on a recognition of the inherent value of a bounded political community. Having said this, however, these arguments are useful in pointing to the common ground between certain aspects of statist and globalist arguments. Statists such as Rawls, Miller and Walzer accept a minimal account of universal human rights. Globalists such as Nussbaum and Pogge accept that cultural sensitivity and democratic process are important to accounts of global justice. None of these thinkers envisages a world state in which the political solution to problems of global justice is to bring all nations under one sovereign order. In spite of their differences, in many respects the mainstream arguments about global justice inhabit the same moral and political vocabulary. This is a vocabulary in which membership of the human species and also of political and economic orders has ethical significance, though in different ways and to different extents.

Reflective exercise

How do you see the relation between global democracy and global justice – can we have one without the other?

The impossibility of global distributive justice

From the postmodernist, pragmatist point of view of Rorty, all of the arguments considered so far incorporate mistakes about humanity and states or peoples as moral communities. In an essay, 'Who are We? Moral Universalism and Economic

Triage', Rorty argues that theories of global distributive justice rest on philosophical universalisms that could only have emerged from a particular western history of material plenty (Rorty 2008: 317) and from a fundamental confusion between moral or political claims about those with whom 'we' identify as part of a common moral community, and supposedly true metaphysical or scientific claims about human nature. On Rorty's account, moral or political claims are not to do with some kind of shared intrinsic essence but with the moral community to which we aspire, and our commitment to that community can only be evident in practice. On his view, it is not at all clear that a commitment to either states/peoples or humanity as inclusive moral communities is actually subscribed to by rich people, whether within the context of their own states or in that of the global economic order. This isn't because rich and powerful people are particularly morally bad but because there simply are not sufficient resources for the rich and powerful to maintain their own moral community and respond adequately to the needs of others and, 'if you cannot render assistance to people in need, your claim that they form part of your moral community is empty' (Rorty 2008: 321). Instead, he suggests, what we find is ongoing economic 'triage' both within and between states in which decisions are constantly made by the rich and powerful, about who qualifies for help and who doesn't, in the interest of preserving the moral life with which the rich and the powerful identify:

> a politically feasible project of the egalitarian redistribution of wealth requires there to be enough money around to ensure that, after the redistribution, the rich will still be able to recognize themselves – will still think their lives worth living. The only way in which the rich can think of themselves as part of the same moral community with the poor is by reference to some scenario that gives hope to the children of the poor without depriving their own children of hope. (Rorty 2008: 323)

Rorty's argument claims to be philosophical and clearly does rely on a particular understanding of the meaning of 'moral community' which is taken to imply an identification with other members of the community as being of equal moral significance, sharing the same moral/political goals, and therefore entitled to the same rights and opportunities as everyone else within it. If we are to take seriously liberal theories of global justice, he argues, this must mean the extension of these same rights and opportunities to all. This means that, to the extent that we differentiate in practice between insiders and outsiders, then our claims to a moral community of humanity are spurious. In this respect he suggests a particularly rigorous understanding of global distributive justice that goes some way beyond even the 'thickest' of the theories considered above, other perhaps than that of the strongest statement of a utilitarian position. In addition, however, Rorty also relies on the empirical claim that global distributive justice could not be possible without a severe negative effect on the position of the global rich and the kinds of democratic and welfare institutions that their wealth has made possible and by which their moral community is defined. This is clearly in contrast with Rawls's argument that liberal polities are not primarily dependent on being resource-rich and with the arguments of theorists such as Singer and Pogge who claim that the meeting of people's needs could be done without putting the achievements of democratic and welfare states in jeopardy. In this respect, Rorty takes us back to issues raised in Hardin's critique of Singer and to the issues of sustainability raised in the previous chapter.

Reflective exercise

- What difference does/should it make to our views about the global distribution of wealth that global resources are finite and shrinking?
- Is the willingness to draw moral distinctions between the claims of humanity and the claims of justice a way of avoiding the implications of what a genuinely just world order would mean for the rich?

Conclusion

Theories of global distributive justice set out principles to govern or regulate the distribution of goods at a global level. These principles provide a yardstick against which current distributions may be judged but also embody goals towards which 'we' (*who?*) ought to strive. Most arguments about global distributive justice operate at a high level of abstraction. Nevertheless, they have concrete implications for practice in that they identify what justice requires (*what*), go some way to specifying the entitlements and responsibilities of different kinds of actor in relation to distributive justice (*who*) and, rather more rarely, specify the sorts of mechanisms through which justice might be achieved (*how*). In most cases the prescriptive implications of the theories cut against the procedures (market relations, inheritance, state welfare schemes in one's country of origin) and outcomes (extreme poverty and extreme affluence, massive inequality) characteristic of the prevailing distribution of goods in the global economic order.

But theorists clearly differ on the question of *what* justice requires and therefore to *whom* it is owed at any given time, from the most minimal requirement to security of property rights, to arguments for a right to a certain level of subsistence, to much more ambitious claims for resources to underpin the development of a range of human capabilities. They also differ on *who* has the responsibility for addressing global injustice and on *how* this should be done. Responsible agencies are identified variously. Theorists such as Rawls and Walzer stress the responsibility of particular political communities and their citizens to look after themselves; theorists such as Singer stress the responsibility of particular individuals (wherever they come from) to do their part; Nussbaum and Pogge argue for the role of international institutions such as the UN or the WTO as well as that of rich states; critical theorists put emphasis on both formal and informal international bodies, including international non-governmental organizations such as charities, as well as individuals. Mechanisms for bringing about justice range from straightforward giving (by individuals or collectives) to making

international aid conditional on economic or political reform, to the imposition of global taxation schemes, to democ-
ratizing the regulation of global markets. In all these
complexities, it is sometimes difficult to disentangle when
theorists have an *ethical* as opposed to a *practical* disagreement. So it is worth reminding ourselves, in conclusion, what
the *ethical* issues are in the debates about global justice which
are always also debates about whether, and if so where, the
line between obligations of *justice* and obligations of *humanity* should be drawn in a global context.

We can identify five ethical issues that are central to debates
about global distributive justice and to the ethics of aid discussed in the previous chapter. First, we have the question of
the *ethical* significance of human individuals. In what does
this significance consist? Deontological, utilitarian and virtue
ethics all give us different answers to this question and the
answers have different implications for requirements of
justice: is it about securing certain fundamental rights, maximizing utility, or enabling human flourishing? And, which-
ever it might be, what exactly do these categories (rights,
utility, human flourishing) mean? For instance, we have the
distinction made by Pogge between interactionist and institutional rights-based approaches. We also have Walzer and
Nussbaum both drawing on aspects of virtue ethics but to
very different effect. Some of these answers allow the retention of distinctions between national as opposed to transnational obligations of justice, whereas others support the
erosion of this distinction. Some make it possible to make a
clear distinction between justice and humanity and some blur
the lines between the two.

Secondly, we have the question of the *ethical* significance
of the individual versus the community. Do communities
(peoples, states, nations) have a distinctive moral status over
and above the sum of the moral value inherent in their
members and, if so, is this status contractually or culturally
grounded? Depending on what one thinks about this question, for instance whether one is more sympathetic to Rawls
or to Nussbaum, one is likely to have a different view on the
obligations of justice owed to those outside of the boundaries
of political community as opposed to those within.

Thirdly, we have the *ethical* question of whether we support what Shue has referred to as 'fault' or 'no-fault' accounts in determining where responsibility rests for fulfilling obligations of justice. A 'fault' account sees the history of relations between actors as morally relevant to the question of who owes what to whom. This view is exemplified by Pogge in his argument that the rich north has profited, and continues to profit, from its unjust economic relations with the poor south and should therefore be obliged to address the problems it has caused. In contrast, outcome-oriented accounts such as Singer's or Nussbaum's link responsibility to address injustice to capability rather than culpability. Fourthly, we have the *ethical* question of whether what matters most for global justice are *procedures* or *outcomes*. Is a situation just if it has been arrived at via the principle of justification, as Forst would argue, or is it only just if it is oriented towards 'what all human beings require to live a richly human life', as Nussbaum would argue? The fifth ethical issue is perhaps less obvious than the other four, but is in some sense fundamental to all of them and is raised by the problem of trying to adjudicate between them. This is the question of the basis of the authority of claims made by theorists of global justice or development ethics. How do we decide which of the above accounts is persuasive, and to what extent does this imply that *everyone* should be persuaded by one ethical position rather than another?

References and further reading

Beitz, C. (1999 [1979]) *Political Theory and International Relations*, Princeton: Princeton University Press. First published in 1979, this was one of the first texts to elaborate a global theory of justice.

Benhabib, S. (2004) *The Rights of Others*, Cambridge: Cambridge University Press. Looks at a range of issues, including those of immigration, from a standpoint informed by discourse ethics.

Brock, G. and Brighouse, H. (eds) (2005) *The Political Philosophy of Cosmopolitanism*, Cambridge: Cambridge University Press. A collection of essays bringing together a variety of contractualist, deontological and virtue ethics approaches to questions of global distributive justice.

Caney, S. (2005) 'Distributive Justice', chapter 4 in *Justice Beyond Borders: A Global Political Theory*, Oxford: Oxford University Press, pp. 102–47. A very thorough overview of the literature, defending a deontological approach to distributive justice.

Carens, J. (2008) 'Aliens and Citizens: The Case for Open Borders', in Pogge and Moellendorf, *Global Justice: Seminal Essays*, pp. 211–33. First published in *The Review of Politics* 49(2) (1987): 251–73. Argues that contractualist and utilitarian theories of justice support open borders.

Cole, P. (2000) *Philosophies of Exclusion: Liberal Political Theory and Immigration*, Edinburgh: Edinburgh University Press. A strong argument for the incompatibility between the assumptions of liberal political theory and restrictive immigration policies.

Forst, R. (2001) 'Towards a Critical Theory of Transnational Justice', in T. Pogge (ed.), *Global Justice*, pp. 169–87. A discourse ethics argument that seeks to mediate between statist and globalist positions on global distributive justice.

Jaggar, A. M. (2008) ' "Saving Anima": Global Justice for Women and Intercultural Dialogue', in T. Pogge and K. Horton (eds), *Global Ethics: Seminal Essays*, St Paul: Paragon House, pp. 565–603. Originally published in A. Follesdal and T. Pogge (eds) (2005) *Real World Justice*, Dordrecht: Springer,: 37–63.

Miller, D. (2008) 'The Ethical Significance of Nationality', in Pogge and Moellendorf, *Global Justice: Seminal Essays*, pp. 235–53. First published in *Ethics* 98(4) (1988): 647–62. An argument that justifies a two-faced approach to thinking about distributive justice.

Miller, D. and Hashmi, S. H. (eds) (2001) *Boundaries of Justice: Diverse Ethical Perspectives*, Princeton: Princeton University Press. An unusual and interesting collection of essays which looks at a variety of different cultural perspectives on the moral status of boundaries, including Christian, Confucian, Islamic, Judaic, as well as at standard statist and globalist arguments.

Nagel, T. (2005) 'The Problem of Global Justice', *Philosophy and Public Affairs* 33(2): 113–47. A defence of the limitation of justice to the context of the state on grounds of enforceability.

Nussbaum, M. (2000) 'In Defence of Universal Values', chapter 1 of *Women and Human Development*, Cambridge: Cambridge University Press, pp. 34–110. This explains Nussbaum's position in contrast to utilitarian, care and postmodernist ethical theories.

Nussbaum, M. (2005) 'Beyond the Social Contract: Capabilities and Global Justice', in G. Brock and H. Brighouse (eds), *The Political Philosophy of Cosmopolitanism*, pp. 196–218. An argument for the superiority of the capabilities approach to social justice over that of utilitarian and rights-based theories.

Okin, S. M. (1989) *Justice, Gender and the Family*, New York: Basic Books.

Okin, S. M. (2008) 'Gender Inequality and Cultural Differences', in Pogge and Horton, *Global Ethics: Seminal Essays*, pp. 233–57. First published in *Political Theory* 22(1) (1994): 5–24. Feminist 'justice' argument for the cross-cultural relevance of universal values of equality.

Pogge, T. (ed.) (2001) *Global Justice*, Oxford: Blackwell. Includes mainly contractualist and deontological contributions to debates over global distributive justice.

Pogge, T. (2008a) 'An Egalitarian Law of the Peoples', in Pogge and Moellendorf, *Global Justice: Seminal Essays*, pp. 461–93. First published in *Philosophy and Public Affairs* 23(3) (1994): 195–224. A critique of Rawls's *The Law of Peoples*.

Pogge, T. (2008b) *World Poverty and Human Rights*, 2nd edn, Cambridge: Polity. Extended version of Pogge's theory of global distributive justice and its practical implications for redistribution.

Pogge, T. (2008c) ' "Assisting" the Global Poor', in Pogge and Horton, *Global Ethics: Seminal Essays*, pp. 531–63. First published in D. K. Chatterjee (ed.), *The Ethics of Assistance: Morality and the Distant Needy* (2004), Cambridge: Cambridge University Press. Reiterating Pogge's argument that there are strict negative duties to address problems of global poverty.

Pogge, T. and Horton, K. (eds) (2008) *Global Ethics: Seminal Essays, Volume II*, St Paul: Paragon House.

Pogge, T. and Moellendorf, D. (eds) (2008) *Global Justice: Seminal Essays, Volume I*, St Paul: Paragon House. This collection and the one above bring together a comprehensive collection of influential essays in Global Ethics. Where I refer to essays in these collections, I have included the original publication details of the article in question.

Rawls, J. (1971) *A Theory of Justice*, Oxford: Oxford University Press. Contractualist theory of justice within the state.

Rawls, J. (1999) *The Law of Peoples*, Cambridge, MA: Harvard University Press. Contractualist theory of justice between political communities.

Robinson, F. (2006) 'Care, Gender and Global Social Justice: "Rethinking Ethical Globalization" ', *Journal of Global Ethics*

2(1): 5–25. Application of care ethics to the question of global distributive justice.

Rorty, R. (2008) 'Who are We? Moral Universalism and Economic Triage', in Pogge and Horton, *Global Ethics: Seminal Essays*, pp. 313–23. First published in *Diogenes* 44 (1996): 5–15. Critique of the idea of global distributive justice on grounds of finitude of resources and lack of political will.

Shue, H. (1980) *Basic Rights: Subsistence, Affluence and US Foreign Policy*, Princeton: Princeton University Press. A founding text on the meaning of basic rights.

Singer, P. (2004) 'One Economy', chapter 3 of *One World: The Ethics of Globalization*, 2nd edn, New Haven: Yale University Press, pp. 51–105. Largely utilitarian argument for global justice.

Walzer, M. (1994) 'Distributive Justice as a Maximalist Morality', chapter 2 in *Thick and Thin: Moral Argument at Home and Abroad*, Notre Dame: University of Notre Dame Press, pp. 21–39. Walzer's application of his contextualist moral thinking to the question of distributive justice.

Walzer, M. (2008) 'The Distribution of Membership', in Pogge and Moellendorf, *Global Justice: Seminal Essays*, pp. 145–77. First published in P. G. Brown and H. Shue (eds) (1981), *Boundaries: National Autonomy and Its Limits*, Totowa: Rowman and Littlefield. Argument for the power of communities to control access to membership.

6
Ethics of War

Introduction

In contrast to the ethics of international humanitarian and development aid or global distributive justice, the ethics of war has been the focus of explicit theological, political and philosophical argument for a long time. Because war has been commonly practised, by most societies, across both time and place for a variety of purposes, most societies have evolved ideas about what war is and how it ought to be conducted. In a world in which international laws of war *claim* global reach and technologies of war *have* global reach, the ethics of war is one of the central concerns of Global Ethics. In this chapter, we will be examining the ethical perspectives at work in contemporary arguments about the ethics of war and the ways in which they have been applied to recent developments in international and global conflicts. As we will see, debates on the ethics of war raise the same issues that were fundamental to the discussion of the ethics of development and global justice in the previous two chapters. Claims about what is or is not ethically permissible in the use of violence for political ends depend on assumptions about the ethical status of the individual, the moral value of community or culture as opposed to the individual, the meaning and implication of moral responsibility, and the relative ethical importance of outcome over procedure. And different views on these issues present us with the same problem of adjudication and therefore with the question of the authoritative ground and reach of ethical claims.

We will begin by unravelling the complex mixture of ethical perspectives embedded in the western tradition of 'just war theory' which has been particularly influential on the development of international laws of war. The most well-known contemporary exponent of the ethics of war is Walzer who draws on the just war theory tradition but reformulates it in terms of modern ethical perspectives and modern accounts of political community. We will move on to examine his position and some of the critical responses to it in the second section, in particular from deontological and feminist perspectives, including ethical arguments for pacifism. Developments since the end of the Cold War have led to a revitalizing of ethical debate about different kinds of uses of collective political violence, including humanitarian intervention, international terrorism and the so-called 'war on terror'. In the third section we will examine these debates: how they rely on different traditions of moral thinking, and their implications for the obligations of collective and individual political actors. In the conclusion we will consider how debates over the ethics of war turn on the same ethical issues as those about aid, development and distributive justice.

Just war theory

'Just war theory' has become the accepted term for a body of thinking that originated in Christianity, once Christianity had abandoned its original pacifism. For early Christians it was clear that their New Testament beliefs implied the rejection of all uses of violence. For this reason, when later Christian thinkers wanted to break the link between Christianity and pacifism, they had to provide justifications, and it was in these justifications that 'just war theory' was born. Over time, two distinct aspects of 'just war theory' were developed. The first dealt with arguments over the circumstances when it might be just for a ruler or people to go to war (still referred to as arguments *ad bellum*). The second dealt with arguments about how war, once undertaken, should be conducted (still referred to as arguments *in bello*) (Clark 1988: 31–50; Elshtain 1991). It isn't possible to do full justice to the complexity of different contributions to 'just war' thinking between the early Christian era and the present. Instead, in order to get a sense of the kinds of argument it involved, we will examine a late twentieth-century summary of Christian 'just war' thinking, *The Challenge of Peace: God's Promise and Our Response* (National Conference of Catholic Bishops 1983), formulated by a conference of Catholic bishops (1983). This revisiting of just war theory reflected the experiences of war and warfare during the twentieth century. In particular the bishops were concerned with the ethical validity of nuclear war and nuclear deterrence. In what follows we will look at each of the just war ethical considerations formulated by the bishops and what kinds of ethical argument underpin them.

Justice ad bellum

1   Just cause: 'War is permissible only to confront a "real and certain danger", i.e. to protect innocent life, to preserve conditions necessary for decent human existence and to secure basic human rights.'
  Ethical reasoning: This account of just cause is strongly deontological in its foregrounding of the value of human life and human rights. It also reflects deontology in its reference to 'innocence', since deontological perspectives see the distinction between innocence and guilt as morally crucial in determining what may be done to others.

2   Competent authority: 'War must be declared by those with responsibility for public order, not by private groups or individuals.'
  Ethical reasoning: This criterion was originally grounded in Christian virtue ethics. It condemned private wars, which undermined the possibility of the stable political order needed to enable each individual to flourish in their role within the community. Challenges to that community undermined the Christian vision of the good life on earth, which was

essentially a preparation for eternal life. In the modern context, competent authority becomes identified with the legitimate authority of the state, or with inter-state bodies (such as the UN), and is ultimately justified on contractualist grounds as deriving from the wills of the peoples that states represent.

3   Comparative justice: In recognition of the fact that there may be some justice on each side, 'every party to the conflict should acknowledge the limits of "just cause" and the consequent requirement to use *only* limited means in pursuit of its objectives.'

Ethical reasoning: This consideration makes sense in Christian terms, because of the comparison of human with divine faculties, the point being that humans are inherently limited; they are not God and they might get things wrong. In terms of ethical perspectives that we have examined, this theme of moral humility is most pronounced in positions that reject rationalist accounts, in particular certain versions of feminist and postmodernist ethics. In secular accounts of the ethics of war, as we will see, it is this criterion that is most likely to disappear in the updating of just war theory. One of the consequences of this in modern just war theory is a detachment of *ad bellum*, from *in bello*, ethical reasoning.

4   Right intention: 'War can be legitimately intended only for the reasons set forth above as a just cause.'

Ethical reasoning: This rests on a strongly deontological argument. As with Kant's account of what counts as a 'moral' action, it must be done on moral grounds. It is immoral to do the right thing for the wrong reasons.

5   Last resort: 'For resort to war to be justified, all peaceful alternatives must have been exhausted.'

Ethical reasoning: This principle suggests that, even though peace is not always ethically preferable to war, it is usually preferable. This position is most obviously underpinned by a consequentialist argument that on the whole more harm is done to more people by using war as a means than by using peaceful mechanisms. In modern contexts, this kind of consequentialist thinking is closest to utilitarian reasoning in its requirement for a kind of cost/benefit analysis of outcomes as the basis of moral judgement.

6   Probability of success: The purpose of this 'is to prevent irrational resort to force or hopeless resistance when the outcome of either will clearly be disproportionate or futile'.

Ethical reasoning: Here again the reasoning is strongly consequentialist in making outcomes, rather than principles or intentions, the reference point for ethical rightness or wrongness.

7   Proportionality: 'The damage to be inflicted and the costs incurred by war must be proportionate to the good expected by taking up arms.'

Ethical reasoning: Consequences are also the reference point for this principle and in modern contexts this is often treated as a utilitarian position. It is important to differentiate between proportionality *ad bellum*, which involves making a cost-benefit analysis about the war as a whole, from proportionality *in bello* (see below).

Justice in bello

1   Proportionality: The damage inflicted in particular military operations (specific battles, bombing campaigns, etc.) during the course of a war should always be proportional to the strategic aims of those particular operations.

2   Discrimination: 'Lives of innocent persons may never be taken directly, regardless of the purpose alleged for doing so. . . . Just response to aggression must be . . . directed against unjust aggressors, not against innocent people caught up in a war not of their making.'

Ethical reasoning: It's clear that whereas the first *in bello* principle involves the kind of cost-benefit analysis typical of utilitarian thinking, the second *in bello* principle is strongly deontological, very much reflecting the Kantian formulation of the categorical imperative that people should never be treated solely as means to others' ends, but always also as 'ends in themselves'. The discrimination principle, which goes back to medieval discussions of justice in the conduct of war, has always posed a problem because of the empirical difficulty of ensuring that 'innocents' (in modern secular just war theory and international law, 'innocents' become defined as 'non-combatants' or 'civilians') never get targeted in war. Traditionally, Christian just war theory dealt with this problem by making the *intention* underlying a particular attack the key to the morality of the actions of the attacker. The double-effect principle acknowledges that a moral act may have unintended regrettable outcomes but argues that this doesn't alter the morality of the act in question (Coates 1997: 239–64). This means that an attack on a military target that also kills non-combatants is still just *in bello* if the killings of the non-combatants were not intended. Clearly tactics like mass bombings, or use of weapons of mass destruction like nuclear or biological weapons, are intended to kill indiscriminately and would therefore not pass the double-effect test.

On the basis of the above, rather brief, analysis, it's already possible to see that the principles and criteria embedded in the just war theory tradition reflect ethical perspectives that are varied and not always compatible with one another. Partly for this reason, just war theory cannot act as a straightforward checklist by which one can decide on the legitimacy of a particular war, either before, during or after the fact. Instead it provides a set of starting points for thinking through the ethical dilemmas inherent in war. Just war theory requires moral actors to face up to the need to make judgements in contexts in which there are no straightforward rules or procedures. In this respect, as a whole, it links most closely to the virtue ethics tradition and the importance of *phronesis*.

Reflective exercise

Examine the list of *ad bellum* and *in bello* principles outlined above.

- Which principles do you find least convincing and why?
- How do you see the relation between *ad bellum* and *in bello* considerations? Could a just war be fought unjustly? If so, does this make it into an unjust war?

Twentieth-century just and unjust wars

At the same time that the Catholic bishops produced their Pastoral Letter, ethical and political theorists were formulating non-theological arguments about the ethics of war. Like the bishops, these arguments reflected the particular experiences of war in the twentieth century, in particular relating to the Second World War, to nuclear deterrence and to the Vietnam war. Walzer's *Just and Unjust Wars* (2006 [1977]) led the way in secular discussions of the ethics of war and continues to be a central reference point in twenty-first century debates. As with his work on principles of distributive justice, discussed in the previous chapter, Walzer's approach to the ethics of war was contextual. He took as his starting point the principles he identified as inherent in the modern international system and, throughout the book, he uses historical illustrations to demonstrate the workings of those principles. On this basis, Walzer elaborated an ethics of war that made a clear distinction between justice *ad bellum* and justice *in bello*. In his view, it was possible for a war to be just in one respect but unjust in another, in contrast to the tradition of just war theory in which the two are necessarily related to each other.

In terms of his *ad bellum* thinking, Walzer follows contractualist, liberal arguments in taking individuals as having certain inherent rights and freedoms that cannot be completely traded off in the social contract that founds the state. He also, however, follows a particular brand of liberalism in making a strong connection between national self-determination, understood as the right of peoples to self-government, and the flourishing of individual rights. This means that rather than individual and state rights being in tension, as in traditional social contract theory, the two are mutually reinforcing. For Walzer the primary 'just cause' for war is the defence of the state against aggression. An attack on the state is simultaneously an attack on the people's right to self-determination and on individuals' rights to survive and flourish. It is therefore perfectly appropriate to use the 'domestic analogy' and treat state self-defence as directly analogous to individuals' rights to defend themselves (Walzer 2006: 58–73).

Although Walzer also argues that extreme violations of individual rights may be a just cause for war (see discussion of humanitarian intervention below), his discussion of justice *ad bellum* always reflects his view that national and individual self-determination are inherently related. The kind of violation of individual rights he sees as most clearly providing just cause are those in which individual and community are literally conflated, genocidal attacks that make no distinction between individual and national, ethnic or cultural identity (Walzer 2006: 251–68). This follows from both his contractualism and his commitment to a virtue tradition of ethical thinking in which moral life, as with thinkers such as MacIntyre, is inherent in shared community and culture. For Walzer, there is a sense in which individual life abstracted from community context is meaningless; the state is not just ethically important because it protects individual rights but because it protects the common identities that give individual life ethical meaning.

Walzer's commitment to the ethical significance of political community inflects his views about the consequentialist elements of traditional just war theory *ad bellum* (probability of success, proportionality). For Walzer, consequences are not just about numbers of individual lives lost and saved. Although they are about this, they are also about the fate of political communities. We are therefore not in a straightforwardly utilitarian position in which costs (to aggregate individual utility) and benefits (to aggregate individual utility) involve comparing like with like. This makes 'probability of success' issues less significant ethically when the weaker party is engaging in a struggle for the identity and survival of a people. And it also makes it more difficult to assess proportionality since there is a special value attached to political community (Norman 1995: 149–53).

When it comes to *in bello* justice, Walzer follows traditional just war theory and its principles of proportionality and discrimination and the ways in which they have been recognized in modern laws of war. In relation to discrimination, he starts from the deontological point of the inviolability of non-combatants. But, as with traditional just war theory, he allows for the argument from double effect. In his case, however, the requirement goes beyond purity of intention in the abstract as the key to the morality of the act of war. In addition, Walzer argues that the soldier must actively minimize unintended damage to non-combatants, even at cost to himself. In other words, soldiers should always take greater risks themselves if this will limit 'collateral damage' (Walzer 2006: 152–9). Having said this, however, Walzer's recognition of the ethical significance of political community affects his views on discrimination in circumstances in which the community is at risk. He notoriously suggests that under conditions of 'supreme emergency', by which he means the point at which the survival of a political community is threatened immediately and as such, discrimination considerations may be overridden (Walzer 2006: 251–68; 2004: 33–50).

A variety of theorists have taken issue with Walzer's arguments. From an ethical rationalist perspective, deontological critics have most often been concerned with the way in which his contractualism and contextualism appear to permit an overriding of the infinite moral worth of individuals. Norman contests Walzer's analogy between individual and political community. He argues that the deaths of human individuals involve the absolute extinction of a unique being whose moral significance is incommensurable with that of any other human. This is strongly dis-analogous with political communities, for whom absolute extinction does not follow as long as some of the members of that community carry on its distinctive cultural traditions, even when its independent political existence has been overcome. Moreover, whereas surviving individuals may retain old or embrace new identities and create new communities, communities cannot bring dead individuals back to life. For Norman this suggests that it must be ethically wrong to treat individuals as means to the end of the survival of communities; the two are not morally equivalent (Norman 1995: 40–62, 132–46).

Caney also argues that Walzer's ethics of war overemphasizes the ethical worth of states and of the principles of sovereignty inherent in the contemporary international system at the expense of the rights of individuals. He argues that Walzer's reliance on the 'domestic analogy' leads him to be insufficiently discriminating between good states and bad states, and therefore to potentially justifying immoral political regimes and underestimating moral grounds for cross-border intervention to protect individual rights. Moreover, he points out that Walzer's view that 'supreme emergency' may justify disproportionate and indiscriminate actions *in bello* contradicts Walzer's own emphasis on the moral weight of respect for non-combatant immunity. Ultimately, Caney sees Walzer's ethical position as inconsistently shifting between the community and the individual as the key ethical reference points. From Caney's point of view, Walzer's *ad bellum* emphasis on the importance of the domestic analogy actively undermines his *in bello* emphasis on individual rights (Caney 2005: 192–9).

Caney's charge of inconsistency suggests that an alternative to Walzer's view could be built either on consistently collectivist or consistently individualist premises, which would ensure an immanent link between justice *ad bellum* and *in bello*. As Walzer points out, a consistently collectivist argument, grounded on a claim to the moral worth of communities as such, would be likely to reduce just war theory to *ad bellum* considerations only since the ends of the state would always outweigh the means used to attain them. Even so, however, there would be a profound difference between a war fought solely to defend the interests of a particular national collective as opposed to one fought to sustain the possibility of a system or society of coexisting peoples. In the former case, there are no arguments for limiting the conduct of warfare as long as the national interest is served (this is the position commonly attributed to 'political realism'; see Walzer 2006: 3–20). In the latter case, however, the need to coexist in the future with present enemies provides good reason to restrict the use of force and suggests *in bello* practices of proportionality, if not of discrimination. However, most attempts to construct an ethics of war alternative to Walzer's have been grounded on consistently individualist rather than collectivist premises, following either utilitarian or deontological lines of argument.

Developing an ethics of war on the basis of either utilitarian or deontological reasoning leads to shifts in the emphases of both *ad bellum* and *in bello* arguments in comparison to

Walzer's hybrid position. In terms of *ad bellum*, it is no longer possible to operate on the domestic analogy in which the political community is treated as analogous to an individual with fundamental rights. The right to self-defence of states can now only rest either on its claim to maximize aggregate individual utility or on its claim to respect the moral worth of human individuals. In both cases, the idea of giving an ethical priority to the state's own citizens, simply because of their national identity, no longer makes any sense. Instead the nature of the state itself becomes a crucial part of the analysis. If a state does not act in accordance with either utilitarian or deontological moral principles, then it is doubtful whether its self-defence matters at all, unless it happens to be the case that not only its members' utility or rights, but also those of the members of the aggressor state or states, is at stake. This might mean that in some cases states had no right to self-defence if their members would actually be better off (in utilitarian or deontological terms) if the state were invaded. In this respect, utilitarian and deontological accounts are likely to be less permissive of traditional inter-state wars and more permissive of humanitarian interventions than Walzer's account.

When it comes to *in bello* justice, then clearly utilitarian and deontological positions generate very different arguments from each other. Whereas Walzer struggles to combine ethical perspectives in his argument in a way similar to traditional just war theory, utilitarian and deontological arguments simplify what is at stake. For utilitarians what matters is the maximization of individual utility. As we have noted before, this means that it is morally acceptable for the utility of a minority to be sacrificed for the greater good. So even if the principle of discrimination *in bello* is generally justifiable in utilitarian terms, as rule utilitarians would argue, it is always possible to encounter a scenario where this is not the case. For classical utilitarians, therefore, the fundamental *in bello* principle is that of proportionality. Proportionality embodies the cost-benefit calculation inherent in the principle of utility itself and ensures impartiality between the different protagonists.

In contrast, from a deontological point of view, discrimination is vital to justice *in bello*. Theorists such as Anscombe

(1981) and Nagel (1972) highlight the ethical importance of respecting the rights of 'innocents' or 'non-combatants', in spite of the inherent difficulty of drawing the line between them in either principle or practice. From a strictly deontological point of view, it can never be justified to intentionally use another human purely as a means to your own ends.

In spite of their differences, however, in the context of modern warfare, both utilitarian and deontological arguments *in bello* threaten to undermine the justice of any war *ad bellum*. In the case of utilitarianism, the disproportionate power of weapons of mass destruction potentially undermines the case for any modern war satisfying the criterion of maximizing individual utility. Norman even suggests that if one takes the consequences of any war seriously in the long term, including the role earlier wars play in creating later ones, and the technologies to fight them, then there is always a strong utilitarian case against war as such – even wars considered to be archetypically just, such as the war of the Allies in the Second World War (Norman 1995: 209–10). For deontologists, the indiscriminate nature of modern weapons potentially undermines the case for any modern war being respectful of each human being as an end-in-themselves (Holmes 1989: 146–82).

It was mentioned at the beginning of this chapter that just war theory originated as a response to the pacifism of the early Christian church. During the twentieth century, pacifist arguments provided a minority counterpoint to both religious and secular just war thinking. And, in particular in the context of the threat of nuclear war and the actuality of nuclear deterrence in the Cold War, deontological arguments against the justice of war have been made. Of these, the most powerful have been those arguments that give priority to the Kantian principle that you should never use other human beings as a mere means for others' ends. To the extent that principles of discrimination are inevitably violated in war, then some people in any war, however just the war may be in *ad bellum* terms, are going to become mere instruments for the purposes of others, which suggests that *in bello* justice is unattainable (Norman 1988). An older deontological approach, one embedded in the pacifism of early Christianity and revived by some modern pacifist thinkers, puts emphasis rather on the wrongness of using violence as such, and on the argument that it is morally better to suffer harm than to inflict it. In this case, the basis of just cause *ad bellum* is undermined (Holmes 1989). This latter position has been countered in turn by equally deontological positions, such as that of Anscombe (1981), which argue that to outlaw war as such is to commit the same crime of indiscrimination as that of utilitarians who permit the torture of the innocent few to maximize the utility of the many. For Anscombe, war is a necessary means to punish the guilty and protect the innocent; to refuse to fight is to collude with the aggressor state in violating its victims.

Aside from deontological arguments, the other main inspiration for pacifism as an ethical position has come from feminism. During the 1980s, in parallel with the Catholic bishops' revisiting of traditional just war arguments, and the attempts of Walzer and others to provide a secular basis for just war thinking, feminist philosophers were also engaged in developing alternative perspectives on the ethics of war. War as a social institution is deeply linked to assumptions about gender. In the western tradition of ethical and political thought, women have been, in general, characterized as more 'pacific' than men, weaker and in need of protection. Women's lack of active participation in armed conflict has historically figured as one of the reasons for excluding women from full citizenship. Partly because of this, as political, ideological positions, feminism and pacifism have been linked together in certain contexts. Nevertheless, there is no connection in principle between feminism and pacifism and only certain strands of feminist thought, such as care ethics, have embraced pacifist arguments. From the point of view of an ethic of care, just war theory, in particular in its secular forms, posed two kinds of problem: first because of its requirements on moral judgement; second, because of the way that the violence of war directly contradicts the values and practices inherent in taking care as an ethical starting point.

Feminist philosophers, such as Ruddick (1990), claimed that the problem with just war theory was that it required that certain people should be able to be defined as 'killable'. This in turn depended on a claim to the capacity to identify the 'killable' which, Ruddick argued, relied on assumptions about 'moral truth' inherent in rationalist traditions of moral theory which were actually unattainable. In addition, the practice of war, however just in its aims or discriminating in its means, relies on inculcating characteristics and practices that are diametrically opposed to the virtues of care. Killing and injuring violate rather than nurture bodies, but they also require the killers and injurers to utterly dissociate themselves from the humanity and vulnerability of those that they are engaged in violating (Ruddick 1990: 198–205). For these reasons, although not embracing a wholly pacifist stance, Ruddick argued for an ethic of non-violence in politics and condemned most utilitarian, deontological and contractarian just war arguments as unconvincing (Ruddick 1990: 160–84).

Reflective exercise

- Do you agree with Walzer that when the survival of the political community itself is at stake, then it is permissible to use any means to fight for it?
- How persuasive are deontological and feminist arguments for pacifism?

Twenty-first century just and unjust wars

The arguments considered above were explicitly related to the experience of war up until the last decade of the twentieth century. The Catholic bishops were particularly concerned about the justice or injustice of nuclear war. Secular theorists, such as Walzer, were concerned about the Vietnam war. All were concerned with the *in bello* questions raised by the development of weapons of mass destruction and the involvement of whole populations in war through mass conscription and mass vulnerability. Although some attention was paid to ethical questions raised by terrorism or by revolutionary or guerrilla conflicts, the main focus of attention was on inter-state wars (Walzer 2006: 176–206). After the end of the Cold

War, different sorts of experiences of collective political violence became more central to the concerns of those interested
in the ethics of war. These have led to a certain amount of
rethinking about both *ad bellum* and *in bello* principles. In
what follows, we will briefly explore some of these issues and
the arguments that have been developed in relation to them.

Ad bellum

Post-Cold War events have provoked new discussion about
two of the traditional *ad bellum* principles in particular: just
cause and competent authority. In relation to 'just cause',
during the 1990s military intervention did not take place to
halt the Rwandan genocide but it did take place to stop ethnic
cleansing in Kosovo. Events such as these sparked a major
debate about the ethics of military humanitarian intervention.
As noted above, traditional just war theory, with its emphasis
on the just cause of protecting the innocent, and modern
deontological and utilitarian arguments, with their emphasis
on the individual as the key ethical reference point, all provide
moral grounds for aggressive action against regimes that
violate their own people. This is in contrast to Walzer's mix
of contractualist and virtue arguments for the ethical significance of political community, which favour humanitarian
intervention only in the most extreme of circumstances and
see state 'self-defence' as the archetypical just cause. Perhaps
the most obvious shift from earlier arguments regarding just
cause has been the growth of popularity of more individualist
positions on the humanitarian issue. Theorists such as Wheeler
have adapted traditional just war theory criteria for cases of
military humanitarian intervention, putting more emphasis
on just cause (gross human rights violations) and probability
of success, and less on just intention and comparative justice
ad bellum, than was the case in traditional just war theory
(Wheeler 2000).

There have also been postmodernist ethical perspectives
brought to bear on the debate over humanitarian justice *ad
bellum*, for instance in the work of David Campbell (Campbell
2001a, 2001b). For Campbell, the established ethical arguments between collectivist and individualist positions on the

ethics of war are all problematic because of their implication that ethical problems can in some way be solved 'without remainder'. Campbell derives his ethical position from Levinas and Derrida, according to whom ethics is oriented by an absolute responsibility to the other that is necessarily always impossible to fulfil. For Campbell, this radical ethical responsibility requires a mode of ethical thinking that does not take established ethical assumptions about the basis of world order, such as the sovereign state, for granted but which also recognizes that whatever ethical choices are made they are going to involve difficulties and dilemmas. In relation to the case of Kosovo, Campbell argues that a failure to intervene would have amounted to a refusal of the international community's ethical responsibility to the other, and the endorsement of a status quo ethics of state right that had made earlier events such as the massacre at Srebrenica in Bosnia in 1995 possible. In this instance, therefore, poststructuralist ethics lined up with the conclusions of many rationalist moral perspectives (Campbell 2001b).

Aside from humanitarian intervention, debates about just cause were also provoked in the early twenty-first century by the 'war on terror' response to the 9/11 attack. In this context, the question of what counts as both aggression (unjust) and self-defence (just) has been revisited in relation to the wars on Afghanistan and Iraq, and in relation to anti-terrorist military and policing actions in many different parts of the world. This is most clear in discussions about 'pre-emptive' and 'preventive' war. At what stage does a state acquire the right to take military action to defend itself? Traditionally the just cause of self-defence was seen to apply either after an attack had actually been made, or in a context in which there were good grounds to see an attack as imminent – troops massing on the border, etc. It has been argued, however, that the nature of the threat of international terrorism is such that it is impossible to wait until an attack is either imminent or has actually happened since by then it would be too late to do anything about it. In this context Bellamy argues for a reworking of the idea of 'imminence': 'The concept of pre-emption detailed here involves reinterpreting imminence. Rather than a temporal imminence, I suggested that a terrorist threat is imminent when a group expresses a clear intention to use terrorism and begins acquiring the means to do so' (Bellamy 2006: 179).

Issues, such as that of preventive war, raised by the invasions of Afghanistan (2001) and Iraq (2003) in the broader 'war on terror' have also prompted new work in the feminist ethics of war. This was particularly the case because the issue of the oppression of women under the Taliban regime in Afghanistan was cited as one of the aspects of the 'just cause' for the post-9/11 invasion. Sjoberg, in her book, *Gender, Justice and the Wars in Iraq*, offers a critique of traditional just war theory and develops a feminist alternative that she calls a feminist security ethic of 'empathetic cooperation' (Sjoberg 2006). This feminist approach draws on aspects of the ethic of care but, in contrast to Ruddick, does so in order to build a theory of just war rather than to argue for an ethic of non-violence per se. Sjoberg incorporates the idea of 'human security' into her theory which means expanding our understanding of what counts as war and as acts of war (Sjoberg 2006: 51). Traditional just war theory, both religious and secular, has treated war as clearly defined, with an identifiable beginning and end and with an identifiable set of (violent) means. The notion of human security, which was developed out of the human capabilities literature discussed in previous chapters, makes the individual's experience of threat and harm central to the meaning of war. This draws attention to the ways in which war is experienced by people on the ground before and after the conflict's supposed beginning and end (for instance in the experience of sanctions, or in injuries resulting from landmine explosions long after the formal cessation of hostilities). It also draws attention to injuries and harms that may not be the direct result of violent means. In relation to the Iraq war, Sjoberg argues that in practice it started in the 1991 Gulf War and the sanctions regime that followed, a long time before the invasion of 2003. One of the things Sjoberg insists on in relation to just cause is that it needs to be linked to the people that will be affected by the war, not just to the 'state' or 'regime' in the abstract. In other words, a just cause for war must mean you have a genuine grievance against the population that the war will harm. To suggest that the protection of women's rights formed part of the 'just cause' for the 2001 invasion of Afghanistan could only be plausible if the population of Afghanistan as a whole (whom the war was going to affect), including women, were themselves responsible for those rights violations (Sjoberg 2006: 77–9).

The examples of humanitarian intervention and the war on terror also raise questions about the ethical value of the just war principle of competent authority. As noted above, traditional just war theory saw competent authority as ethically important because of its basis in an idea of the virtuous political community. The limiting of the right to use violence to sovereign power was derived from deeper ethical foundations and not simply from the legal status of the sovereign. In contractualist accounts of sovereign authority, however, the emphasis shifts to state sovereignty as a *sui generis* ground of the right to make war. It follows from this that sovereign powers have rights to create international law and institutions, such as the UN, in which their sovereign rights to make war are pooled. At the time of the Kosovo intervention, international law and institutions had formalized a set of rules about *legitimate* authority in the case of wars other than those of self-defence and the only international institution in which such authority resided was the UN Security Council. The decision of NATO (North Atlantic Treaty Organization) powers to intervene in Kosovo without explicit UN sanction prompted a new discussion about legitimate authority and its ethical foundations.

From the NATO point of view, legitimacy was linked back to its deeper ethical foundations and argued to be a question of competence (the capacity to restore order within the state) plus just cause (the absence of order within the target state and the consequent threat to its members), rather than a matter of legal right. Thus, it was argued that, even if *illegal*, the action to intervene in Kosovo had nevertheless been *legitimate* because it was based on the ethical principles that underlie international law, even if they are not always fully reflected in international law. In opposition, it was argued that this move undermined respect for the sovereign authority of states and was overly permissive in its implications for what strong powers could do to weak ones on the grounds of their own competence and capacity to identify just cause. Here we find an argument about legitimate authority becoming an argument about the ethical basis on which the sovereignty of states should be respected. In traditional just war theory, the right of sovereign power to be respected was always conditional. If a ruler persecuted the innocent, then this provided ethical grounds on which invasion to protect the innocent and punish the guilty perpetrator could be permitted. The discussion of legitimate authority in relation to Kosovo revived this argument and led to the formulation of a new doctrine, 'responsibility to protect', which formalized (though not necessarily actualized) the idea of a duty of the international community to protect populations against their own regimes in certain circumstances (Bellamy 2008).

9/11 and the 'war on terror' raised issues about legitimate authority in a different way but with similar implications. The focus on international terrorism drew attention back to the question of whether non-state actors could ever be seen as having the right to use violence for political ends. This was not a new question. Various kinds of campaigns of violence over the past two hundred years, whether for national liberation or for ideological, revolutionary ends, have laid claim to legitimate authority in the name of the people they represent or humanity as such. According to one line of thinking, non-state actors can never be counted as having a right to use violence. This argument relates back to the traditional just war grounds for *ad bellum* competent authority. By disrupting the order of political community, violent non-state actors are disrupting the way of life through which human beings are able to flourish. To allow them legitimacy is to threaten the basis of human virtue. The argument can also be defended on contractualist grounds, in that membership of a state is taken to imply a trade-off between the individual's right to use violence in the state of nature which is given up in exchange for protection by sovereign power. However, both of these arguments imply that the legitimate authority of states to monopolize the use of violence is conditional rather than absolute. In other words, if states don't maintain order or don't represent or protect their people, then they forfeit their legitimacy. Sjoberg, drawing on a feminist principle of consent as the basis of legitimacy, makes a different version of a conditionality argument in relation to the question of legitimate authority. She argues that legitimate authority should be identified not with 'the political position of an authoritative agent' but with the process through which the decision to go to war is arrived at. This implies the need for some kind of democratic input into states' decisions to go to war (Sjoberg 2006: 70–2).

However, if it is argued that the legitimate authority of states is conditional on either their mode of political organization or political participation in the actual decision to go to war, then it becomes possible to argue that the legitimacy or illegitimacy of non-state organizations cannot be established in an absolute sense either. In other words, non-state actors may be able to claim an ethical basis for their authority in a way analogous to state actors. It is precisely this kind of argument that non-state groups engaged in violent struggles for political ends tend to deploy. If they do so, however, this implies that, as with states, the legitimacy of their authority as political actors would necessarily be undermined if they acted in such a way as to violate the ethical basis on which they purport to act. Bellamy, for instance, argues that at some point the use of terrorist tactics which, following Coady, he defines as the 'deliberate targeting of non-combatants for political purposes' must have an impact on the legitimacy of the organizations responsible (Bellamy 2006: 139).

Reflective exercise

Think about the following examples of pre-emptive military action considered by Bellamy (2006: 158–79): US and NATO invasion of Afghanistan, 2001; US missile attacks on terrorist targets in Yemen, 2002; US and allied invasion of Iraq, 2003.

- Which of these attacks was justified in your view, and on what grounds?
- How does it affect your ethical assessment of the 2003 invasion of Iraq if you see it, like Sjoberg, as part of an ongoing war rather than as the beginning of a new one?

In bello

One of the general tendencies in discussions of justice *ad bellum* in the post-Cold War period has been to stress the interconnection between *ad bellum* and *in bello* justice. We can see this in relation to both the 1999 Kosovo intervention and the 'war on terror' examples discussed above. From the point of view of humanitarianism in general, if the just cause is to stop the abuse of human rights, it would seem either contradictory or hypocritical to engage in extensive violations of human rights in the process of the intervention. Largely for this reason, there was a great deal of criticism of the tactics of aerial bombing from height in the Kosovo campaign. This prevented any NATO casualties but was an inherently more indiscriminate method than either flying lower or using ground troops. In this respect, it cut against Walzer's double-effect position in which the military are obliged to accept more risk to themselves in order to minimize noncombatant casualties (Walzer 2006: 152–9).

Somewhat paradoxically, at the same time as humanitarian intentions were seen to limit the range of acceptable *in bello* actions in the case of Kosovo, in the case of the 'war on terror', the survival of certain sets of values or ways of life was seen to permit that range to be broadened. After 9/11, it was argued that the extremity of the threat to certain states or ways of life was such as to justify not only the invasions of Afghanistan and Iraq but also the breaching of various international conventions concerning the treatment of prisoners of war, including the permissibility of torture as a method of interrogation. This in turn provoked responses from a range of ethical perspectives, from utilitarian to postmodernist, that argued for the condemnation of such tactics. The issues raised by the cases of Kosovo and the 'war on terror' about the *ad bellum–in bello* relation have led most of those moral theorists commenting on the ethics of war to reiterate the importance of the *in bello* criterion of discrimination as a touchstone for the overall ethical assessment of particular kinds of violent action (Burke 2005; Butler 2004, 2009; Elshtain 2004, 2005; Falk 2003; Jabri 2007).

Traditionally, a key aspect of the principle of *in bello* discrimination is the prohibition of the intentional targeting of civilians. In relation to this principle, Bellamy examines the use of aerial bombing in *Operation Enduring Freedom* in Afghanistan in 2001 and its ongoing aftermath. He acknowledges that the nature of this particular conflict complicates ethical requirements of discrimination because of the ways in which the war is fought on the ground and the difficulties of distinguishing combatant from non-combatant. This is not a war in which the 'enemy' is in uniform, or on a battlefield, but rather one in which fighters are located, often deliberately, in civilian areas. One way of responding to this has been to argue that, in these circumstances, the responsibility for non-combatant deaths rests with the 'enemy' ('terrorists', 'insurgents') rather than with the invading force. However, Bellamy rejects this:

> A balance has to be struck between rigid adherence to the rules and the instrumental requirements of waging successful wars. There are, nevertheless, some moral absolutes that are fundamental to the Just War tradition and can never be breached. The most fundamental of these is the commitment not to deliberately kill, maim or otherwise harm non-combatants and the additional requirements to take active steps to minimize potential harm to them. (Bellamy 2006: 181)

On the basis of the above position, which leans heavily on Walzer's adjustment to the double-effect principle, Bellamy argues that we can distinguish between unjust and just uses of violence *in bello*.

In contrast to Bellamy, Sjoberg, on the basis of her feminist just war ethics, argues that traditional understandings of the principle of discrimination *in bello* are morally inadequate (Sjoberg 2006: 89–102). First, she suggests that the way in which lines between combatant and non-combatant are normally drawn is ethically ungrounded and pretends to a degree of certainty in distinguishing between the two categories that is not actually available. A robust moral grounding for the distinction, she argues, would be one in which 'combatants' were both participants in war and had meaningfully consented to that participation. This is clearly a much more demanding way of drawing the line than is common in just war theory, though it does hark back to the original Christian emphasis of 'innocence' as the key criterion for immunity in war. Even if we take a less demanding view, however, for Sjoberg the pretence of certainty has a permissive effect and leads to the occlusion of actual harm that war always does to non-combatants. Sjoberg's second critique of the principle of non-combatant immunity follows on from this in that she argues that the concept of 'immunity' is an insidious abstraction in the case of war. Not only is it the case that 'non-combatants' always get killed and injured in war (excused under the double-effect principle) but also no one in a war zone is immune from the harmful effects of war, even if they are not directly killed or injured: 'The humanitarian impacts of war are so far reaching that it is not possible to be *immune* to them' (Sjoberg 2006: 101). Sjoberg's third argument against the traditional formulation of the meaning of discrimination *in bello* relates specifically to how, she argues, it perpetuates gender subordination by neglecting the gendered harms that war routinely inflicts, including sexual violence and economic harms. These harms do not even get included in terms of double-effect arguments since they do not register as injuries consequent on acts of war. 'Empathetic cooperation moves away from reactive combativeness and focuses on intersubjective connections between persons. As a motivating morality for a feminist reformulation of the ethics of targeting, empathetic cooperation provides a focus on real people's *physical* and *social/emotional* lives' (Sjoberg 2006: 102).

Reflective exercise

- Are there any circumstances in which you think it would be permissible to violate *in bello* principles of discrimination in a war like the wars in Afghanistan (2001) and Iraq (2003)?
- Does the principle of non-combatant immunity as it is currently understood do any good? Should it be rewritten along the lines suggested by Sjoberg?

Conclusion

Although systematic thinking about the ethics of war has been going on for much longer than thinking about the ethics of international development aid or of global distributive justice, the *ethical* issues at stake in debates over just war are strongly reminiscent of those we encountered in previous chapters. Here again, we find different arguments as to the basis of the ethical value of individuals, as well as the issue of the ethical value of the individual as opposed to the community. We also find divisions over the meaning and moral significance of guilt (responsibility) and innocence, procedure and outcome. Does the individual have a unique moral worth and, if so, why? The answer to this affects your view as to whether it is ethically acceptable for the deaths of individuals to be traded against each other and, if so, for what purposes. To the extent that individuals do have unique moral value, then is this the basis of an argument for pacifism or for discrimination *in bello*? Does the survival of political community provide ethical justification for the slaughter and injury of individuals? The answer to this affects your view as to whether in conditions of 'supreme emergency' we enter a world of 'emergency ethics', in which the necessity of the survival of *a* people trumps the individual survival of many people. How much does active involvement in war alter the moral status and entitlements of an individual? The answer to this question determines your view of whom it is permissible to kill and injure in war. Does it matter ethically that your *intentions* were principled, even if the unintended outcomes of your actions violated those principles? The answer to this determines how much it matters ethically that one did not intentionally target civilians, even if civilians nevertheless die. In each of these cases we are encountering dilemmas that are parallel to those we encounter when trying to work out whether individual rights should be the ground of global distributive justice, whether we have different kinds of ethical obligations to our fellow citizens than to strangers, whether the polluter should pay and so on.

As is the case with theories of global economic justice, different just war theories imply different responses to *who* and *how* questions in the ethics of war. In the post-Cold War context, deontological, utilitarian and feminist theories have put into question the automatic correlation between the state and legitimate authority. In some cases this implies a scaling up of sources of legitimacy in war to international law and institutions, such as the UN, in others an emphasis on the importance of meaningful consent on the part of citizens in the authorization of war and an opening up of the question of whether non-state actors may be legitimate users of violence. In terms of *how*, as opposed to for what purposes or by whom, war may be used, the meaning and implications of traditional *in bello* principles is understood very differently from a utilitarian as opposed to a deontological, or a feminist as opposed to a contractualist, perspective.

At the beginning of this chapter, I introduced traditional just war theory as a complex amalgam of different types of ethical reasoning which could not act as an algorithm for determining the justice of war. Instead it provided a series of starting points for the exercise of *phronesis*, or moral judgement. In contemporary arguments about just war there has been a tendency to want to turn just war theory into something much more like an algorithm. Predominant debates surrounding the justice of humanitarian intervention and the recent wars in Afghanistan and Iraq have sought to refine and apply just war theory so as to be able to pronounce on the rights and wrongs of specific events and they have been deeply entangled with questions about the ethical grounds of international law and with the desire to create laws of war appropriate to the contemporary age. This reflects the predominance of rationalist moralities, in particular deontology and contractualism, both of which presume the possibility of a *right* answer to the question of justice. The most significant opponents of the presumption of moral truth to be found in recent debates are in feminist and postmodernist work. The arguments of both Campbell and Sjoberg question a range of ways in which moral certainty in thinking about the ethics of war is grounded, from the premises of the moral priority of the individual or of the community to the combatant/non-combatant distinction, to drawing the line between what counts as war and what doesn't, to the ethical significance of the mistakes we know will happen. In doing so they bring us back to the old *ad bellum* principle of comparative justice: the need for moral humility in the face of our own limitations. And they remind us that the fifth ethical issue identified in debates over development ethics and global distributive justice, the issue of the grounds of authority of ethical claims, is also fundamental to arguments concerning the ethical justification of using violence as a means to resolve political conflict.

References and further reading

Anscombe, G. E. M. (1981) 'War and Murder', in *The Collected Philosophical Papers of G. E. M. Anscombe, Volume III*, Oxford: Blackwell. A deontological, Christian critique of both indiscriminate warfare and of pacifism.

Atack, I. (2005) *The Ethics of Peace and War*, Edinburgh: Edinburgh University Press. Provides an overview of ethics of war.

Bellamy, A. (2006) *Just Wars: From Cicero to Iraq*, Cambridge: Polity. Includes both an account of the history of just war thinking and the development of just war theory for the twenty-first century.

Bellamy, A. (2008) 'The Responsibility to Protect and the Problem of Military Intervention', *International Affairs* 84(4): 615–39. A largely empirical account of the difficulties facing attempts to act on the UN 'Responsibility to Protect' principles.

Burke, A. (2005) 'Against the New Internationalism', *Ethics and International Affairs* 19(2): 73–89. Critique of uses of war for humanitarian and regime change purposes.

Butler, J. (2004) 'Violence, Mourning and Politics', in *Precarious Life: The Power of Mourning and Violence*, London: Verso. Poststructuralist reflections on the ethical significance of the ways in which some lives are recognized as worthy of mourning and some are not.

Butler, J. (2009) *Frames of War: When is Life Grievable?* London: Verso. An extension of the arguments made in Butler (2004); the final chapter looks at the ideal of non-violence from a rather different angle than Ruddick or Norman, one that draws on Levinas's ethics.

Campbell, D. (2001a) 'Why Fight? Humanitarianism, Principles and Poststructuralism', in H. Seckinelgin and H. Shinoda (eds), *Ethics and International Relations*, Basingstoke: Palgrave, pp.

132–60. Making the argument that poststructuralist ethics does not rule out forcible intervention on humanitarian grounds.

Campbell, D. (2001b) 'Justice and International Order: The Case of Bosnia and Kosovo', in J.-M. Coicaud and D. Warner (eds), *Ethics and International Affairs: Extent and Limits*, Tokyo: United Nations University Press, pp. 103–27. Applies poststructuralist ethical thinking to the cases of Bosnia and Kosovo.

Caney, S. (2005) 'Just War' and 'Humanitarian Intervention', chapters 6 and 7 of *Justice Beyond Borders: A Global Political Theory*, Oxford: Oxford University Press, pp. 189–262. Good overview of range of ethical positions, defending an essentially deontological stance.

Clark, I. (1988) 'Doctrines of Just War', chapter 2 in *Waging War: A Philosophical Introduction*, Oxford: Clarendon, pp. 31–50. A useful introduction to the just war tradition from its origins.

Coates, A. J. (1997) *The Ethics of War*, Manchester: Manchester University Press. Deals thoroughly but accessibly with the traditional questions of just war theory.

Dower, N. (2007) 'Peace and War', chapter 7 in *World Ethics: The New Agenda*, 2nd edn. Edinburgh: Edinburgh University Press, pp.123–47. Overview of ethics of war.

Elshtain, J. B. (ed.) (1991) *Just War Theory*, Oxford: Blackwell. Useful collection of articles by just war theorists – reflects concerns of latter stages of Cold War in the 1980s.

Elshtain, J. B. (2004) *Just War Against Terror: The Burden of American Power in a Violent World*, 2nd edn, New York: Basic Books. An argument in support of the US interventions in Afghanistan and Iraq.

Elshtain, J. B. (2005) 'Against the New Utopianism', *Ethics and International Affairs*, 2(19): 91–5. Critique of Burke's position on the 'new internationalism'; see above.

Falk, R. (2003) *The Great Terror War*, New York: Olive Branch Press. Critique of US 'war on terror'.

Holmes, R. (1989) *On War and Morality*, Princeton: Princeton University Press. Good engagement with just war issues in the 1980s. Contends that modern wars are necessarily unjust, using both utilitarian and deontological arguments and argues for investment in non-violent modes of resistance.

Jabri, V. (2007) *War and the Transformation of Global Politics*, Basingstoke: Palgrave Macmillan. Critique of 'war on terror', informed by a poststructuralist ethical perspective.

Nagel, T. (1972) 'War and Massacre', *Philosophy and Public Affairs* 1(2): 123–44, also reprinted in Nagel (1979), *Mortal Questions*, Cambridge: Cambridge University Press, pp. 53–74; and C. Beitz et al. (eds) *International Ethics* (1985), Princeton: Princeton University Press, pp. 53–74. Critical engagement with the combatant/non-combatant distinction.

National Conference of Catholic Bishops (1983) *The Challenge of Peace: God's Promise and Our Response*, at www.usccb.org/ sdwp/international/TheChallengeofPeace.pdf, accessed December 2009. Detailed statement of modern Christian just war theory, reflecting 1980s' Cold War concerns.

Norman, R. (1988) 'The Case for Pacifism', *Journal of Applied Philosophy* 5(2): 166–79. A careful philosophical argument that makes a case for pacifism but with some reservations.

Norman, R. (1995) *Ethics, Killing and War*, Cambridge: Cambridge University Press. Argues for the inadequacy of most moral arguments that justify war and makes a case for pacifism but sees this as limited by the lack of alternative non-violent means of resistance to aggression.

Orend, B. (2000) *Michael Walzer on War and Justice*, Cardiff: University of Wales Press. Useful, detailed account of Walzer's work.

Ruddick, S. (1990) *Maternal Thinking: Towards a Politics of Peace*, London: Women's Press. Feminist argument against just war thinking and for non-violent modes of conflict resolution.

Sjoberg, L. (2006) *Gender, Justice and the Wars in Iraq: A Feminist Reformulation of Just War Theory*, Lanham, MD: Lexington Books. Develops a feminist just war theory using the example of the Iraq wars.

Steinhoff, U. (2007) *On the Ethics of War and Terrorism*, Oxford: Oxford University Press. Argument for the need for consistency in positions on the ethics of war and the ethics of terrorism.

Walzer, M. (2004) *Arguing About War*, Yale: Yale University Press. Collection of a variety of essays relating to the ethics of war, including essays on Kosovo, Israel/Palestine, 9/11 and 2003 invasion of Iraq.

Walzer, M. (2006 [1977]) *Just and Unjust Wars*, 4th edn, New York: Basic Books. Classic formulation of modern, secular just war theory.

Wheeler, N. (2000) *Saving Strangers: Humanitarian Intervention in International Society*, Oxford: Oxford University Press. Most thorough attempt to elaborate a just war theory for humanitarian intervention but also an argument that international norms on intervention shifted in the 1990s.

7
Ethics of Making and Sustaining Peace

Introduction

According to traditional just war theory, in order for a war to be just it must have a just peace as its aim. However, arguments surrounding the ethics of war, as explored in the previous chapter, do not necessarily give us clear answers as to what a 'just peace' means or to the ethical problems inherent in dealing with the aftermath of violent conflict, whether intra- or inter-state, in such a way as to deliver a just peace. Yet this has become a matter of central importance for Global Ethics in the context of a world characterized by the global ramifications of ongoing civil conflicts and violent regime transitions of various kinds and by an increasingly explicit commitment to international peacemaking and peacekeeping operations. The aim of this chapter is to map out the terrain of debates surrounding the ethics of making and keeping peace which, according to some theorists, constitutes a third aspect of just war theory, *jus post bellum*. The chapter falls into three sections. In the first section we will examine the ethics of peacemaking, with peacemaking here being understood as the processes through which, and the terms on which, conflicts should be ended. In the second section we will examine the ethics of transitional justice and the question of what are the ethically appropriate ways to treat victims of conflict and to deal with individual and collective responsibility for *ad bellum* and *in bello* wrongdoing. In the third section we will examine the ethics of longer-term processes of building and sustaining peace and will note the way in which this returns us to ethical arguments relating to development and distributive justice issues. In conclusion, we will note how debates over the ethics of peace turn on the same ethical issues identified in previous chapters. And it will be argued that moral debates about the meaning of just peace make it clearer than ever that the issue of the authority of ethical claims is an *ethical* issue that is at the heart of Global Ethics.

Making peace justly

It would be misleading to suggest that traditional just war theory offers no guidance as to what making peace justly involves, since both *ad bellum* and *in bello* principles have implications for the outcome of war. Just cause and just intention both imply that the 'just peace' which war aims towards must be one that addresses the wrong that has been done. However, this also means that a great deal depends on what counts as just cause and just intention. On Walzer's account, for instance, the most obvious just cause for war is self-defence in response to aggression. The implication here would be that a just peace would be one in which the *status quo ante* was restored, plus one in which measures were taken to prevent future aggression, such as disarmament of the aggressive power (restoration plus). Something like the outcome of the 1991 Gulf War might exemplify just peace in this respect since the peace was made so as to restore pre-war borders and destroy capacity for future aggression. And it did not take the further step of imposing regime change on Iraq, therefore apparently continuing to respect principles of non-intervention and self-determination in the case of the defeated state (Jackson 1992).

If one takes a more deontological position than Walzer, however, and identifies just cause and just intention with defence of the innocent and punishment of the guilty, then making peace justly would seem to involve more than 'restoration plus', at the very least requiring the removal of the guilty from power and the entrenchment of protection of the innocent from harm. This might well involve a considerable amount of intervention in reshaping the unjust state after war. *Ad bellum* principles of comparative justice and proportionality and *in bello* principles of discrimination and proportionality also have implications for what a just peace could involve since they all suggest the importance of limiting righteous violence in order to enable the possibility of peaceful relations between warring parties in the future. If they are taken seriously, then unconditional surrender, such as was insisted on by the Allies in relation to the Axis powers in 1945, could not count as a justly made peace (Bass 2004; Orend 2002).

Orend, building on Walzer's arguments, has attempted to produce a systematic set of principles to govern *jus post bellum* which are guided by the following understanding of just cause and just intention: 'the just goal of a just war, once won, must be a more just state of affairs than existed prior to the war' (Orend 2002: 44). This principle, he argues, takes account of the fact that the *status quo ante* must have harboured in it the seeds of unjust war in the first place and that therefore what is needed is 'restoration plus'. At the same time, the individual and collective rights of the defeated population should still be respected as much as is compatible with the 'more just' outcome. Although Orend formulates these principles in relation to traditional inter-state war, he argues that they are generalizable to other sorts of conflicts, including the contemporary 'war on terror'. We will use his principles as a starting point for discussing the different aspects of the ethics of making and sustaining peace in the rest of this chapter. The first three principles *post bellum* that he formulates relate to the nature of the peace as such which he argues must be: proportional and public; rights-vindicating; and discriminate.

This means that, firstly, the peace settlement should be 'measured and reasonable' as opposed to revengeful or an unconditional surrender. The victors should not be entitled to do anything they like to the defeated population and regime. In addition, the terms of the peace settlement should be public so that the population of the defeated regime *know* the terms and are aware that they will not simply be victimized by the victors. Orend's second *post bellum* principle requires that the peace settlement restores and reinforces individual and community entitlements that have been violated by unjust war. So, for instance, individual human rights are protected and collective borders rewritten to restore rights of national self-determination which may involve return to *status quo ante* borders, or in cases of secessionist conflicts, of new borders being put in place. The third *post bellum* principle of discrimination states that the peace settlement must discriminate between different classes of people in the defeated population, for instance political leaders as opposed to soldiers or civilians. In particular, Orend argues that civilians must be immune from harmful effects of the peace settlement. There should be no sweeping sanctions that will affect the civilian population such as happened after the 1991 Iraq war.

If we examine Orend's first three principles, they clearly reflect a mixture of deontological and contractualist reasoning. As with Walzer, Orend is attempting to establish *post bellum* justice on the basis of a respect for both individual and collective rights, with the latter following from a contractualist understanding of the relation between the individual and the collective. As with Walzer also, therefore, there are potential tensions in Orend's account, in principle and practice, between individual and collective rights, as well as problems of how to restore and reinforce the individual and collective rights of victims without affecting the individual and collective rights of the defeated. It isn't clear, for instance, how the principle of self-determination can be fully vindicated in the aftermath of a conflict that leaves a foreign regime in occupation in order to respect the rights of the population. Moreover, restoring the individual rights of the victims of war may require violating the immunity of civilians in the defeated state in order to help fund the economic reconstruction of the victim state.

From the point of view of deontological critics, Orend could be argued to be giving too much ground to a trade-off between individual and collective rights. Williams and Caldwell formulate their definition of a just peace in wholly individualist terms: 'A just peace is one that vindicates the human rights of all parties to the conflict' (Williams and Caldwell 2006: 317). This clearly involves a commitment to equal consideration for the human rights of both victors and vanquished. From a utilitarian perspective, however, both deontological and contractualist *post bellum* arguments pose ethical problems. As Bellamy points out, treating *post bellum* justice as necessarily implied in *ad bellum* justice could well dissuade potential interveners from taking action against injustice because of the extent of the *post bellum* obligations that would be being taken on. Moreover, he suggests that Orend's attempt to establish a single set of *post bellum* principles is insufficiently sensitive to the different kinds of action that may be needed to sustain peace following different types of conflict, from wars of liberation to humanitarian interventions to territorial inter-state wars. For these reasons, Bellamy argues that *post bellum* justice should not be treated as a third branch of just war theory but rather as a separate ethical arena in which moral discourses other than those inherent in just war theory have a place (Bellamy 2008).

The arguments considered so far are focused on the *outcome* of the conflict. From the points of view of discourse, feminist and postmodernist ethics, this neglects the ethical significance of the *processes* that underlie arrival at peace agreements. Traditionally, peacemaking after war has been an inter-elite process, negotiated secretly and as a trade-off between the interests of elite actors in conditions usually of a clear hierarchy of power. However, from a Habermasian perspective, a peace agreement could only be just if it were arrived at through a free and fair discussion between all those that are affected by the outcome. In principle this suggests that peace processes must be substantially democratized and that they might need to involve not only representatives of the regimes and populations directly involved but also of those 'bystanders' in the international community who nevertheless have an interest in the outcome of the conflict. Even if this were not to be possible in practice, discourse ethics requires that the peace agreement at least aspire to meet the test of being something that *would have been agreed to under conditions of fair argumentation by all affected*. This means that Orend's requirement that a peace be 'measured and reasonable' if it is to be genuinely just needs to be tested against a range of relevant perspectives, that is to say, not just the perspectives of ruling regimes and militaries but also those of different sectors of the populations of both aggressor and victim states or communities, as well as broader international publics (Murithi 2009: 113–35).

The claim that there is an intrinsic link between process and outcome in the context of peacemaking suggests that there may be distinct ethical standards involved in the ethics of peacemaking that do not simply relate to the principles of just cause and intention. Murithi, drawing on discourse ethics, stresses the importance of moral inclusion in conflict resolution processes which, he argues, necessitates a shift in the moral stance of all participants from self-interest towards being able to see from the standpoint of others (Murithi 2009: 126–7). This draws our attention to factors, more commonly central to virtue, feminist and postmodernist ethics, to do with the *who* and *how* questions of peace negotiations as opposed to the *why* and *what*. Outside of a situation of unconditional surrender, in which peace terms are simply dictated by the victor, peacemaking always involves interaction between parties that have been, and may still be, engaged in killing each other. Peacemaking presupposes decisions about who is allowed to be party to the process and how non-violent inter-subjective communication is to be made possible. These decisions, in turn, necessarily feed into the outcomes of the process. From the point of view of postmodernist ethics, Campbell criticizes the peacemaking process that led up to the formulation of the Dayton Accords which settled the terms of the peace in Bosnia-Herzegovina in 1995. This was a complex set of processes, mediated by the international community and resulting in a settlement in which representation of different ethnic identities in the new regime was entrenched and long-term international assistance and peacekeeping commitments were made. Crucial to Campbell's argument is his critique of the way in which the peace process failed to challenge the terms in which the conflict itself was defined, that is to say, terms in which ethnic identities were understood to be essential, mutually exclusive and the basic principle on which political community rested. The result, on Campbell's account, was a settlement in which ethnic tensions were institutionalized rather than addressed, making peace and politics a continuation, rather than a resolution, of war (Campbell 1998).

The point being made here is that if parties to peace processes hold onto mutually exclusive identities, then this will be reflected in the peace. Were parties to peace processes to be more willing either to identify with each other, or to understand themselves in relation to each other, then a different, more enduring, peace might be the result. It would, of course, be absurd to suggest that this is in any sense easy but feminist ethics, in particular, has suggested that an ethical approach to peace would necessitate precisely such an alternative starting point. One of the ways in which it has been suggested that this should work is through bringing a care ethics perspective into *post bellum* considerations. At the heart of such an approach is the recognition of *dependence* and *interdependence* rather than *independence* as the basic ethical condition. Where a peace process is premised on its participants representing closed identities with exclusive interests, then peace can only ever be a bargaining process in which each party seeks to maximize its advantage. But if peace processes start from the acknowledgement of the mutual entwinement of the identities and interests of the parties involved, then it is much more difficult to model the peace process in zero-sum terms. This implies that the ethical requirements of peace processes involve those facilitating peacemaking in challenging the assertion of closed identities (Ben-Porath 2008).

One of the ways in which feminists have suggested that this can be done is through bringing a greater range of perspectives into the peace process itself to include parties that may not be entirely identified with warring factions but who have a deep interest in the outcome of the process. Traditionally, women have played very little role in formal peace processes, although they have frequently been involved in grass-roots peace movements that cross boundaries of warring groups (e.g. Northern Ireland, Bosnia, Israel/ Palestine). From the feminist point of view, greater involvement of women in peacemaking would be one way to challenge the closed understanding of identities that war reproduces, and to point up mutual dependencies and common interests that cross partisan boundaries. In addition feminists argue, in common with discourse ethicists, this would also make a difference to the justice of the outcome of the process. Because women have been largely excluded from peacemaking, their vulnerabilities and needs have not been at the forefront of the concerns of post-war settlements. Bringing them in would make it more likely that 'gender justice' was part of the 'more just' outcome that just war theorists such as Orend require. From the point of view of feminist ethics, therefore, there is often good reason to see the requirements of a just peace as going above and beyond addressing *ad bellum* just cause (Eide 2008; Helms 2003; Rooney 2007).

In contemporary conflicts, peace is usually brokered through the mediation of others in a way that sets up ethical issues and problems for the mediator, as distinct from the warring parties themselves (Murithi 2009: 71–112). In terms of the immediate context in which peace is made, one of these areas of ethical obligation is that of military peacekeeping. Peacekeeping operations work in a grey zone between war and peace in which traditional just war thinking does not straightforwardly apply. Firstly, peacekeepers are often required to keep warring parties apart, to guard 'safe havens', or to protect convoys carrying humanitarian aid, without themselves abandoning neutrality or engaging in aggressive action. Secondly, peacekeepers are required to cooperate with and win the trust of civilians and civilian authorities, often in contexts in which they are not familiar with the culture and customs of the people they are protecting. In both cases peacekeepers are soldiers required to act in ways that are not fully consistent with what they have been trained to do as soldiers. These different rules of engagement raise different ethical problems from those familiar to soldiers *in bello*, in particular when it comes to the relation between soldiers and civilians. In the context of war, the soldier's duty is to discriminate as far as possible between combatant and non-combatant and minimize civilian casualties. In peacekeeping, the soldier's duty is to collaborate with civilians, and often also with hostile forces, and in contexts in which the local population is uneasy with the peacekeeper presence. Within this context there is a potential for corruption and for the exploitation of the local population.

As Whitworth has shown in her discussion of certain peacekeeping scandals, there can be a link between peacekeepers' sense that their work is not 'proper' soldiering and both racist and sexist contempt for the local population (Whitworth 2004). This calls attention to the importance of issues highlighted by both virtue and feminist ethics about character and empathy. The predominant ethical discourse underpinning peacekeeping operations is a deontological human rights discourse but one in which the recipients of the operation, as with humanitarian aid, are identified as incapable of looking after themselves. This can easily become mapped onto a paternalistic, or not so paternalistic, hierarchical understanding of the relation between the protector and the protectee, in particular if the protector already identifies protecting with something less than what it means to be a real soldier. The deontological thinking that identifies the *why* and *what* of respect for the human rights of all does not address the question of *how* it is possible for soldiers to become successful peacekeepers in gendered and raced hierarchical contexts. In order to address this question, attention needs to be paid to the kinds of characteristics, knowledge, skills and emotions that enable good peacekeeping practice.

Orend's first three principles of *post bellum* justice appear initially to be quite straightforward. A just peace should be proportional and public, rights-vindicating and discriminate. But as soon as we begin to look at what this means, a whole host of ethical issues emerge to do with the process as well as the outcome of attaining just peace. So far we have looked only at the ethics of some of the aspects of the settlement itself and of the process leading up to it. For Orend, just peace involves further principles that address directly the appropriate treatment of both victims and aggressors after war. In the following section, we will examine the arguments surrounding transitional justice.

Reflective exercise

- Compare the positions of Orend and Bellamy on the meaning of a just peace: which do you prefer and why?
- Are peace agreements based on respecting exclusive identities unethical?
- UN Security Council Resolution (UNSCR) 1325 (2000) calls for the mainstreaming of gender into all aspects of peacemaking, peacekeeping and peacebuilding. Do you think this will make peace processes more ethical? See www.iwtc.org/1325_word.pdf for a summary of UNSCR 1325, accessed December 2009.

Transitional justice

Traditionally, the aftermath of war was simply a matter for the 'winner' to decide. There was no expectation that either punishment of the guilty or compensation for the innocent would be part of the aftermath of war, except insofar as the verdict of battle happened to bring those things about. From the Christian just war point of view, war itself was the mechanism for punishment of the guilty and protection of the innocent. During the twentieth century, however, in parallel with the development of international laws of war and peace, the notion that just peace required distinct post-war processes, in which the guilty were called to account and reparations were made to the injured and innocent, took hold. The peace settlement following the First World War exemplified this trend in one way, that following the Second World War in a rather different way. In the case of the First World War, although there were calls for the trial of the German emperor, what happened was a process of collective punishment, in which Germany (the German state and therefore the German population) was required to make reparations that took the form of territorial concessions and financial payments. In the case of the Second World War, there was the holding of particular individuals to account for *ad bellum* and *in bello* crimes. The Nuremburg and Tokyo trials set a precedent for the idea of individual war guilt but also raised important questions about the meaning of both individual and collective responsibility for and in war, and about the generalization of the principle of responsibility to conquering as well as conquered forces.

Of all the ethical perspectives discussed in this book, it is only utilitarianism that does not accord major ethical significance to the idea of responsibility, though the other perspectives have rather different views on what it means and implies. From the utilitarian point of view, recognizing responsibility for actions through reward and punishment is only ethically right to the extent that it works so as to maximize utility. Most utilitarians agree that on the whole it is the case that rewards and punishments encourage or deter ethically appropriate action, so from this point of view they might well argue that holding individuals or collectives to account post war might be a good thing. However, to the extent that such accounting brings about harmful effects, as did, one could argue, the settlement after the First World War, then in utilitarian terms the principle of responsibility should give way to the more important principle of maximizing good outcomes. This view opposes deontological and contractualist arguments. From the deontological point of view, the moral responsibility of individuals is what defines them as uniquely ethically significant. It is therefore part and parcel of respect for each individual that they are held to account for what they do, otherwise you are treating them as equivalent to animals. Contractualist arguments assume individual responsibility as a starting point but also see it as directly connected to collective responsibility since it is the will of individuals that grounds the rights of political communities. On this account, both individual and collective 'holding to account' may be justified, depending on the nature of the connection between people and regime but the fundamental foundation of responsibility is individual. Moral responsibility is written into the definition of contractualist and deontological accounts of what it means to be human as such.

As might be expected, virtue, feminist and postmodernist ethics think about responsibility differently. In the case of virtue ethics, rather than the responsible individual being taken as foundational, the emphasis is on what it means to be *ethically* responsible as a person. From this point of view, ethical responsibility is an aspect of moral character that needs to be nurtured but which is also relative to role and context. This means, for instance, that the ethical responsibility of soldiers for their actions may be seen to vary, depending on their rank or role. This socializing of the meaning of responsibility is also characteristic of feminist thinking which emphasizes the relational nature of ethical identity and therefore works against the atomized understanding of the individual characteristic of contractualist and deontological thought. Of course, this doesn't mean that either virtue or feminist ethicists deny the possibility of individuals being held to be ethically responsible but it does mean that the context in which individuals were socialized and in which they acted is also ethically important and must be taken into account. Moreover, both virtue and feminist arguments draw attention to the significance of the collusion of many others in the contexts in which morally wrong actions are perpetrated. The rape of men and women is an act that most people find ethically abhorrent but gendered hierarchies of value that make sexual violence a way to humiliate and subdue an enemy contribute to the likelihood of such war crimes. These are collectively shared and reproduced and cannot be traced to any individual wrongdoer.

For postmodernists, even more than for virtue and feminist ethics, ideas of individual and collective responsibility pose problems because they presuppose a self-identical coherent subject. Postmodernists draw attention to the danger of the imputation of individual and collective responsibility in the aftermath of war. This is because it can undermine the justice of the peace by reproducing a myth of essentialized subjects that is itself one of the key contributors to war in the first place. From the postmodernist point of view, ethical responsibility is a discourse that tends to support rather than to challenge processes of 'othering' which fuel conflict. In this sense, paradoxically, 'responsibility' to the other may require not holding the other 'responsible' but rather trying to unpick the conditions that rendered the wrongs done possible. Here postmodernists share some pragmatic ground with utilitarianism; before one can decide whether and how to use the discourse of moral responsibility, one must think very carefully about what it *does* rather than how it is justified.

As a practice, just war (in spite of principles of discrimination and proportionality) is premised on the idea of collective responsibility since it presumes that it is reasonable to kill and injure members of a particular political community and destroy their property and infrastructure, in spite of the fact that they are not directly, individually responsible for initiating unjust aggression. In the aftermath of war, also, collective responsibility is assumed to the extent that policies imputing responsibility are followed, with implications for the citizens of the defeated political community as a whole. Two examples of this would be requirements for defeated communities to pay reparations, effectively taxing all citizens of the state, as in Germany after the First World War, and the more recent example of the sanctions regime against Iraq in the 1990s, designed to enforce compliance with UN resolutions. Both of these cases raise the question of the ethics of identifying states or regimes with their population as a whole. From a contractualist point of view, this might be reasonable to the extent that the population as a whole freely supported the regime's aggression. From a deontological point of view, such an equation is problematic since it involves the idea that collective rights trump those of the individual. Unless every individual explicitly endorsed what their leaders were doing, it is hard to see how every citizen can be held responsible by effectively suffering the consequences of another's actions. It is even harder to see how infants or the mentally ill, who will also suffer from the consequent impoverishment, can be held responsible.

In a book written in the aftermath of the Second World War, the philosopher Karl Jaspers addressed this issue in his book, *The Question of German Guilt* (Jaspers 1995 [1948]). Here he distinguished between four categories of guilt: criminal; political; moral; and metaphysical. Jaspers's argument is strongly deontological. The categories of criminal and moral refer straightforwardly to individual responsibility. Criminal guilt refers to guilt carried by those responsible for committing criminal acts. Moral guilt refers to guilt carried by those who have acted immorally, even if they have done so under orders or in circumstances in which they cannot be held criminally responsible because of unjust laws. Both criminals and sinners deserve to be held responsible for what they have done. Political and metaphysical guilt are categories that refer to co-responsibility rather than individual responsibility but they nevertheless imply individuals' accountability for collusion in, or apathy towards, wrongdoing. According to Jaspers, all citizens bear co-responsibility for the ways in which they are governed, whatever the nature of the regime. This means that even if citizens in general should not be seen as criminally guilty, they do participate in a common political guilt and it is reasonable that they should bear some of the costs incurred by the criminal and immoral actions of their government. Metaphysical guilt is a universal category that applies to all human beings and refers to our collective co-responsibility for all human injustice. This kind of guilt, Jaspers argues, is impossible to specify in criminal, political or moral terms but is shared by all humans insofar as all humans are bystanders of evils that they do nothing to prevent. Clearly, metaphysical guilt may implicate not only citizens of the aggressor community but also outsiders who knew what was happening and did nothing about it.

Orend's *post bellum* principles for a just peace follow up the requirements for the peace to be proportional and public, rights-vindicating and discriminate with three further requirements that relate to the issues raised by Jaspers: punishment one; punishment two; and compensation. Punishment one refers to punishment for crimes *ad bellum*, punishment two to crimes *in bello* and the principle of compensation relates to Jaspers's category of political guilt. The latter principle calls for financial restitution to the victims of the aggressive regime but with the proviso that any such scheme should not entirely bankrupt the aggressor, thereby limiting the severity of the implications of collective responsibility. In the case of punishments one and two, Orend argues for the need for criminal trials as the appropriate mechanism of transitional justice. For crimes *ad bellum*, this would involve indicting individual leaders responsible for aggression, trying them for war crimes in fair and public international tribunals and imposing proportional punishments. In the case of *in bello* crimes, Orend is insistent that perpetrators from all sides of the preceding conflict must be equally liable to criminal proceedings and punishment.

There are a variety of ethical issues raised by the idea that war crimes tribunals are the most appropriate ways of holding people to account for their actions. The notion that political or military leaders should be held to account personally for actions undertaken in their public role has been questioned. Nagel, for instance, argues that there are differences between the ethical standards governing private and public conduct and that this means that the actions of politicians cannot be judged in equivalent terms to those of a private person. Would it, for instance, be appropriate to regard Churchill as a murderer because he sanctioned indiscriminate bombing in the Second World War? Nagel suggests that the morality governing public figures is more utilitarian and outcome oriented than private morality and that public actions should be judged in those terms (Nagel 1979). There are also utilitarian arguments against holding leaders accountable in war crimes trials. Echoing Bellamy's point about the problem of overdemanding requirements for *jus post bellum*, it can be argued that this may undermine the possibility of peacemaking since a leader who knows he or she will be arraigned if defeated may be more likely to fight to the end, and there will be less possibility of trade-off in peace negotiations (Bellamy 2008). These kinds of argument often pit deontological and utilitarian moral theorists against each other, with deontologists arguing for the importance of absolute moral principles and utilitarians giving priority to consequences. However, beyond this familiar debate is another argument, one that relates to the meaning of *post bellum* transitional justice more generally. This is the debate as to the relative moral importance of *retributive* as opposed to *restorative* justice (Murithi 2009: 136–59).

Retributive justice punishes the guilty because they deserve to be punished. It is essentially backward looking. Restorative justice, in contrast, is concerned with doing justice to the victims, addressing the harms they have suffered and enabling them to start afresh. It is essentially forward looking. The two notions of justice are not necessarily contradictory; it may even be the case that victims need to see the guilty punished as part of having justice done to them. But if we look at war crimes tribunals as a mechanism for transitional justice, then it is clear that they are primarily retributive rather than restorative, and perpetrator rather than victim oriented. For some critics, the ethical problem with war crimes trials is not to do with holding political leaders to personal account but to do with the way in which the ethical requirements of victims are inadequately met by these kinds of proceedings. This can be in two different ways: first, because there is not necessarily any restitution for victims built into criminal proceedings and, second, because in their role as witnesses victims are effectively forced to relive the violence perpetrated against them. Feminist theorists have been particularly concerned to criticize the effects on victims of trials for sexual violence offences (Campbell 2004; Mertus 2004). More generally, however, for virtue, feminist and post-modernist ethics perspectives, as well as for utilitarianism, the war crimes trial gives an ethical priority to the perpetrator that draws attention away from other ethical issues, including the issue of how best to enable transition beyond conflict.

Over the past decade, critics of retributive mechanisms of transitional justice have been particularly interested in alternatives that have been developed in contexts other than that of inter-state war. These mechanisms include most famously 'truth' and 'truth and reconciliation' commissions. Truth commissions were pioneered in a variety of South American countries in the aftermath of transitions from authoritarian regimes, often following civil conflict. The essential idea of the truth commission was that 'truth' about what the authorities had done, including what happened to people who had 'disappeared', was traded for amnesty for perpetrators. Truth commissions reflected utilitarian moral reasoning in that they reassured those giving up power that they would not be prosecuted and therefore enabled political transition. However, they were also inspired by restorative justice, in that they made public the suffering of victims and of relatives of victims and allowed people to grieve for those whose deaths had been hidden. Truth and reconciliation commissions (TRCs), of which the South African tribunal is the central example, are more ambitious than truth commissions and are explicitly inspired by an ideal of restorative justice (Crocker 1999).

As with truth commissions, a large part of what went on in the South African TRC involved the exchange of testimony for amnesty (within limits – only 'political' acts could be given amnesty). In many cases this involved direct communication between perpetrator and victim in a way very different from the relation between accused and witness in a standard criminal court. In addition, the TRC called in representatives of collective institutions, such as churches or the South African Medical Association, to witness to their collusion with the apartheid regime. And it had a committee that dealt with reparation and rehabilitation for victims. Overall, therefore, the TRC sought to encompass aspects of collective and individual accountability for wrongdoing as well as giving priority to restoration over retribution. Above all, however, rather than establishing the truth about the past, its role was identified with the need to produce a new narrative for post-apartheid South Africa that would allow the nation to go forward. For this reason, the TRC had to be even-handed and include the ANC as well as representatives of the apartheid regime in those to whom it applied.

Many problems have been identified with the way in which the South African TRC operated (Crocker 1999; Fletcher and Weinstein 2002). In terms of the ethical issues it raised, however, three matters have been especially prominent. The first related to the question of whether there are certain acts that should not be permitted to go unpunished. From a deontological point of view, to allow torturers to go free is not only to fail to respect the absolute nature of each human being's right to bodily integrity but is also a failure of respect for the torturer as a rational human being who deserves to be held accountable for his or her actions. In addition, it has been argued that amnesty granted to perpetrators fails to meet the need of victims to see justice done retributively as well as restoratively. The second problem related to lack of comprehensiveness; not all perpetrators obeyed the summons to come and bear witness and legal proceedings have been slow to catch up with those who refused to testify, including some of the major players in the apartheid regime. Again, from a deontological point of view, this allows certain individuals to get away with behaviour for which they ought to be held to account. The third problem related to the inadequacy of the provision for reparation and rehabilitation. It can be argued that without a much more extensive redistribution of resources, the majority population lacked the means to move on with their lives in a constructive fashion. This problem shifts us away from the terrain of transitional justice towards the question of what is needed in the longer term to sustain a just peace in a context that has been deeply affected by ongoing exploitation and distributive injustice as well as violent conflict (Kutz 2004).

Reflective exercise

- How do you understand the concept of 'collective responsibility'? If there is such a thing as collective responsibility, then does it justify collective punishment?
- Do you need retributive justice in order to have restorative justice?

Sustaining peace

Orend's final principle of justice *post bellum* is a principle of rehabilitation. Essentially this refers to the requirement to reform the aggressor in the case of inter-state war or to rebuild political community in the aftermath of civil conflict. Within the list of possible things that this might include, Orend lists: demilitarization and disarmament; police and judicial retraining; human rights education; and 'even deep structural transformation toward a peaceable liberal democratic society'. There are a variety of ethical problems that surround the project of what Orend calls rehabilitation and which underpin ethical debates about the *why*, *what*, *who* and *how* of sustaining peace. Before we move on to look at these in more detail, we should note that our discussion of the ethics of peace has, throughout this chapter, moved between two different kinds of understanding of the term: negative and positive. Negative peace is peace understood as the absence of war; positive peace is peace understood as a state of affairs in which the conditions of violent conflict have been addressed and it becomes possible for former enemies to live in harmony with one another (Dower 2007: 143). In the previous sections, the emphasis on these different understandings of peace has varied, with some ethical positions being more focused on negative and others on positive. When it comes to the matters that Orend includes under 'rehabilitation', however, the implication is that sustainable peace has to be more than a truce between warring parties and that negative peace ultimately rests on positive peace. If this is accepted, the meaning of a just peace expands to encompass a whole range of issues that relate to the structural conditions of war and not just the specificities of particular conflicts between warring groups.

On what grounds is rehabilitation an ethical requirement of *post bellum* justice? From Orend's point of view, the requirement follows from *ad bellum* justice, in that the aim of a just war should be to achieve an outcome that is 'more just' than the situation prior to war, and this can only be brought about if the aggressor is reformed as well as defeated. In this context, 'more just' means the vindication of individual and collective rights. This position is susceptible to two different kinds of criticism. On the one hand, it can be argued that it results in contradictory requirements in that it suggests that the collective and individual rights of the aggressor community and population can be vindicated by coercion. This seems particularly problematic in the case of the collective right to self-determination which is hard to make compatible with an imposed social and political regime. From a contractualist point of view, such an imposition breaches both collective and individual rights since the legitimacy of the state essentially derives from the consent of the people.

On the other hand, a different kind of critique of Orend's view takes issue with the claim that the aim of a 'more just' outcome for war should always be understood to include the reform of the aggressor party. Bellamy argues that taking this 'maximalist' position is morally questionable, depending on the kind of war that is involved, the potential contestability of its justice, the relation between *jus post bellum* and *jus ad bellum*, and the degree of consensus that exists about what counts as just social and political order (Bellamy 2008: 619–21). In relation to the first point, Bellamy distinguishes between aggressive just wars and just wars of self-defence. Aggressive just wars, which would include humanitarian interventions or wars on unjust regimes, do seem to imply rehabilitation as part of meeting the requirements of *jus ad bellum*. However, it isn't clear why a war of self-defence entails a moral obligation to sort out the problems of the aggressor in the aftermath of war, in particular on the part of the community that was attacked in the first place. Even with aggressive wars that claim to be just, if this justice is widely contested, then this would seem to limit the right of the victor to extensive interference in the affairs of the allegedly unjust state. Bellamy is also concerned that by making *jus post bellum* rehabilitation a requirement entailed by *jus ad bellum*, one would be committed to condemning an intervention that stopped genocide but failed to reform the state in question as unjust. His final objection to maximalist *post bellum* justice is that it has to presume a particular understanding of a just social and political order that is itself contestable (Bellamy 2008).

Bellamy's argument is partly a consequentialist one that seeks to undermine overambitious accounts of *post bellum* justice in order to maintain the possibility that wars of self-defence or to stop genocide will still count as just wars, and states will continue to be willing to engage in them. He also draws on contractualism in his insistence on linking responsibilities *post bellum* to the moral commitments implicit in *ad bellum* reasoning and in his focus on the lack of consensus about just forms of social and political order. In doing so, he links the question of why rehabilitation may be a requirement of justice to *what* that rehabilitation involves, *who* is responsible for it and *how* it should be brought about.

A rehabilitated political community is one that is no longer liable to engage in violent conflict, whether external or internal. In order for a polity to be transformed in this way, Orend, and an extensive literature on peacebuilding, suggests that a variety of ideational, political and economic transformations need to take place (Murithi 2009). In order to get rehabilitation right, then, we need to understand the ideational, political and economic conditions that facilitate war and sustain peace. Different understandings of these conditions have different implications for the meaning of just peace. A frequently cited example of rehabilitation is that of the Allied occupation and reconstruction of West Germany after the Second World War. In this context disarmament, demilitarization, de-Nazification, political regime change and massive economic investment have been credited with creating the conditions for sustainable peace. On the basis of this example, sustainable peace would appear to require community and individual identities of a certain kind, a democratic polity and some level of distributive justice.

On this account, tackling the capacity for war-making involves something more than taking weapons away; it involves changing hearts and minds, in part through socialization processes, in part through democratization and in part through removing poverty as a ground of grievance. In the case of the first, the reliance on re-socialization raises profound problems for the model of moral agency at work in deontological and contractualist ethical thinking since it is difficult to reconcile the idea of a free moral subject with an agent whose moral thinking is shaped by external processes. From these points of view, re-socialization is conceptualized as a reintroduction to moral truth which will be apparent to rational agents that are no longer being manipulated by false prophets. This truth has to be independently understood and accepted; if it is simply imposed, then moral agency is not being respected. From a utilitarian point of view, re-socialization is a matter of altering the incentives of ethical thinking by rewarding adherence to one set of values as opposed to another. What matters for the utilitarian is outcomes rather than beliefs. There is no intrinsic ethical problem with beliefs being manipulated or coerced since this is the nature of how all beliefs are internalized in the first place.

Discourse, virtue, feminist and postmodernist ethics all already assume the inter-subjectivity of ethical thinking, and for them the idea that moral values are grounded in socialization rather than derived from abstract reasoning or human nature is already taken for granted. For discourse ethics, reorienting values that have supported violent conflict requires a democratic process in which all affected by those values are able to weigh them up in conditions of fair argumentation and, by implication, find them wanting. This means involving both sides of the preceding conflict in the conversation. From the virtue perspective, reorientation of moral values is only possible through building on the resources inherent in the moral tradition in which those in need of reform participate and it should therefore be thought of as a process of renewal rather than the replacement of one set of values by another. For both feminists and postmodernists, rethinking the values and identities that have fuelled violent conflict involves a process of self-questioning in which the commonalities and mutual dependencies between enemies become a basis on which to transform an essentialized antagonistic self–other relation.

These different ways of thinking about the meaning of moral re-education clearly reflect different ethical starting points but also different implications for the question of on whom the moral responsibility for conducting or facilitating such processes should rest. Contractualism, utilitarianism and deontology suggest a paternalistic model, in which it is the duty of the victorious power or of some third party to put right the mistaken values of an aggressor population. Bellamy argues strongly that it would be wrong to insist that the victorious power should have to take responsibility for such long-term processes. In the case of all processes that require long-term interference in building and sustaining peace, he argues that the international community needs to accept a collective responsibility. This both protects winners of just wars from having to commit massive amounts of resources to the defeated party and is more legitimate, in particular in cases where the justice of the war was itself in question. The implication is that inter-state bodies in conjunction with international non-governmental organizations will have to take on the role of enabling sustainable peace (Bellamy 2008).

In different ways, discourse, virtue, feminist and postmodernist ethics suggest that processes of re-socialization need to be 'bottom up', not on grounds of effectiveness but because this is what makes them genuinely ethical. In the case of discourse, feminist and postmodernist arguments, in addition such processes need to involve not just the 'aggressor' but also erstwhile enemies – very much in the manner of the TRC discussed above (Murithi 2009: 160–80). Whilst this is not incompatible with the idea that the international community has moral responsibilities to facilitate these processes, it suggests that other kinds of local, grass-roots actors may be more likely to enable appropriate ethical transformation. In the case of discourse, feminist and postmodernist ethics it also spreads responsibility for ethical transformation to all participants in and sufferers from conflict, including 'winners' whose rights and righteousness the outcome of the conflict may have been taken to have vindicated.

Ethical arguments surrounding regime change echo some of the themes encountered in relation to changing hearts and minds. All of the ethical perspectives with which we are concerned raise problems for the morality of imposing a political regime upon a people, even when this is a democratic regime. Even in the case of utilitarianism, the rightness of democratization depends on its working to maximize utility. To the extent that imposed democratization exacerbates the likelihood of instability and collapse back into violence, then this would make a strong utilitarian case against it. More complex ethical problems are encountered by contractualism and deontology on this question. In both cases these are moral perspectives that are sympathetic to the idea of self-determination that underpins both democratic political forms and the protection of individual rights inherent in liberal democracy. From these perspectives, the setting up of a liberal democracy in the aftermath of war could be seen as entailed by 'rights vindication'. On the other hand, both contractualism and deontology have a conception of human freedom at their heart that sits uneasily with the idea of a coercively imposed regime. It is therefore ethically significant from these points of view that a distinction can be drawn between 'regime' and 'people' in respect of the defeated party or parties. If it can plausibly be argued that the two are not identifiable with each other, and that regime transition has broader support within the population as a whole, it becomes more ethically acceptable. From the contractualist point of view in particular, if a genuinely democratic regime is set up, then this means that the people will have an opportunity to make their 'will' known which will counteract coercive elements in the setting up of that opportunity. Moreover, for both perspectives, it matters that liberalism and democracy are ethically superior forms of political organization. When this is assumed to be true, then it is also assumed that the people, insofar as they are rational moral agents, will eventually appreciate this truth.

Discourse ethics shares contractualist and deontological commitments to democracy and the protection of individual rights as the political and legal arrangements that best reflect the requirements of morality. From the discourse ethics point of view, the conditions of fair argumentation themselves are intrinsically both democratic and rights-respecting. So there is a sense in which democratization is the sine qua non of just peace, when that justice depends on that to which all affected would agree. Here again a distinction is drawn between what may have been the immoral proceedings of a previous regime and what the *people* themselves want, or would want if they understood the ethical assumptions underlying communication. In addition, if all affected are entitled to be involved in the discussion, discourse ethics appears to require a broadening of democratization beyond the party being reformed to encompass other parties to the conflict and third parties with an interest in the outcome. In some ways, therefore, discourse ethics has more powerful implications than contractualism or deontology, requiring cosmopolitan levels of legal and political organization to enable appropriate conditions for ethical argument (Murithi 2009: 160–80).

The standpoint of virtue ethics presents more problems for the idea of forcible regime change towards liberal democracy, in particular where the virtues are identified with contextually specific 'thick' values, as in the work of someone like Walzer. 'Democracy' and 'rights' are arguably terms in ethical discourse that are more culturally specific in their historical development than the term 'justice'. Is it possible to extrapolate a 'thin' common meaning of these terms from the 'thick' morality in which they have been embedded in a way that is genuinely inclusive? In this respect, certain kinds of virtue ethics arguments come to similar conclusions to contractualism, though for rather different reasons. Whereas a contractualist would condemn coercive democratization processes on the ground that they negate the value of liberty, contextualist virtue arguments condemn such processes because they claim that political arrangements, if they are to take root, must be justifiable in terms that are available within the existing ethical vocabularies of those to be reformed. In the case of more universalist versions of virtue ethics, there is still a problem with forcible democratization imposed from above, without the inculcation of appropriate moral development through more 'bottom-up' moral education processes.

There is nothing in feminist and postmodernist ethics that condemns democratization as such but, as with the arguments relating to socialization processes, in both cases there is also a problem with this taking a top-down form. Contractualism, deontology, and discourse ethics all suggest that there are modes of legal and political organization that are morally superior. For feminists and postmodernists, not only is this kind of certainty itself morally problematic but it also tends to lead to a disregarding of contexts, not only culturally but also politically. For example, the identification of some democratization processes with a continuation of colonialism in the post-Cold War period reflects the experience of political communities and peoples who have historically had their polities shaped and reshaped by external and more powerful actors. What is, in all honesty, proposed as a process of liberation may be experienced as a process of subjection. Feminist and postmodernist critics argue that rationalist moral theories overlook this fact because they understand ethics in contradistinction to power, and then try to apply ethical principles in a world in which ethics is inextricable from power. In relation to this, feminist and postmodernist ethics raise questions about democratization processes that take for granted a particular understanding of relevant identities and interests. New constitutions in which recognition of ethnic groups is enshrined may do more to perpetuate conflict than to resolve it. Formal parliamentary systems that set up structures for bargaining between groups may exclude less powerful actors. Human rights provisions that reflect one set of understandings of crucial vulnerabilities, for instance on grounds of ethnicity, may fail to encompass other crucial vulnerabilities related to age or gender. One of the ways to counter these possibilities is to listen to and invest in 'bottom-up' democratization processes.

In thinking about the conditions for sustainable peace, along with shifts at the level of individual attitudes and identities and changes in political institutions and structures, changes at the economic level have also been identified as important. As noted earlier in the chapter, one of the requirements of a just peace is supposed to be restitution for the people victimized by war. In the case of inter-state war, this has traditionally been taken to mean restitution to the victims of aggression by the aggressor, though in Orend's case this is with the proviso that the guilty state is not entirely impoverished. This is complicated by cases of aggressive just wars for regime change and by civil wars, where identifying who has the *post bellum* responsibility to pay, and quite what that payment entails, is a matter of contestation. These debates link to the broader question of how distributive justice considerations are bound up with the ethical requirements for just peace. Is it the case that a peace can only be just if requirements of distributive justice guide our thinking about both victims *and* aggressors, just *and* unjust regimes and their populations? And if we are guided by the requirements of distributive justice, then what theories of distributive justice do we follow?

Without rehearsing the arguments already encountered in chapter 5, we can see immediately that contractualist and deontological reasoning might give us very different stories about the principle of distributive justice appropriate for guiding *post bellum* arrangements. From a contractualist point of view, ethical responsibilities are inherent in agreements undertaken. This might well imply that the economic sanctions following the end of the 1991 Iraq war were not unjust in terms of the commitments made by the international community. Rather, the Iraqi regime was unjust in persisting in behaviour that perpetuated them. From a deontological point of view, the violation of minimal welfare rights to food and health care that could have been avoided by abandoning the sanctions policy makes the justice of the international community much more questionable. This argument is reminiscent of the debate about global distributive justice between theorists, such as Rawls, for whom political communities must take responsibility for their own populations in determining who owes what to whom, as opposed to needs-based virtue or deontological theories, such as those of Nussbaum or Caney, for whom what matters morally is the need itself and who has the capacity to meet it, regardless of explicitly contracted obligations. However, both contractualism and deontology would be likely to agree that the powers invading Afghanistan in 2001 and Iraq in 2003 should be obliged to make major economic investments in the region – for contractualists because this is implied by the regime-changing commitments made by those powers, and for deontologists because not to do so would involve major violations of basic economic human rights.

For contractualists and deontologists, innocence and guilt matter for the distributive principles governing a just peace. Neither of them would argue for retention of goods by owners that had expropriated them in the first place, and in this sense both would support restitution and reparation to injured parties after war. Nevertheless, one can argue on deontological grounds there is a basic level of distributive justice that is absolutely inviolable, regardless of the guilt or innocence of the individuals involved. This suggests that peacebuilding requires mechanisms for addressing distributive justice issues that go beyond a language of restitution or reparation. Similarly, from a utilitarian point of view, distributive justice comes into just peace insofar as it can be demonstrated that economic redistribution maximizes utility by making peace more sustainable. Since there is considerable evidence that extremes of poverty and inequality fuel violent conflict and vice versa, there is a powerful utilitarian case for making distributive justice central to sustainable peace (MacGinty and Williams 2009). For the utilitarian, what matters is that the cycle of violence is broken, regardless of the guilt or innocence of the parties to the conflict. From the point of view of discourse, virtue, feminist and postmodernist ethics, the ethics of *post bellum* distributive justice depends, though in rather different ways, on the extent to which the principles underpinning it are acceptable to those affected by it. All of the ethical perspectives, therefore, accept the idea that distributive justice is significant for just peace and take us back to the question of the meaning of distributive justice itself. What begins as a discussion about justice *post bellum* ends as a much broader discussion about global justice as such.

Reflective exercise

- Feminist and postmodernist critics have argued that collective violence is sustained by gendered and raced identities. If this is true, then what is it ethically permissible to do in order to change such identities in the interests of peace?
- Is the imposition of democracy on an undemocratic regime ethically permissible? Give reasons for your answer.

Conclusion

Short-term and long-term questions about the meaning of just peace return us to the issues familiar from other debates within Global Ethics. Here again we have encountered opposing views about the ethical value of individuals, the meaning and comparative ethical significance of individual and community, the meaning and implications of ethical responsibility, the comparative ethical importance of process in relation to outcome. Alternative utilitarian and deontological views about retributive and restorative justice reflect different assumptions about the basis of the moral significance of the individual. The ways in which contractualists see the moral significance of consent and political community affect their conclusions about the legitimacy of collective punishment or rehabilitation. Postmodernist understandings of ethical responsibility suggest a different way of going about peace-building than we find in either contractualist or deontological accounts. And discourse, feminist and postmodernist theorists give priority to the ethical inclusion of affected parties as opposed to the utilitarian emphasis on outcomes when it comes to peace processes. As always, we are presented with the problem of adjudicating between alternative theoretical frameworks and the range of prescriptive consequences that follow from them. In this respect, working out the meaning of just peace highlights the clashes between rationalist and non-rationalist accounts of ethics – and therefore the question of the ground and reach of the authority of ethical claims – particularly starkly. This is because, in the aftermath of conflict, settlements are made on the basis of power relations that give some parties the capacity to *impose* their views on others.

The principles of *post bellum* justice articulated by contemporary theorists predominantly reflect utilitarian, contractualist and deontological accounts of ethics, in which the question of what counts as a just peace are seen to be resolvable in a way acceptable to all right-thinking people (Murithi 2009). Discourse, virtue, feminist and postmodernist ethical theorists cast doubt on this possibility but also point to the ethical implications of imposing a particular resolution that is not acceptable to at least some of those who are its recipients and who cannot be immediately dismissed as either immoral or mistaken. Views about the nature and basis of the authority of ethical claims have implications for the ethical relation between the ethical theorist and his or her interlocutors, as well as for the kinds of mechanisms of coercion or persuasion that count as legitimate when it comes to implementing particular ethical prescriptions. For example, utilitarian, contractualist and deontological theorists of just peace are positioned in relation to those engaged in peacemaking and peacebuilding activities as authoritative experts, offering guiding principles for peacemakers and peacebuilders to follow. To the extent that these guiding principles are not being followed, then the implication is that this needs to be put right by those practitioners with the power to make things happen. This may be through mechanisms of education and training for people on the ground or it may be through the coercive effect of carrots and sticks, such as the provision or withholding of aid.

The question of the moral authority of ethical claims is therefore an *ethical* question, a question about how the ethical theorist relates to his or her audience (as teacher, as expert, as peer) and about what the ethical theorist is suggesting it may or may not be permissible to do to others in the service of morality. At the beginning of this book, we raised the question of whether Global Ethics involves the extension of existing moral knowledge and ways of knowing to the global arena, or whether it is the construction of novel ethical responses to challenges posed by new globalized levels of hierarchical interdependence. Implicit within this question is a contrast between a view of moral theory as a body of knowledge that can be acquired by individuals and a view of moral theory closer to the idea of *phronesis* in virtue ethics, as a set of tools rather than a set of answers. In the following chapter we will explore what is at stake between these different understandings and how this affects Global Ethics as a distinct field of ethical inquiry.

References and further reading

Bass, G. (2004) '*Jus Post Bellum*', *Philosophy and Public Affairs* 32(4): 384–412. Thorough overview of *post bellum* justice issues – makes an argument for early exit as the most just option for a victorious, occupying state.

Bellamy, A. (2008) 'The Responsibilities of Victory: *Jus Post Bellum* and the Just War', *Review of International Studies* 34(4): 601–25. Extremely helpful critical account of existing *jus post bellum* arguments; argues for a nuanced and limited approach to post-war justice and for the detachment of post-war justice from just war theory as such.

Ben-Porath, S. (2008) 'Care Ethics and Dependence: Rethinking *Jus Post Bellum*', *Hypatia* 23(2): 61–71. Makes the case for a care ethics approach to issues of post-war justice.

Campbell, D. (1998) *National Deconstruction: Violence, Identity and Justice in Bosnia*, Minneapolis: University of Minnesota Press. A poststructuralist-inspired critique of the international community's response to the war and peace process in Bosnia-Herzegovina.

Campbell, K. (2004) 'The Trauma of Justice: Sexual Violence, Crimes against Humanity and the International Criminal Tribunal for the Former Yugoslavia', *Social and Legal Studies* 13(3): 329–50. Feminist poststructuralist critique of the model of justice at work in the ICTY.

Crocker, D. (1999) 'Reckoning with Past Wrongs: A Normative Framework', *Ethics and International Affairs* 13: 43–64. An attempt to combine retributive and restorative justice in an overarching model of the requirements for transitional justice.

Dower, N. (2007) *World Ethics: The New Agenda*, 2nd edn, Edinburgh: Edinburgh University Press. See pp. 142–7 for a consideration of the meaning and implications of peace.

Eide, M. (2008) '"The Stigma of Nation": Feminist Just War, Privilege and Responsibility', *Hypatia* 23(2): 48–60. Argument that a feminist ethics of war should be focused on justice *post bellum*.

Fletcher, L. E. and Weinstein, H. M. (2002) 'Violence and Social Repair: Rethinking the Contribution of Justice to Reconciliation', *Human Rights Quarterly* 24: 573–639. Critical examination of the role of war crimes trials in bringing about national reconciliation.

Helms, E. (2003) 'Women as Agents of Ethnic Reconciliation? Women NGOs and International Intervention in Postwar Bosnia-Herzegovina', *Women's Studies International Forum* 26(1): 15–33. Examines role of women and grass-roots groups in peace-making in Bosnia-Herzegovina.

Jackson, R. (1992) 'Dialectical Justice in the Gulf War', *Review of International Studies* 18: 335–54. A thorough just war theory analysis of the 1991 Gulf War.

Jaspers, K. (1995 [1948]) 'The Question of German Guilt', in N. J. Kritz (ed.), *Transnational Justice*, Volume I, Washington, DC: United States Institute of Peace Press. Exploration of the facets and bearers of responsibility and guilt involved in Germany's actions in the 1930s and 1940s.

Kutz, C. (2004) 'Justice in Reparations: The Cost of Memory and the Value of Talk', *Philosophy and Public Affairs* 32(3): 277–312. Looks at the cases of Central and Eastern Europe and the role of economic reparations in aiding or preventing restorative justice.

MacGinty, R. and Williams, A. (2009) *Conflict and Development*, Abingdon: Routledge. Explores the interrelation in contemporary world politics between violent conflict and development, including chapters on conflict resolution and post-conflict reconstruction.

Mertus, J. (2004) 'Shouting from the Bottom of the Well: The Impact of International Trials for Wartime Rape on Women's Agency', *International Feminist Journal of Politics* 6(1): 110–28. Critical account of the negative effects on victims of the ICTY trials of perpetrators of crimes of sexual violence.

Murithi, T. (2009) *The Ethics of Peacebuilding*, Edinburgh: Edinburgh University Press. A systematic exploration of the ethics of peacemaking and peacebuilding which draws on aspects of discourse ethics to make an argument for a morally inclusive approach.

Nagel, T. (1979) 'On Ruthlessness in Public Life', in *Mortal Questions*, Cambridge: Cambridge University Press, pp. 75–90. An argument for the need to distinguish between the kinds of moral responsibility carried by political leaders as opposed to private individuals.

Orend, B. (2000) 'Terms of Peace: Walzer's Theory of *Jus Post Bellum*', chapter 6 in *Michael Walzer on War and Justice*, Cardiff: University of Wales Press, pp. 135–52. A useful extrapolation of Walzer's argument about justice *post bellum*.

Orend, B. (2002) 'Justice after War', *Ethics and International Affairs* 16(1): 43–56. An attempt to systematize principles of justice *post bellum* derived from a Walzerian take on just war theory.

Rooney, E. (2007) 'Engendering Transitional Justice: Questions of Absence and Silence', *International Journal of Law in Context* 3(2): 93–107. Examines the case of Northern Ireland and the implications of the exclusion of women from the peace process.

Walzer, M. (2004) 'The Question of Responsibility', Part V of *Just and Unjust Wars*, 4th edn, New York: Basic Books, pp. 287–327. Focuses specifically on the accountability of leaders and of soldiers for crimes *in bello*.

Whitworth, S. (2004) *Men, Militarism and UN Peacekeeping*, Boulder, CO: Lynne Rienner. A feminist critique of peacekeeping operations.

Williams, R. E. and Caldwell, D. (2006) '*Jus Post Bellum*: Just War Theory and the Principles of Just Peace', *International Studies Perspectives* 7(4): 309–20. An account of *jus post bellum* based on a human rights argument.

8

Global Ethics in a Glocal Context

Introduction

The last four chapters have focused on issues that are generally agreed to be global, in the sense that questions about
distributive justice, war and peace are embedded in the ways
in which different parts of the world share significant commonalities or are reciprocally interconnected and mutually
dependent, or both. As we have seen, different ethical perspectives offer different accounts of global economic justice,
just war and just peace. But whatever their account, and
however certainly it is held, all of these ethical approaches
are being developed in a world in which ethical consensus
cannot be taken for granted. All attempts to address questions in Global Ethics are, therefore, confronted with the
challenge of how to respond to this lack of consensus. The
significance of the ways in which this challenge is met became
particularly evident in the previous chapter when considering
ethical issues involved in establishing a just peace, where
certain agents have the power to impose their particular
vision of justice on those that do not share it but are supposed
to benefit from it. In this concluding chapter, I want to suggest
that, in spite of the deep differences between them, all of
the ethical perspectives with which we have been concerned
converge on the need to establish ethically appropriate means
of mediating between ethical convictions that clash but
are sincerely held. As we will see, what counts as 'ethically

appropriate means' depends on assumptions different perspectives hold about the authoritative status of their moral claims.

In this chapter, we will be focusing on the ways in which the challenge of global ethical disagreement (dissensus) can be met, from the point of view of the different perspectives with which we have been concerned. In order to do this, we will turn to explore ethical issues that arise at the level of the 'glocal'. Glocal is the term that has been coined to capture the ways in which globalization processes are not uniform but are always locally experienced and transformed by, as well as transformative of, local contexts. One of the effects of globalization is an increase in the number of situations in which apparently incommensurable ethical values clash in contexts that reproduce, at the local level, global diversities of both culture and power. The chapter will proceed in three sections. In the first section, we will rehearse the ethical issues at stake between the ethical theories we have been considering and how they point to the need to think about the ethics of mediating ethical dissensus. The second section will focus on the response of rationalist perspectives in Global Ethics to problems posed by glocal clashes of values. The third section will examine the responses to these kinds of clashes of anti-rationalist ethical perspectives. The conclusion will suggest that debates concerning glocal ethical issues set an important future agenda for Global Ethics, one that requires a greater engagement with the *who* and *how* questions central to virtue, feminist and postmodernist ethics. Returning to the question raised in the first chapter of this book, it will be argued that, although we may not need to entirely reinvent our ethical theories in order to contribute to the field of Global Ethics, theorists such as Appiah and Parekh are right to suggest that Global Ethics requires a different theoretical orientation than fields of ethical inquiry that, implicitly or explicitly, take commonalities in their target audience as given.

Revisiting the ethical issues at stake

At the beginning of this book, we raised the question of whether Global Ethics could be premised on existing ethical perspectives applied to global ethical issues or whether Global Ethics required the invention of new ways of thinking about ethical problems. In the preceding chapters we have mapped the ground of contemporary ethical debates on global questions about aid, development, distributive justice, just war and just peace. In each case we have seen the implications of the application of existing ethical frameworks to these questions. And we have also seen how the application of existing ethical perspectives to global questions is never entirely straightforward. Even where moral approaches are clear about the relevant principles or outcomes involved, difficulties arise in working out responses to the *who* and *how* questions. In other words, we may have established in principle that the polluter should pay, but who is the polluter? Is it states, corporations, citizens, those polluting now or the heirs of those who polluted in the past? We may have established that a massive global redistribution of wealth is morally required but what are the ethically appropriate mechanisms for doing this, and how do we do it without perpetuating new injustices? And in any of these cases, who is 'we'? In this context, tensions already embedded in traditions of moral thought that have been developed without paying explicit attention to the scope of the relevant moral community become particularly acute.

We can see this if we return to the ethical issues fundamental to the debates that we have traced during the course of this book. For example, individualist moral theories, such as utilitarianism, contractualism and deontology, have debated with each other for centuries about the basis of the grounding moral significance of the human individual. But the scale and significance of the implications of their different accounts becomes greater as the ethical questions being addressed involve a larger range of actors and realms of action such as in aid and development policies, the management of immigration, the legitimation of collective political violence or the appropriate mechanisms for transitional justice (Brock and Brighouse 2005; Pogge 2001). Similarly, the question of the significance of community and context in grounding the validity of ethical claims has been at stake in debates between universalist moral theories, such as deontology or utilitarianism on the one hand and contractualist or virtue ethics on the other, for a very long time. But it *matters* much more when the questions being asked are about ethical responses at a global level. In western political theory, so-called liberal (universal) and communitarian (contextualist) thinkers have debated with each other for years about the *why* question, whilst agreeing substantially on a range of ethical values characteristic of liberal social, economic and political orders (Mulhall and Swift 1996). But once this debate is globalized across different types of political community, each with its own complex of moral traditions, then disagreement over the *why* question also becomes disagreement over *what* ethical values count as genuinely global (Benhabib 2002; Caney 2005; Caney and Jones 2001).

Questions of moral responsibility (fault/no fault) and of how and whether reciprocal relations are relevant to justice and injustice have always been important for thinking about ethical relations between individuals or between individual and collective actors or structures. But when it comes to *global* concerns about poverty or violence, where it is much more plausible for responsibilities to be untraceable and reciprocity to be deniable, it can make the difference between something and nothing. To redistribute from wealthy to poor across national boundaries, or to invest economically in a defeated state, may be an ethical obligation, a work of supererogation, ethically neutral, or even ethically wrong. And just as the *who* question takes on greater complexity in a global context, so too does the *how* question. The amount to which procedures for reaching decisions about what is ethically right, and processes for implementing what is ethically right, themselves matter *ethically* is multiplied many times when you are dealing with a global context in which both diversity of moral traditions and hierarchies of power separate individual and collective actors in decisive ways.

Implicit in all of these debates and their implications for ethical judgement and action is the stake of moral authority implicit in different answers to the *why* question. As we have seen, rationalist moral theories think of their moral claims on analogy with knowledge claims. This analogy is particularly strong in the case of utilitarian and contractualist arguments that ground their moral position in claims to empirical truths about human nature and rationality. Deontology denies the idea of a natural basis for claims to moral truth but it argues nevertheless that there are ways in which moral truths may be discerned by reasonable human beings through reference to the universal ground and scope of moral claims. The question of how to convince others of the validity of a particular ethical position is central to modern philosophical ethics. This is because that validity has been understood as key to the justifiability of ethical prescriptions about what individuals should think and do, and how social, economic and political arrangements should be structured. But the question bites particularly hard in Global Ethics, where it isn't clear that there is a common moral vocabulary in which to pose the *why* question in the first place and the idea of the overriding authority of truth can be countered by evidence of the lack of global recognition for any of the claimants to that authority within ethical rationalism. This is not to claim that there are no global commonalities in ethical values but rather to claim that there are no global commonalities in the reasons for why those values are held. In this respect, even those ethical perspectives that are most certain of the universal ethical validity of their claims are obliged to think much more seriously about the ethical problems involved in the *global* application and implementation of the principles or values they hold to be morally right since this will necessarily involve dealing with large populations that hold to mistaken (from the rationalist perspective in question) views about the ground and meaning of justice, as opposed to being wilful wrongdoers.

Discourse ethics builds on deontology and contractualism, but also on Habermas's consensus theory of truth, to argue that justice can be identified with the agreed position of those affected, following discussion under conditions of fair argumentation. But even though discourse ethics follows a rationalist path, it already signals a departure from the model of moral knowledge implicit in utilitarian, contractualist and deontological arguments. This is because it denies that moral knowledge is attainable and demonstrable on the basis of the rational inquiry of an individual moral agent, or that moral truth can exist independent of people's agreement with it. As we have seen, this puts discourse ethics in some respects part-way between rationalist and anti-rationalist ethical theories since the latter also share both the view that ethics is fundamentally inter-subjective and that the ethical worth of values and principles can't be divorced from the ways in which the understanding of ethical worth has been arrived at and applied. In this respect, therefore, for discourse, virtue, feminist and postmodernist ethics, the application and implementation of justice presupposes some kind of inter-subjective process in the working out of what justice means. And in the case of feminist and postmodernist ethics in particular, this process is embedded in a context in which those who disagree are understood to be differentially placed in terms of economic, cultural and political power as well as moral identity and tradition.

As approaches to Global Ethics, discourse, virtue, feminist and postmodernist ethics start where utilitarianism, contractualism and deontology end, that is to say with the problem of identifying and achieving justice in a context in which right-minded people disagree. This means that anti-rationalist, just as much as rationalist, approaches have to be able to give an account of how to respond to this problem if they are to be a plausible basis for establishing Global Ethics as a distinctive branch of ethical inquiry, let alone for establishing global ethical values and principles. In order to examine the kinds of response implicit in the different approaches, we will now move on to look at the resources they offer for dealing with 'glocal' clashes of ethical values.

Reflective exercise

We have identified five issues in debates in Global Ethics that are particularly significant: the moral significance of human individuals; the relative moral significance of individual versus community or culture; the question of the ethical importance of 'fault'; the ethical significance of procedure vs. outcome; and the question of the basis of the authority of moral claims. Which of these issues do you think is most important for Global Ethics and why?

Addressing glocal ethical dissensus from a rationalist perspective

Clashes of ethical values did not originate with the effects of globalization. Most cultures and traditions harbour divergent views about moral rights and wrongs. Nevertheless, most cultures and traditions also restrict the permissible scope of explicit moral diversity and enshrine predominant views in custom and law. In addition, debates within cultures and traditions share at least some common reference points both substantively and procedurally. Think, for instance, about how arguments for and against abortion in liberal countries, which reflect deep ethical disagreement, nevertheless are both often formulated in the language of rights. In the case of glocal dissensus, debate isn't framed by a pre-existing context in which majority and minority, prevailing and subversive moral views, and certain common moral reference points are already identifiable. This means that we do not have a pre-existing map of the shape and potential outcomes of glocal moral disputes in the way that we do of moral arguments that are closer to home. This isn't to suggest that parties to glocal disputes necessarily live in incommensurable ethical universes but rather to emphasize that whether they do or not is an open question.

It is important to recognize that not all apparent disagreements over moral values and principles actually reflect ethical dissensus. Debates over global issues to do with human rights, the moral significance of culture, the problems of poverty and immigration often reflect the immediate priorities of particular interested actors rather than deep moral difference. For example, the refusal of the USA to sign up to the International Criminal Court does not necessarily reflect moral disagreement with the values of retributive and restorative justice that the court embodies. It may reflect a different ranking of moral priorities between the collective and the individual than that embodied in the court or it may just as easily be a strategic judgement that signing up to the court may put US citizens at risk. But if we examine ethical arguments for and against the USA signing up to the court, the arguments for and against are conducted in very much the same ethical vocabulary and in relation to the same kinds of values. Even issues such as child labour, which has been a major focus of human rights transnational campaigning over past decades, have increasingly been identified as to do with socio-economic context and not with some fundamental disagreement with the idea that the care, nurture and education of children should be morally valued. This became apparent when policies of boycotting firms that used child labour resulted in a serious deterioration of their conditions (Pierik 2007). One therefore needs to exercise some care in identifying ethical disagreements and not jump to the conclusion that, because practices in different contexts are different, this implies the inhabitation of distinct moral universes.

There are two contexts for glocal clashes of value that, although they both have a much longer history, have become particularly prominent in today's globalizing world. The first kind follows patterns of migration, where the values of immigrant peoples differ from those of predominant opinion in the recipient society. The second kind follows patterns of international or transnational intervention, where the values of interveners, such as aid workers or peacekeepers, differ from those of the society, or groups within the society, in which they are operating. In both cases, this is rarely a straightforward insider/outsider clash since not all actors will line up with the prevailing views associated with the majority position of their own culture. Such clashes are experienced most powerfully in relation to intimate aspects of how people live their lives. They centre on the body, on punishment, on the treatment of children, on religious observance, on the ethical legitimacy of choices and practices in relation to sex, marriage and sexuality. Clearly such issues have to be addressed by policy makers and legislators, but our concern here is not with the political or legal response but with how ethical theories deal with the question of how to respond to these glocal ethical clashes *ethically*. Issues of this kind that have gained a lot of attention in recent years have included: female circumcision (termed female genital mutilation by its critics); women's dress; punishments such as amputation or stoning; birth control; abortion; forced marriages; arranged marriages; attitudes towards homosexuality; responses to

HIV AIDS (Barry 2001; Benhabib 2006; Jaggar 2008; Okin 2008; Parekh 2000).

What would be the utilitarian response to being confronted by opposing positions on these kinds of issue? As a rationalist moral theorist, the first task for the utilitarian would be to work out which position was morally right, that is to say which of the positions maximized utility to the greatest possible extent. In order to do this, the utilitarian would be obliged to abstract from the particular context and consider the issue at a general level in terms of the implications for pleasure or pain for every individual counting as one. Having done this and arrived at conclusions, the utilitarian would then have to consider the prescriptive consequences of these conclusions and their implications for action. These in themselves would then have to be assessed in utilitarian terms. If we take something like female circumcision (FGM), given the pain involved for half of the human population in relation to uncertain gains for both men and women as individuals, it seems likely that the utilitarian cost-benefit calculation would identify female circumcision as morally wrong. What matters, in utilitarian terms, are outcomes. Given this, the prescriptive implications are clear; the practice should be stopped as soon as possible. The ethical question then becomes 'what is the most effective way to stop the practice within utilitarian limits?'– that is to say, without generating more disutility than was generated by the practice in the first place.

From the utilitarian point of view, whether the way to stop the practice turns out to be through moral education, major social change, legislation, bribery or physical coercion does not matter as long as the gains outweigh the losses. But in making this judgement, the utilitarian would have to take careful account of the actual practice, the ways in which it is or isn't interconnected to other aspects of people's lives, the knock-on effects for the individuals concerned and so on. For instance the fact that circumcision ensured the eligibility of some women for marriage would not affect the utilitarian judgement of the wrongness of the practice but would have to be taken into account in the question of how to eradicate it. This suggests that, in order to stop the practice, a whole set of other assumptions about women (as individuals that count as one) and marriage as a social institution would need to be addressed in order to change the incentive structure for an unjust practice. In keeping with its history as a moral approach with a critical cutting edge, the implication of utilitarianism would appear to be that change consequent on moral judgements is likely to have to be root and branch, creating a world in which utility does not arise out of practices that are fundamentally contrary to the utility of each person counted equally. In this context the *means* through which change is engendered are necessarily subservient to the *ends*.

How would a contractualist moral theory respond to glocal ethical disputes about the morality of punishments for adultery or murder? As with the utilitarian, the first move the contractualist moral theorist would make would be to attempt to identify what was morally acceptable or not on contractualist grounds. As we know, two elements are involved in how this is worked out: the specification of the precontractual individual and of the, usually hypothetical, circumstances in which the contract is agreed. Because of this, different contractualist theorists will be more or less permissive on the issue of the parameters of what realms of behaviour count as private (and therefore immune from punishment, if not from censure) and on appropriate modes of punishment in the public realm. However, because of the emphasis of all contractualist moral theory on the constraining role played by the natural rights of individuals on what they would agree to, and because of a philosophical anthropology linked to the utilitarian model of humans as pleasure seeking and pain avoiding, there is a strong connection between contractualism and liberal views about the distinction between private and public spheres of action and about extremes of physical punishment. Most contractualists would regard punishment for adultery as inappropriate and, even if accepting capital punishment as appropriate for murderers, would want executions carried out in ways that were not, in their terms, 'cruel and unusual'.

Given a contractualist position that punishment for adultery is morally wrong, and that the infliction of intense physical pain as part of punishments for acts in the public sphere is morally wrong, what follows for contractualist

prescriptions about what should be done about those with
opposing views and practices? The implication presumably is
that these views and practices should be stopped. But in
thinking about *how* this should be done, the contractualist is
faced with two puzzles. At the heart of contractualist thought
is the individual as 'rational chooser'. It is because this is how
the individual is seen that his or her consent to extremes of
punishment cannot be assumed, even where individuals do
implicitly or explicitly consent. This must therefore mean that
at some level those endorsing these kinds of practices are
rational but in error, irrational or wicked. Yet clearly one's
response to the ongoing wrongness of these punishment
practices will be different, depending on the diagnosis. If it is
error on the part of rational beings that is in question, then
it would seem that argument is the way forward. However,
if it is irrationality or wickedness, rather than error, then
this would suggest the need for immediate and forcible intervention. This might involve the re-socialization of those
committed to irrational views because of the ways they have
been acculturated, or the use of force to prevent deliberate
wickedness. The first puzzle is how one works out how to
account for immoral views and practices in the first place.
The second puzzle arises in relation to how it is possible
to reconcile coercive, interventionist mechanisms for changing existing views and practices with a model of the human
being as having a natural right to freedom, in particular
where the offending practice is located in another political
community.

Two possible contractualist justifications for coercive intervention in the affairs of other communities are possible: first,
that the violations of right in question are so fundamental as
to be impossible to trade off contractually; or, second, that
there is a lack of consent to these practices in the communities
in which they exist. In such situations coercion is itself a
response to coercion and so the paradox is resolved, though
only if one accepts the foundations of contractualist thought
in the first place. In contrast to utilitarianism, contractualism
gives moral relevance to consent. For this reason coercion,
even when it leads to good (in contractualist terms) outcomes,
is harder to justify where opinions are held in good faith by
rational people but easier to justify to the extent that certain

opinions are by definition ones that no rational or good human being could hold.

Deontological moral theory is not tied so closely to liberalism as utilitarian and contractarian ways of thinking. Nevertheless, as with utilitarianism and contractualism, the deontological response to how to deal with glocal ethical disputes, such as those discussed above, would also depend on first working out the rightness or wrongness of the views and practices in question. Once that is known, the deontological position is clear: what is morally right must be pursued regardless of consequences. This means, in the case of many contemporary deontological theories, that respect for fundamental human rights is a bottom-line requirement for all moral traditions. To the extent that moral traditions do not respect such human rights, then there is a requirement to ensure that respect, providing that in doing so one is not also engaged in rights violation. In a similar way to contractualism, in thinking about the ethics of implementing what is right, deontologists must discriminate between the different reasons why right is being violated in the first place. Is it straightforward error, in which case rational demonstration is all that is needed? Is it a deeper level of irrationality or false consciousness, in which case paternalistic intervention and moral education may be necessary? Or is it wickedness? In that case, violators need to be held fully responsible for their actions and be called to account if they are to be given their due respect as human beings.

There are several points to note about the ethics of tackling ethical dissensus in the perspectives discussed so far. The first point is that all of the perspectives put limits on a 'live and let live' approach to glocal clashes of value. Although none of them require uniformity across the whole range of ethical views and practices, all of them permit diversity only to the extent that it does not violate fundamental values and principles. All of them, therefore, make room for intervention and change as an ethically required response to ethical dissensus. The second point is that all of the perspectives claim to be detached from anchorage in any particular majority view. Instead they represent universally accessible moral truths. This means that, thirdly, opinions contrary to moral truth are categorized as 'opinion', and therefore as inferior points of

view, however sincerely held. Fourthly, such 'opinions' have
to be further categorized: they may be mistakes, they may be
fundamentally irrational or they may be straightforwardly
wicked. In this context, fifthly, holding immoral opinions
reflects more or less powerfully on the moral status of the
holders of these opinions. At best they are mistaken, perhaps
through their own fault, perhaps because of the machinations
of others; at worst they are either failing to live up to their
humanity by identifying with an irrational moral position or
are morally bad individuals committed to wrongdoing.

Precisely because of their individualist basis, utilitarianism,
contractualism and deontology have trouble working out
why human beings persistently do the wrong thing when they
all have the capacity to know and do right. If rational demonstration is not enough to convince wrongdoers that that is
what they are, then the answer has to be either that people
are at some level coerced (they are moral dupes or they are
operating under threat) or that they are subhuman or morally
bad (possibly the same thing). Regardless of the specifics of
what such theorists may want to say about any glocally contentious ethical issue, their deliberations are bound to place
large amounts of the global population as morally inferior.
This is because on these accounts it is precisely your capacity
to know what is right that determines your moral status.
Some moral convictions are right and some are wrong. To
the extent that the moral theorist knows what is right, then
he or she can claim moral superiority in having worked out
the implications of nature, reason or the moral law.

Rational demonstration, moral education, re-socialization
and coercion all emerge as permissible mechanisms for
addressing glocal ethical dissensus from the point of view of
rationalist moral theories. On the basis of having answers to
the *what* question when it comes to what an ethical response
to moral dissensus involves, utilitarianism, contractualism
and deontology pay relatively little attention to *how* and by
whom these processes should be conducted, except to place
certain moral limits, such as that they should not generate
disproportionate harm or violate fundamental rights. What
does discourse ethics, which is also rationalist in its inspiration, have to say to this discussion? The obvious difference
is that, from the point of view of discourse ethics, the answer

to the question of which glocal moral opinion is right needs itself (along with its prescriptive consequences) to be practically and provisionally authorized by actual engagement between proponents of different opinions. From a discourse ethics perspective, glocal ethical dissensus can only be dealt with through argument, under fair conditions, including all those affected by the issue in question.

The kind of argument involved in discourse ethics requires mutual respect and honesty amongst the participants and would therefore, it is claimed, make clear where the commitment to a particular ethical view is genuinely universally defensible (moral) as opposed to a reflection of specific identities (ethical) or operating in the particular interests of certain parties (strategic). As we saw in chapter 2, discourse ethics is commonly criticized on grounds of plausibility and practicability. Even the determination of who counts as a member of the all-affected group is difficult to work out and the process, as well as posing massive logistical problems, requires a major effort of detachment on the part of the participants from their given identities and prejudices. Moreover, critics argue that the condition of fair argumentation effectively institutionalizes liberal norms in such a way as to predetermine the outcome of the conversation. If we take something like the issue of female circumcision, which is a practice embedded in hierarchical assumptions about sexual and kinship relations, then the very involvement of all affected as equal parties in a conversation about it undermines those assumptions. This means that those in favour of the practice could not treat relations between participants in discussion about the morality of the practice as being between equals. If they did so, they have already effectively abandoned a key pillar of the practice that they were supposed to be defending.

On the basis of the above reasoning, it can be argued that discourse ethics suffers from a kind of circularity in which we already know from the conditions of argumentation what principles will pass the discourse version of the universalization test that distinguishes between the right and the good. These will be principles that reflect an understanding of individuals as equal, free and rational. This latter understanding, as with utilitarian and contractarian views about human nature and deontological views about the form of the moral law, floats free of anchorage in any particular community or way of life. It implies that ethical views and practices that clash with assumptions about individuals as equal, free and rational reflect at best mistakes and at worst wilful immorality. This therefore returns discourse ethics, once the right is established through actual or virtual argumentation, to the alternatives for responding to glocal ethical dissensus implied by other rationalist theories. Within Habermas's own thought, moral education is the crucial way of changing mistaken moral viewpoints and practices.

Reflective exercise

Think about your most fundamentally held moral values or positions on issues such as abortion, capital punishment, arranged marriages or homosexuality. What do you to think would be necessary in order for you to change your mind on these issues? Would rational demonstration do it? What are the prescriptive implications of your moral certainties for others?

Addressing global ethical dissensus beyond rationalism

Some proponents of discourse ethics have criticized Habermas's view that the conditions for fair argumentation are in some sense 'free floating'. Benhabib has argued that these conditions in fact reflect the normative horizons of modernity and cannot be treated as 'outside' contexts of culture and community (Benhabib 1990, 1992). She also criticizes Habermas for putting too much emphasis on the *outcome* of universalization procedures and thereby falling back into the errors of rationalism. From the point of view of discourse ethics, Benhabib argues, outcomes are only ever principles that may be universalized in general. The results of argumentation therefore always underdetermine the substantive principles that should be adopted for action in a particular situation. They rule certain things out but do not positively determine what it must be right to do. The significance of the discursive procedure for Benhabib, therefore, does not lie in it as a way of arriving at a definitive account of what is right but rather in the values and principles embedded in the procedure itself.

In following up this insight, Benhabib moves on to question again the over-rationalism of Habermas's account of argumentation, with its assumption of disembodied, rational participants, detached from their concrete identities and interests in communication with one another. In place of this vision, Benhabib argues for an understanding of the moral point of view as involving seeing from the other's point of view in a double sense. This means not only operating according to assumptions of universal respect and equality in relation to the others involved in moral conversation but also using one's imagination and empathy to understand others' positions as concrete, embodied subjects, with particular identities, histories and needs. In effect, Benhabib argues that discourse ethics is not a way of 'cutting like a knife' between claims that can be accorded universal validity and those that cannot but is rather a form of moral judgement that combines respect for a principle of universalizability with the capacity to recognize and be sensitive to difference. For Benhabib, therefore, the response to glocal ethical dissensus is to keep moral conversation of this kind ongoing. This is a distinct departure from the rationalist theories considered so far, where the point of moral engagement is to arrive at a conclusion rather than to embed a process (Benhabib 1990: 359).

Benhabib's modification of discourse ethics is influenced by virtue and feminist ethical theories but seeks to hold on to aspects of rationalist, deontological moral thinking. The response of virtue ethics to glocal ethical dissensus goes further along the path of abandoning the idea of the *answer* to the question of what is morally right being necessary in order to work out what to do about clashes of moral views and practices. This is because, from the virtue ethics point of view, the answer to the question of what is right is always embedded in a network of existing practices and ways of life that may not be commensurable with one another. At first sight, this suggests that virtue ethics can offer no answer to the question of how to deal ethically with mediating between different glocal views since there is no common set of practices or way of life that characterize the space between different moral traditions. On this account, glocal proponents and opponents of particular forms of punishment for adultery or murder would simply have to settle for the fact of plurality and their inability to talk to each other.

However, this is to underestimate the degree to which virtue ethics does not give priority to the question of the rightness or wrongness of moral views in the first place. For virtue ethics, the rationalist theories are asking the wrong question. We need to move from starting with questions about moral knowledge (how to attain it and its prescriptive implications) to questions about how to live a flourishing life in specific contexts, questions of moral character and virtue. In answering these questions, we can assume neither a 'view from nowhere' nor a definitive epistemological resolution to glocal ethical clashes. The question instead becomes a question of how to live together well in a context of plural ethical commitments that, for all parties, arose in one ground and are now transplanted to another.

Following Walzer's argument in *Thick and Thin* (1994), the first thing for the moral theorist to do is not to establish what is right but to examine the resources available within his or her own moral tradition for forging common ground with others. These resources may turn out to be substantive in that this exploration turns up commonalities in ethical qualities and commitments between different ways of life (e.g. parents' obligation to do their best for their children, the moral value of honesty, the rejection of murder), or they may turn out to be more 'procedural', that is to say, qualities that enable communication with strangers or innovations in ethical thinking (sympathy, kindness, humility, scepticism, creativity). The second thing for the moral theorist to do is to examine the implications of the new ground of ethical life: what does it mean to live well in a world in which plurality is embedded? Precisely because virtue ethics is contextual, virtue theorists cannot simply assert the integrity of one way of life over another. To suggest that a way of life grounded in one set of social relations must be retained at all costs when those social relations are no longer in place in the same way is to misunderstand ethics by detaching it from what makes it meaningful in the first place. What follows from the examination of existing moral traditions and changing context isn't something that can be known in advance. It may or may not enable building bridges between antithetical views. But it is the only *ethical* way to proceed in relation to glocal ethical clashes from a virtue ethics point of view.

For rationalist theories, the virtue ethics way is both too slow and in danger of arriving at the wrong answer concerning what is the right thing to do. From the standpoints of feminist and postmodernist ethics, they are in sympathy with the decentring of moral authority inherent in a glocalized virtue ethics but suspicious of the neglect of questions of power in its treatment of ways of life. Like virtue ethics, care and postmodernist ethics do not give priority to moral knowledge in their responses to glocal ethical plurality but they complicate that plurality by pointing to the ways in which predominant ethical positions are entwined in relations of hierarchy and subordination.

From the perspective of the feminist ethic of care, taking the context of power into account leads to the questioning of *both* sides of standard glocal ethical debates surrounding issues that affect women. As these are commonly constructed, for instance in relation to female circumcision, the debate is understood as one of giving ethical priority to culture versus giving ethical priority to individual rights to bodily integrity (Galeotti 2007; Li 2007). For care theorists, however, both sides of the debate need to be concretely deconstructed in the light of values implicit in the practice of care. In this respect, there are problems both with proponents of the practice of female circumcision, in that it causes ongoing pain and perpetuates patriarchal social systems, and with the opponents, in that they detach the specific practice from its context, don't take account of its actual impact on women or of women as active agents in its perpetuation and are using a liberal human rights discourse that is located in the cultures with the most global power and reach. In troubling the accounts of both sides of the debate, feminist ethicists look to open up pathways for immanent critique and change for both parties, and in the meantime favour compromise over coercion in mediating between different ethical positions. From the care point of view, an ethical approach to glocal ethical dissensus could not be straightforwardly coercive or one-directional. As with virtue ethics, it requires the attempt to think through the ethical implications of a new relational context of deep plurality.

Postmodernist ethics pushes the deconstruction of claims to moral knowledge further even than virtue and feminist ethics. In general, this makes postmodernist positions highly resistant to strategies for dealing with glocal ethical dissensus that are based on a claim to the ethical authority of knowing the right. However, this clearly has implications not only for rationalist positions but also for communitarian positions in which the 'rightness' of respect for cultural difference is given an overarching authority. Given that this is so, the *ethical* postmodernist response to ethical dissensus would appear to have to be a persistent questioning of the claims to authority of all sides in ethical disputes, and resistance to the emergence of hegemonic positions on ethical values and principles. In opposition to all of the preceding views, therefore, the resolution of glocal ethical disputes is neither possible nor desirable from the postmodernist perspective. What would be desirable would be to enable such disputes to flourish without imposing permanent exclusions on who counts morally and *how* they count. This would seem to require an ethic of openness and humility in glocal ethical debate (Butler 2000, 2004).

From Benhabib's revision of Habermas's discourse ethics through virtue, feminist and postmodernist accounts, the appropriate *ethical* approach to glocal ethical dissensus emphasizes the need for glocal interaction not based on a prior assumption of moral authority. If we go back to the mechanisms for responding to ethical dissensus in rationalist theory, they are all essentially one way, in that the morally authoritative position is in control because of its monopoly on truth but also because truth legitimates power and force. When opposing moral positions are construed as either 'wrong' (in error) or 'wrong' (immoral), the people who hold them are construed as oppressed, in need of enlightenment, stupid or bad. Either way, a hierarchy is set up before any interaction takes place and it shapes the nature of the interaction. The critics of ethical rationalism treat the meaning of ethical dissensus, its extensiveness and depth, as something to be discovered rather than assumed. For them what is in question are not simply opposing propositions but how it is that particular propositions come to be held, which may sometimes turn out to reflect profound ethical division and sometimes not. To the extent that profound ethical divisions are at work, they put argument, self-reflection, self-questioning, listening, immanent critique and constructing new ways of living in place of rational demonstration, moral education and coercion. They pay attention to who people are, rather than to what they know, as central to the possibility of forging common ways of dealing with complex and plural ethical commitments. And they draw attention to the *politics* of ethical debate and its rootedness in concrete social relations and conditions.

Reflective exercise

Think about your most fundamentally held moral values or positions on issues such as abortion, capital punishment, arranged marriages or homosexuality. What would it mean to have a debate about these issues with people of opposing views if you take your starting point from virtue, feminist or postmodernist ethics?

Conclusion

The anti-rationalist traditions of ethical thinking remind us that Global Ethics, as a branch of academic inquiry that has implications for how individuals should live their lives as well as for domestic and transnational institutional arrangements, cannot be studied or understood in a vacuum. Global Ethics is necessarily bound up with global politics and economics, with international law and the globalization of culture and communication. For this reason, even if one is confident of one's ethical position in the abstract, that confidence is hard to translate to a consistent set of behaviours in our personal lives, let alone to the behaviours of collective actors such as states, international organizations or international charities. Anyone involved in a pension scheme in the affluent world is likely to be investing in companies with policies and practices that contravene their ethical commitments. Anyone scraping a living in conditions of urban poverty is likely to contribute to the undermining of sustainable development. In these contexts, even if one is sure that the rights of the individual trump the rights of the collective, or that ethical obligations follow from 'fault', it isn't clear how these moral certainties should be translated into practice.

The above discussion is not intended to suggest that moral theories preoccupied with the question of what is morally right are somehow inappropriate in the context of Global Ethics. Rather it is to suggest that all participants in debates in Global Ethics must be sensitive to the ethical issues raised by processes of justification and application of values and principles that are claiming a worldwide scope. To know what is right is one thing but to act rightly is another. Acting rightly is not just about doing what is right in the substantive sense of putting one's moral convictions into practice. It involves thinking about how one is acting and of the range of impacts that one's actions may have, above and beyond the explicit intended outcome of doing the right thing. In the peculiarly complex and hierarchically structured world in which we live, acting rightly may sometimes involve putting one's moral convictions on one side or rethinking them in the light of not living in the best of all possible worlds. It will always involve a degree of risk because it is so easy to mis-understand what is at stake in ethical conflict and because we cannot control all of the consequences of our actions, however well intended. In this respect, as well as needing well worked-out views about what the best of all possible worlds might look like, we also need to cultivate in ourselves capacities for responsibility, sympathy, generosity, kindness and humility as qualities that will enable us to live well with others and work to recognize shared values where they exist, and to recognize when and how it may or may not be possible to construct them when they do not.

At the beginning of this book, when examining the meaning of Global Ethics as a field of academic inquiry, we raised the question of whether Global Ethics should be understood as introducing a new field of application (the global) for existing moral theories, or whether it required the development of new modes of moral theorizing. Based on the previous chapters, the answer to this question is 'both/and' rather than 'either/or'. Existing moral theories, in particular the rationalist theories that currently dominate the field, are powerful tools for addressing *why* and *what* questions, and can do a great deal to clarify the basis of alternative ethical positions on issues such as global warming or the justice of war. At the same time, the resources provided by these theories for making connections between strangers tend to reinforce rather than challenge moral exclusion because of the way in which they set up the relation between the experts in Global Ethics and those who are to benefit from this expertise. In this respect, we also need to learn from theorists such as Appiah and Parekh who argue that Global Ethics is as much about invention as it is about discovery. And that thinking about the ethical *who* and *how* questions involved in this *process* of invention as well as discovery is ultimately what makes the field of Global Ethics especially distinctive and challenging (Appiah 2007; Parekh 2005).

References and further reading

Appiah, K. A. (2007) *Cosmopolitanism: Ethics in a World of Strangers*, London: Penguin Books. Argues that we need new modes of ethical thinking to respond properly to the changing nature of our ethical existence in a globalizing world.
Barry, B. (2001) *Culture and Equality: An Egalitarian Critique of Multiculturalism*, Cambridge: Polity. A robust critique of multiculturalism based on a strong argument for the moral and political equality of individuals.
Benhabib, S. (1990) 'Communicative Ethics and Current Controversies in Practical Philosophy', in S. Benhabib and F.

Dallmayr (eds), *The Communicative Ethics Controversy*, Cambridge, MA: MIT Press. Sets out how Benhabib differentiates her view from that of Habermas.

Benhabib, S. (1992) *Situating the Self: Gender, Community and Postmodernism in Contemporary Ethics*, Cambridge: Polity. A collection of essays in which Benhabib develops her modified version of discourse ethics.

Benhabib, S. (2002) *The Claims of Culture: Equality and Diversity in the Global Era*, Princeton: Princeton University Press. The application of Benhabib's perspective to debates over multiculturalism within and between states.

Benhabib, S. (2006) *Another Cosmopolitanism*, Oxford: Oxford University Press. Sets out Benhabib's arguments for how to respond to particular transnational issues surrounding migration and glocal clashes of value.

Brock, G. and Brighouse, H. (eds) (2005) *The Political Philosophy of Cosmopolitanism*, Cambridge: Cambridge University Press. A collection of essays bringing together mainly rationalist approaches to questions in Global Ethics and illustrating the 'expertise' approach to ethical theory.

Butler, J. (2000) 'Restaging the Universal: Hegemony and the Limits of Formalism', and 'Competing Universalities', in J. Butler, E. Laclau and S. Žižek, *Contingency, Hegemony, Universality: Contemporary Dialogues on the Left*, London: Verso. Sets out a poststructuralist argument for how to use the category of 'universal' in ethical thinking.

Butler, J. (2004) 'Beside Oneself: On the Limits of Sexual Autonomy', in *Undoing Gender*, New York and London: Routledge. An example of a poststructuralist ethical approach in which the meaning of 'human' in human rights is always in question.

Caney, S. (2005) *Justice Beyond Borders: A Global Political Theory*, Oxford: Oxford University Press. Particularly strong on examining debates between different types of ethical rationalism.

Caney, S. and Jones, P. (2001) *Human Rights and Global Diversity*, London: Frank Cass. Collection of essays engaging with the question of whether there can be universal human rights in a context of global pluralism, which includes examining the issue of what to do about clashes of value in a glocal context.

Galeotti, A. (2007) 'Relativism, Universalism, and Applied Ethics: The Case of Female Circumcision', *Constellations* 14(1): 91–111. A critique of moral certainties about female circumcision offers a modified critique of rationalist, universalist arguments.

Gehring, V. V. (ed.) (2007) *The Ethical Dimensions of Global Development*, Plymouth: Rowman and Littlefield. A collection of essays that addresses a variety of issues in Global Ethics, most of which point to the importance of thinking about Global Ethics 'glocally' and interactively, rather than through the application of already existing ethical frameworks.

Jaggar, A. (2008) ' "Saving Anima": Global Justice for Women and Intercultural Dialogue', in Pogge and Horton (eds), *Global Ethics: Seminal Essays*, St Paul: Paragon House, pp. 565–603. Originally published in A. Follesdal and T. Pogge (eds), *Real World Justice* (2005), Dordrecht: Springer. A critique of the feminist critique of multiculturalism pioneered by thinkers such as Nussbaum and Okin.

Li, X. (2007) 'Tolerating the Intolerable: The Case of Female Genital Mutilation', in V. Gehring (ed.), *The Ethical Dimensions of Global Development*, Lanham: Rowman and Littlefield. Makes a liberal case for the toleration of certain practices of female circumcision.

Mulhall, S. and Swift, A. (1996) *Liberals and Communitarians*, Oxford: Blackwell. An account of the debates splitting Anglo-American political theory in the 1970s and 1980s which prefigured the ways in which debates over international or global ethics have been framed in cosmopolitan vs. communitarian terms.

Okin, S. M. (2008) 'Gender Inequality and Cultural Differences', in Pogge and Horton (eds), *Global Ethics: Seminal Essays*, St Paul: Paragon House, pp. 233–57. Originally published in *Political Theory* 22(1) (1994): 5–24. Feminist critique of multiculturalism.

Parekh, B. (2000) *Rethinking Multiculturalism: Cultural Diversity and Political Theory*, Basingstoke: Macmillan. An argument for multiculturalism, one of the targets of Barry's critique.

Parekh, B. (2005) 'Principles of a Global Ethic', in J. Eade and D. O'Byrne (eds), *Global Ethics and Civil Society*, Aldershot: Ashgate. An argument for a global ethic based on difference and dialogue.

Pierik, R. (2007) 'Fighting Child Labour Abroad: Conceptual Problems and Practical Solutions', in V. Gehring (ed.), *The Ethical Dimensions of Global Development*, Lanham: Rowman and Littlefield. Demonstrates how the debate over child labour is much less morally clear-cut than has previously been supposed.

Pogge, T. (ed.) (2001) *Global Justice*, Oxford: Blackwell. Includes mainly contractualist and deontological contributions to debates over global distributive justice, and again illustrates an 'expertise' approach to ethical theory.

Pogge, T. and Horton, K. (eds) (2008) *Global Ethics: Seminal Essays, Volume II*, St Paul: Paragon House.

Pogge, T. and Moellendorf, D. (eds) (2008) *Global Justice: Seminal Essays, Volume I*, St Paul: Paragon House. This collection and the one above bring together a comprehensive collection of influential essays in Global Ethics. Where I refer to essays in these collections, I have included the original publication details of the article in question.

Walzer, M. (1994) *Thick and Thin: Moral Argument at Home and Abroad*, Notre Dame: University of Notre Dame Press. Walzer's attempt to show the implications of a contextual ethical position for moral engagement across cultural and political boundaries.

Glossary

act utilitarianism The original **utilitarian** theory that required that all acts should be justified on the basis that they maximize individual happiness (see discussion in chapter 2).

anthropocentrism Literally, this means human-centred. Most of the ethical theories considered in this book are anthropocentric but there are ethical approaches in environmental and ecological ethics that argue against ethical anthropocentrism (see discussion in chapter 4).

autonomy Literally the capacity to legislate for yourself, more generally it refers to the ethical value of individual freedom, this is something particularly important to **contractualist** and **deontological** moral theories (see chapter 2).

categorical imperative Kant's term for genuinely moral principles. They had to be categorical, which means absolutely obligatory, and they took the form of imperatives or commands because of humanity's inherent weakness which meant that, unlike angels, we didn't necessarily always *want* to do the right thing (see chapter 2 for discussion on Kant).

communitarianism This refers to ethical and political theories that give moral priority to the community rather than the individual. In contemporary debates in Global Ethics, it encompasses moral positions influenced by both

contractualism and **virtue ethics**. It is commonly contrasted with **cosmopolitanism** (see discussion in chapter 1).

consequentialism Theories that give moral priority to outcomes (consequences) rather than to either moral principles (**deontology**) or procedures (**discourse ethics**). The main consequentialist theory considered in this volume is **utilitarianism**, discussed in chapter 2.

contextualism The view that moral values, principles and judgements are only meaningful in relation to context. Moral contextualists include **communitarian** versions of **virtue ethics**, as well as **feminist** and **postmodernist** positions. See discussions in chapter 3 and Walzer's view of **distributive justice** in chapter 5 for examples of contextualist moral thinking.

contractualism Ethical theories based on consent, building on a view of humans as naturally free and rational and therefore possessed of certain **natural rights**, often using the device of a hypothetical contract between individuals. The most famous modern exponent of ethical contractualism is Rawls, discussed in chapters 2 and 5.

cosmopolitanism This means literally a belief in the idea of world citizenship. In contemporary debates in Global Ethics, it refers to ethical theories that are morally **universal** in implication and take the individual rather than the community as the primary source and location of moral value. It is commonly contrasted with **communitarianism** (see discussion in chapter 1).

deontology The view that moral rules hold absolutely and without exception. See the discussion in chapter 2 of Kantian deontology and Habermas's **discourse ethics** for examples of deontological moral thinking.

dependency theory A theory about global economic relations that was developed as a critical counter to **modernization theories** in the 1960s and 1970s (see discussion in chapter 4).

development A heavily contested term in Global Ethics. It is sometimes used to refer solely to economic development, with industrialized countries being counted as 'developed' in contrast to 'underdeveloped' agrarian economies. More recently, its meaning has been expanded to cover a range of non-economic goods, such as in the **human capabilities**

approach pioneered by thinkers such as Sen and Nussbaum (see discussion in chapter 4).

dialogical   A term coined by **discourse ethics** to refer to inter-subjective, communicative processes for grounding ethical claims. It is contrasted with **monological** modes of theorizing (see discussion of Habermas in chapter 2).

difference principle   Rawls's term for one of the principles of **distributive justice** that he thought people in the **original position** would recommend for liberal political communities. It states that any economic inequality within the community must operate so as to improve the position of the worst-off citizens; in other words they must be better off than they would have been had there been a straightforwardly egalitarian distribution (see chapters 2 and 5).

discourse ethics   The view that the presuppositions of morality are present in the presuppositions of successful, non-coercive communication with others. Examples of discourse ethics theorists considered in this book include Habermas (discussed in chapter 2), Forst (discussed in chapter 5) and Benhabib (discussed in chapters 5 and 8).

distributive justice   Concerns the moral rightness or wrongness of different patterns of distribution of material wealth and other goods (see discussions in chapters 4 and 5).

domestic analogy   Treating the state or nation as analogous to an individual moral actor, with analogous capacities, responsibilities and value. Walzer relies on the domestic analogy in his version of just war theory (see discussion in chapter 6).

double effect   The principle that unintended bad outcomes do not reflect negatively on the moral worth of an action. It is most commonly appealed to in the context of war and 'collateral damage', that is to say the damage to civilians or infrastructure that is a side effect of attacks on military targets. Double-effect arguments make sense for moral approaches that stress the significance of intention or **procedure** over that of outcomes (see discussion in chapter 6).

essentialism   The view that something has an essence, for instance that there are certain qualities present in all humans in virtue of them being human, or of all women in virtue of them being women. **Postmodernist** ethical theories object to **rationalist** moral theories on the grounds that they are essentialist about human nature and to **feminist care ethics** on the grounds that it presumes that all women share a common essence (see chapter 3).

felicific calculus A term coined to refer to the cost-benefit analysis necessary for **utilitarians** to work out the right thing to do (see chapter 2).

feminism Refers both to political movements for overcoming of injustices embedded in gendered relations of power, and to forms of scholarship that approach doing ethical theory from a feminist standpoint. The most well-known feminist ethical theory is **feminist care ethics** (for example Ruddick and Robinson) but feminist ethics also includes thinkers such as Okin, who combines **contractualist** and **deontological** elements in her thought; Nussbaum, who combines **virtue** and **deontological** elements in her thought; and Butler, who takes a feminist **postmodernist** stance (see discussions in chapters 3, 5 and 6).

feminist care ethics Inspired by the work of Carol Gilligan, this is the most influential branch of feminist moral theory (examples discussed in this book include the work of Ruddick and Robinson). Care ethics sees moral judgement and action as based on embedded relations of care and responsibility rather than abstract universal rules (see discussions in chapters 3, 4 and 6).

formalism Ethical theories based on the idea that the form of moral principles (for instance the form of a universal, categorically binding rule) is the key to their moral authority and meaning. Kant's and Habermas's theories are both formalist in this sense, and because of this put emphasis on the ethical importance of **procedure** as opposed to **context** or **consequences** when making moral judgements (see chapters 2 and 3).

foundationalism Theories that claim to have established an authoritative ground or foundation for moral claims. The question of foundations is one of the issues that divides **rationalist** moral theories from other alternatives (see chapters 2 and 3).

global/globalization Increasing commonality and interdependence of the world's population as a whole. As a process it may be more or less advanced at the current time in different sectors: the economy, politics, technology,

media and communications or culture. Sociologists, economists and political scientists differ over the extent, depth
and novelty of globalization processes. These debates are
discussed briefly in chapter 1.

glocal/glocalization   A term made up out of a hybrid of
global and 'local'. It refers to the ways in which globalization processes are experienced and transformed at the level
of the local (see chapters 1 and 8).

human capabilities   The idea of human capabilities emerged
out of criticism of economistic theories of development
(see discussion in chapter 4). Thinkers such as Sen and
Nussbaum built on the human capabilities idea to critique
both economism and crude utilitarian approaches to
aid and to global distributive justice (see chapters 4 and
5). Human capabilities theory is premised on an ideal
of human flourishing that owes a debt to **virtue ethics,**
and it is used by Nussbaum as the basis of a **feminist**
theory of global justice (see discussion of Nussbaum in
chapter 5).

human rights   The innate, inalienable rights of all human
beings in virtue of being human, the successor to the earlier
idea of **natural rights** in the **contractualist** tradition (see
chapter 2). The idea of international human rights was
institutionalized after the Second World War by the
Universal Declaration of Human Rights (UDHR) in 1948.
See chapter 1 bibliography for a variety of different Human
Rights declarations, and see discussions of Shue and Pogge
in chapters 4 and 5 for examples of theorists resting their
arguments about global justice on the idea of inalienable
human rights.

humanitarianism   Used to refer to all different kinds of
responses to emergency situations by the international
community, from economic aid to military intervention
(see chapters 4 and 6).

incommensurability   Two views are incommensurable when
they are mutually exclusive; that is to say that they could
not both be true at the same time (see discussions in
chapter 8).

liberalism   Political ideology based on a **contractualist**
account of ethics which comes in more or less **libertarian**
versions. Liberalism in contemporary moral theory is most

closely related to Rawls's **contractualism** but it also encompasses **deontological** arguments that make the discourse of **human rights** central (see for instance, Pogge and Shue, discussed in chapter 5, or Orend, discussed in chapter 7).

libertarian A form of **contractualist liberal** theory that stresses the moral significance of 'negative' rights, such as the right not to have your property stolen or the right to freedom of movement, as opposed to 'positive' rights, such as the right to food or other forms of welfare (which might entail taking someone else's property, via taxation, in order to pay for them – see discussion of Shue in chapters 4 and 5). Within Global Ethics, libertarian forms of liberalism are less influential than ones with a stronger **deontological** element.

metaphysical/metaphysics Refers literally to what is beyond the material, physical world. Metaphysics is the branch of philosophy that has traditionally sought to investigate questions that go beyond the material universe, for instance about the existence of God or the meaning of truth. The moral theories discussed in chapters 2 and 3 all claim not to be reliant on metaphysical assumptions.

modernization theory The theory, popular in the 1950s and 1960s, that all economies would and should develop along the same lines as the advanced industrialized economies and that economic development was the key to solving problems of global poverty and inequality (see discussion in chapter 4).

monological A term coined by **discourse ethics** theorists to describe philosophical theories that are premised on the reasoning of a single individual. It is contrasted with **dialogical** ethical theories that rely on intersubjective communication to ground substantive moral claims (see discussion of Habermas in chapter 2).

multiculturalism The policy of encouraging cultural diversity within states. Many of the ethical debates surrounding multiculturalism have been transferred into debates in Global Ethics about ethical responses to **glocal** clashes of value (see discussion in chapter 8).

natural rights Rights innate to human individuals regardless of the actual legal and political rights they may possess. In the twentieth century, the idea of natural rights was an important inspiration for the idea of fundamental **human rights**.

original position   The term Rawls uses to describe the hypothetical situation of his **contractors** in *A Theory of Justice*. The original position builds in assumptions about the rationality and motivation of the **contracting** parties, as well as the fact that they are choosing behind a **veil of ignorance**. See discussion of Rawls in chapter 2.

pacifism   The political and ethical condemnation of the use of violence to attain political ends, most commonly based on **deontological** or **feminist** ethical arguments (see discussion in chapter 6).

particularism   The view that morality and moral judgement are relative to specific contexts and practices. In this sense **communitarian** versions of **virtue ethics** (for example Walzer, see chapters 5 and 6) and **feminist care ethics** (for example Robinson or Ruddick; see chapters 4 and 6) are morally particularist because they both embed the meaning of moral values and principles in specific social and institutional practices that are not shared by all humanity. Moral particularism overlaps with moral **contextualism** and is opposed to moral **universalism**.

performative contradiction   A term used by Habermas to describe what happens when you make a claim that is contradicted in the making of it, the most well-known example of which is the liar's paradox: 'I am lying'. Habermas argues that those who claim that morality is purely subjective are in performative contradiction because, in order to make and defend the claim, they rely on certain objective truths about the presuppositions of communication (see discussion of Habermas in chapter 2).

phronesis   Aristotle's term for moral reasoning, a kind of practical reasoning that he distinguished from other forms of logical deduction or induction. *Phronesis* is a kind of ethical skill that is acquired through experience and can be drawn on in order to tackle novel moral issues and dilemmas. **Virtue ethics** give *phronesis* a central place in moral theory, but we also find similar concepts in **feminist care ethics**, for instance in Ruddick's work (see chapters 3 and 6).

postmodernism   Any theoretical perspective that is dubious about **foundationalist** moral theory. It includes a variety of theories, some of which draw on Derrida's work (**poststructuralist** ethics) and some of which is more influenced by ethical **pragmatism** (for example Rorty); see discussion in chapter 3.

poststructuralism   Theoretical perspectives that reject **universalist** and **foundationalist** approaches to ethics. Important influences on poststructuralist ethics are Levinas and Derrida (see discussion in chapter 3). Examples of poststructuralist approaches in Global Ethics include the work of Edkins (chapter 4) and Campbell (chapter 6).

pragmatism   A tradition of ethical theory that identifies what is morally valuable with what *works* within the contexts of particular social practices rather than with a set of substantive principles or values. Pragmatist moral perspectives have a lot in common with **virtue** and **postmodernist** theories. Rorty's ethical perspective, discussed in chapters 3 and 5, combines pragmatism with insights from **virtue** and **postmodernist** ethics.

pre-emptive war   A war fought in response to an actual and imminent threat from an aggressor. Traditionally just war theory has allowed for the *ad bellum* justice of pre-emptive wars (see discussion in chapter 6).

preventive war   A war fought to prevent a future, nonimminent threat from another party, traditionally just war theory has not seen preventive war as morally justifiable. Much of the discussion of the morality of the invasions of Afghanistan (2001) and Iraq (2003) has been about whether the prohibition of preventive war in just war theory needs to be revisited (see discussion in chapter 6).

proceduralism   Theories that justify moral judgements or actions by reference to procedure (Habermas in chapter 2 and Forst in chapter 5) rather than *substantive values* (Nussbaum in chapter 5), *context* (Walzer in chapter 5) or *consequences* (Singer in chapter 5).

rationalism   This term has a variety of meanings in philosophy. Within this text, it is used to refer to ethical theories that give reason an important role in the foundations of morality (see chapter 2).

restorative justice   An approach to **transitional justice** that gives the needs of the victim moral priority, rather than the punishment of the perpetrator (see discussion in chapter 7).

retributive justice   An approach to **transitional justice** that gives priority to the punishment of perpetrators, individual and collective (see discussion in chapter 7).

rule utilitarianism   The moral theory that justifies obedience to moral *rules* or principles, such as 'stealing is wrong' or 'lying is wrong' on the grounds that they promote the greatest happiness of the greatest number of people. This is in contrast to **act utilitarianism**, which requires that every individual *act* is justified in terms of whether it maximizes the greatest happiness of the greatest number of people (see discussion in chapter 2).

social contract   The contract to which individuals in a **state of nature** agree in order to establish social institutions, norms and laws (see discussion of **contractualism** in chapter 2).

sovereignty   The principle of state control over their own populations and territories. One of the key issues in contemporary ethics of emergency aid and armed conflict is the question of the ethical basis of state sovereignty (see chapters 4 and 6).

state of nature   The situation of humanity in a natural condition, abstracted from any social institutions, norms and laws, the context for the **social contract**. One of the most famous examples of an imagined state of nature is in Hobbes's political theory (discussed in chapter 2). Contemporary moral theorists, such as Rawls, substitute a hypothetical **original position** for the idea of the state of nature.

supererogation   Ethical actions above and beyond the call of duty. The distinction between obligatory and supererogatory actions is particularly clear in **deontological** moral theories (see discussion of Kant in chapter 2, the distinction between justice and humanity in chapter 4 and Pogge's institutionalist account of economic human rights in chapter 5).

supreme emergency   Walzer's term for the situation in which the survival of state or nation is immediately at stake (see discussion in chapter 6).

sustainable development Economic and human development that takes account of the limits on the earth's resources and capacity to absorb the implications of industrialization and mass consumption (see discussion in chapter 4).

transitional justice Ways of addressing moral wrongs committed before and during armed conflict in the aftermath of the conflict. Some theories of transitional justice emphasize **retributive** and others **restorative** conceptions of justice. Mechanisms for delivering transitional justice include criminal tribunals, TRCs and reparations, all discussed in chapter 7.

universalism Universalist ethical theories are applicable to all moral agents and are grounded on supposedly universal truths about humanity, regardless of context, community or culture. Examples of ethical universalism (**utilitarianism, contractualism, deontology, discourse ethics**) are discussed in chapter 2. Some versions of **virtue ethics**, discussed in chapter 3, are also universal in their grounding and implications; see, for instance, Nussbaum's theory of human capabilities (chapter 4). Moral universalism is normally contrasted with moral **contextualism** and moral **particularism**.

universalization test Refers to Kant's moral theory and his view that only principles that are capable of universalization (in other words could be turned into a **categorical imperative** for all rational beings) are genuinely moral principles (see discussion of Kant in chapter 2).

utilitarianism The most well-known **consequentialist** ethical theory. It is based on the principle that to act morally is to act so as to maximize the happiness of each human being counted as one, discussed in chapter 2.

veil of ignorance Rawls's term for the limits on the information available to his contractors in the **original position**. They do not know anything specific about who they are or what position they will occupy in the society they are constructing (see discussion of Rawls in chapter 2).

virtue ethics Moral theories that give greater priority to qualities of character (virtues such as honesty, prudence, courage, kindness) and practical reasoning (*phronesis*) than to moral rules (as with **deontology**) or outcomes (as with **utilitarianism**); see discussion in chapter 3. Some contemporary versions of virtue ethics emphasize the importance of local contexts and practices to the meaning of virtue (for example, Walzer, discussed in chapters 5 and 6); others link the idea to a broader notion of human flourishing that applies to all of humanity (for example, Nussbaum, discussed in chapters 4 and 5).

Index

238   *Index*